THE CROWN OF CHIEF MOUNTAIN FROM THE SOUTHEAST.

Hunting

In Many Lands

The Book of the Boone and Crockett Club

EDITORS

THEODORE ROOSEVELT
GEORGE BIRD GRINNELL

NEW YORK
FOREST AND STREAM PUBLISHING COMPANY
1895

Contents

	Page
Hunting in East Africa	13
W. A. Chanler.	
To the Gulf of Cortez	55
George H. Gould.	
A Canadian Moose Hunt	84
Madison Grant.	
A Hunting Trip in India	107
Elliott Roosevelt.	
Dog Sledging in the North	123
D. M. Barringer.	
Wolf-Hunting in Russia	151
Henry T. Allen.	
A Bear-Hunt in the Sierras	187
Alden Sampson.	
The Ascent of Chief Mountain	220
Henry L. Stimson.	
The Cougar	238
Casper W. Whitney.	
Big Game of Mongolia and Tibet	255
W. W. Rockhill.	

5

Hunting in Many Lands

	Page
Hunting in the Cattle Country.	278
Theodore Roosevelt.	
Wolf-Coursing.	318
Roger D. Williams.	
Game Laws	358
Charles E. Whitehead.	
Protection of the Yellowstone National Park	377
George S. Anderson.	

———

The Yellowstone National Park Protection Act	403
Head-Measurements of the Trophies at the Madison Square Garden Sportsmen's Exposition.	424
National Park Protective Act	433
Constitution of the Boone and Crockett Club	439
Officers of the Boone and Crockett Club	442
List of Members	443

List of Illustrations

Crown of Chief Mountain . .   Frontispiece

From the southeast. One-half mile distant. Photographed by Dr. Walter B. James.

Facing page

A Mountain Sheep   55

Photographed from Life. From Forest and Stream.

Rocky Mountain and Polo's Sheep . . .   75

The figures are drawn to the same scale and show the
difference in the spread of horns. From Forest and
Stream.

A Moose of the Upper Ottawa   85

Killed by Madison Grant, October 10, 1893.

How our Outfit was Carried   123

Photographed by D. M. Barringer.

Outeshai, Russian Barzoi   151

Winner of the hare-coursing prize at Colombiagi
(near St. Petersburg) two years in succession. In
type, however, he is faulty.

Fox-hounds of the Imperial Kennels . . .   177

The men and dogs formed part of the hunt described.

Hunting in Many Lands

Facing page

The Chief's Crown from the East. . . 229
Photographed by Dr. Walter B. James. Distance, two
miles.

Yaks Grazing 255
Photographed by Hon. W. W. Rockhill.

Ailuropus Melanoleucus 263
From Forest and Stream.

Elaphurus Davidianus 271

The Wolf Throwing Zloeem, the Barzoi . 319
From Leslie's Weekly.

Yellowstone Park Elk 377
From Forest and Stream.

A Hunting Day 395
From Forest and Stream.

In Yellowstone Park Snows 413
From Forest and Stream.

On the Shore of Yellowstone Lake . . 419
From Forest and Stream.

NOTE.—The mountain sheep's head on the cover is from a photograph
of the head of the big ram killed by Mr. Gould in Lower California, as
described in the article "To the Gulf of Cortez."

Preface

The first volume published by the Boone and Crockett Club, under the title "American Big Game Hunting," confined itself, as its title implied, to sport on this continent. In presenting the second volume, a number of sketches are included written by members who have hunted big game in other lands. The contributions of those whose names are so well known in connection with explorations in China and Tibet, and in Africa, have an exceptional interest for men whose use of the rifle has been confined entirely to the North American continent.

During the two years that have elapsed since the appearance of its last volume, the Boone and Crockett Club has not been idle. The activity of its members was largely instrumental in securing at last the passage by Congress of an act to protect the Yellowstone National Park, and to punish crimes and offenses within its borders, though it may be questioned whether even their efforts would have had any result had not the public interest been aroused, and the Congressional conscience pricked, by the wholesale slaughter of buffalo which took place in the Park in March, 1894, as elsewhere detailed by Capt. Anderson and the editors. Besides this, the Club has secured the passage, by the New York Legislature, of an act incorporating the New York Zoölogical Society, and a considerable representation of the Club is found in the list of its officers and managers. Other efforts, made by Boone and Crockett members in behalf of game and forest protection, have been less successful, and there is still a wide field for the Club's activities.

Public sentiment should be aroused on the general question of forest preservation, and especially in the matter of securing legislation which will adequately protect the game and the forests of the various forest reservations already established. Special attention was called to this point in the earlier volume published by the Club, from which we quote:

If it was worth while to establish these reservations, it is worth while to protect them. A general law, providing for the adequate guarding of all such national possessions, should be enacted by Congress, and wherever it may be necessary such Federal laws should be

Preface

supplemented by laws of the States in which the reservations lie. The timber and the game ought to be made the absolute property of the Government, and it should be constituted a punishable offense to appropriate such property within the limits of the reservation. The game and timber on a reservation should be regarded as Government property, just as are the mules and the cordwood at any army post. If it is a crime to take the latter, it should be a crime to plunder a forest reservation.

In these reservations is to be found to-day every species of large game known to the United States, and the proper protection of the reservations means the perpetuating in full supply of all the indigenous mammals. If this care is provided, no species of American large game need ever become absolutely extinct; and intelligent effort for game protection may well be directed toward securing through national legislation the policing of forest preserves by timber and game wardens.

A really remarkable phenomenon in American animal life, described in the paper on the Yellowstone Park Protection Act, is the attitude now assumed toward mankind by the bears, both grizzly and black, in the Yellowstone National Park. The preservation of the game in the Park has unexpectedly resulted in turning a great many of the bears into scavengers for the hotels within the Park limits. Their tameness and familiarity are astonishing; they act much more like hogs than beasts of prey. Naturalists now have a chance of studying their character from an entirely new standpoint, and under entirely new conditions. It would be well worth the while of any student of nature to devote an entire season in the Park simply to study of bear life; never before has such an opportunity been afforded.

The incident mentioned on page 421 was witnessed by Mr. W. Hallett Phillipps and Col. John Hay. Since this incident occurred, one bear has made a practice of going into the kitchen of the Geyser Hotel, where he is fed on pies. If given a chance, the bears will eat the pigs that are kept in pens near the hotels; but they have not shown any tendency to molest the horses, or to interfere in any way with the human beings around the hotels.

These incidents, and the confidence which the elk, deer and other animals in the Park have come to feel in man, are interesting, for they show how readily wild creatures may be taught to look upon human beings as friends.

THEODORE ROOSEVELT,
GEORGE BIRD GRINNELL.

NEW YORK, August 1, 1895.

Hunting in Many Lands

Hunting in East Africa

In the month of July, 1889, I was encamped in the Taveta forest, 250 miles from the east coast, and at the eastern foot of Mt. Kilimanjaro. I was accompanied by my servant, George Galvin, an American lad seventeen years old, and had a following of 130 Zanzibaris. My battery consisted of the following weapons: one 8-bore smooth, using a cartridge loaded with 10 drams of powder and a 2-ounce spherical ball; one .577 and one .450 Express rifle, and one 12-bore Paradox. All these were made by Messrs. Holland & Holland. My servant carried an old 12-bore rifle made by Lang (intended to shoot 4½ drams of powder, but whose cartridges he recklessly loaded with more than 7) and a .45-90 Winchester of the model of 1886.

Taveta forest has been often described by pens far abler than mine, so I will not attempt to do this. It is inhabited by a most friendly tribe of savages, who at the time of my visit to them possessed sufficient food to be able to supply the wants of my caravan. I therefore made it a base at which I could leave the major part of my following, and from which I could with comfort and safety venture forth on shooting trips, accompanied by only a few men.

The first of these excursions was made to the shores of Lake Jipé, six hours' march from Taveta, for the purpose of shooting hippos. I took with me my whole battery and thirteen men. This unlucky number perhaps influenced my fortunes, for I returned to Taveta empty handed and fever stricken, after a stay on the shores of the lake lasting some days. However, my experiences were interesting, if only because they were in great measure the result of ignorance. Up to this time my sporting experience had dealt only with snipe and turkey shooting in Florida, for on my road from the coast, the little game seen was too wary to give me a chance of putting a rifle to my shoulder.

The shores of Lake Jipé, where I pitched my tent, were quite flat and separated from the open water of the lake by a wide belt of swamp growth. I had brought with me, for the purpose of constructing a raft, several bundles of the stems of a large palm growing in Taveta.

These were dry and as light as cork. In a few hours' time my men constructed a raft, fifteen feet in length and five feet in width. On trial, it was found capable of supporting two men, but even with this light load it sank some inches below the surface of the water. I fastened a deal box on the forward end as seat, and instructed one of the men, who said he understood boatman's work, to stand in the stern and punt the craft along with a pole. During the night my slumbers were constantly disturbed by the deep, ominous grunting of hippopotami, which, as if to show their contempt for my prowess, chose a path to their feeding grounds which led them within a few yards of my camp. The night, though starlit, was too dark for a shot, so I curbed my impatience till the morning.

As most people are aware, the day begins in the tropics as nearly as possible at 6 o'clock and lasts twelve hours. Two hours before dawn I was up and fortifying myself against the damp morning air with a good breakfast of roast chicken, rice and coffee. My men, wrapped in their thin cotton shirts, lay about the fires on the damp ground, seemingly unmindful of rheumatism and fever, and only desirous to sleep as long as possible. I awoke my crew at a little after 5, and he, unassisted, launched the raft. The swamp grass buoyed it up manfully, so that it looked as if it disdained to touch the yellow waters of the lake. When it had been pushed along till the water was found to be two feet deep, I had myself carried to the raft and seated myself on the box. I was clad only in a flannel shirt, and carried my .577 with ten rounds of ammunition. As we slowly started on our way, my men woke up one by one, and shouted cheering words to us, such as, "Look out for the crocodiles!" "If master dies, who'll pay us!" These cries, added to the dismal chill of the air and my boatman's only too apparent dislike of his job, almost caused me to turn back; but, of course, that was out of the question.

Half an hour from the shore found me on the edge of the open water, and, as if to endorse my undertaking, day began to break. That sunrise! Opposite me the rough outlines of the Ugucno Mountains, rising several thousand feet, lost their shadows one by one, and far to the right towered Mt. Kilimanjaro, nearly four miles high, its snowy rounded top roseate with the soft light of dawn. But in Africa at least one's higher sensibilities are dulled by the animal side of his nature, and I fear I welcomed the sun more for the warmth of its rays than for the beautiful and fleeting vision it produced. Then the hippos! While the sun was rising my raft was not at rest, but was being propelled by slow strong strokes toward the center of the lake, and as the darkness lessened I saw the surface of the lake dotted here and there by spots, which soon resolved themselves into the black, box-like heads of my game. They were to all appearance motionless and appeared quite unconscious or indifferent to the presence, in their particular domain, of our strange craft and its burden.

I approached them steadily, going more slowly as the water grew deeper, and more time was needed for the pulling out and dipping in of the pole. When, however, I had reached a position some 150 yards from the nearest group, five in number, they all with a loud snort faced me. I kept on, despite the ardent prayer of the boatman, and when within 100 yards, and upon seeing three of the hippos disappear beneath the surface, I took careful aim and fired at the nearest of the remaining two. I could see the splash of my bullet as it skipped harmlessly along the surface of the lake, and knew I had missed. At once all heads in sight disappeared. There must have been fifty in view when the sun rose. Presently, one by one, they reappeared, and this time, as if impelled by curiosity, came much closer than before. I took aim at one not fifty yards away, and could hear the thud of the bullet as it struck. I thought, as the hippo at once disappeared, that it was done for. I had not yet learned that the brain of these animals is very small, and that the only fatal shot is under the ear.

After this shot, as after my first, all heads vanished, but this time I had to wait much longer ere they ventured to show themselves. When they did reappear, however, it was too close for comfort. One great head, blinking its small eyes and holding its little horselike ears at attention, was not twenty feet away, and another was still closer on my other side. While hesitating at which to shoot I lost my opportunity, for they both ducked simultaneously.

I was riveted to my uncomfortable seat, and I could hear my boatman murmuring "Allah!" with fright, when slowly, but steadily, I felt the raft rise under my feet. Instinctively I remembered I had but one .577 rifle, and hastened, my hands trembling, to fasten it with a loose rope's end to the raft. My boatman yelled with terror, and at that fearful cry the raft splashed back in the water and all was again still. One of the hippos, either with his back or head, must have come in contact with the bottom of the raft as he rose to the surface. How far he would have gone had not the negro screamed I do not know, but as it was it seemed as if we were being held in mid air for many minutes. I fancy the poor brute was almost as frightened as we were, for he did not reappear near the raft.

I now thought discretion the better part of valor, and satisfied myself with shooting at the animal from a somewhat greater distance. I hit two more in the head and two—who showed a good foot of their fat bodies above the water —in the sides. None floated on the surface, legs up, as I had been led to expect they would do; but the men assured me that they never come to the surface till sundown, no matter what time of day they may have been shot. This, needless to state, I afterward found, is not true. My ammunition being exhausted, and the sun blazing hot, I returned to camp. I awoke the next day feeling anything but energetic; nevertheless, I set out to see what game the land held ready for the hunter, dissatisfied with his experiences on water. The country on the eastern side of Lake Jipé is almost flat, but is dotted here and there with low steep gneiss hills, stretching in an indefinite line parallel to the lake and some three miles distant from it. I made my way toward these hills. On the way I put up some very small antelope, which ran in such an irregular manner that they presented no mark to my unskilled arm.

We reached the hills, and I climbed one and scanned the horizon with my glasses. Far to the northwest I spied two black spots in a grassy plain. I gave the glasses to my gunbearer and he at once said, "Rhinoceros!" I had never seen these beasts except in a menagerie, and the mention of the name brought me to my feet eager to come to a closer acquaintance with them. The wind blew toward me and the game was too far for the need of caution, so I walked rapidly in their direction. When I got to within 250 yards, I could quite easily distinguish the appearance of my quarry. They were lying down and apparently oblivious to my approach—perhaps asleep. My gun-bearer (a Swahili) now began to show an anxiety to turn back. This desire is, in many cases, the distinguishing trait of this race. On we went, but now cautiously and silently. The grass was about two feet high, so that by crawling on hands and knees, one could conceal most of his body. But this position is not a pleasant one with a blazing sun on the back, rough soil under the knees and a thirteen-pound rifle in the hand.

We got to within fifty yards. I looked back for the negro with my .577. He was lying flat on his stomach fifty yards to the rear. I stood up to beckon him, but he did not move. The rhinos did, and my attention was recalled to them by hearing loud snorts, and, turning my head, I saw the two beasts on their feet facing me. I had never shot an 8-bore in my life before, so it is not to be wondered at that the shock of the recoil placed me on my back. The animals were off before I could recover my feet, and my second barrel was not discharged. I ran after them, but the pace of a rhino is much faster than it looks, and I soon found pursuit useless. I returned to the place where they had lain, and on looking about found traces of fresh blood. My gun-bearer, as an explanation for his behavior, said that rhinos were devils, and were not to be approached closely. He said I must be possessed of miraculous power, or they would have charged and slain me. The next day, fever laid me low, and, though the attack was slight, some days elapsed before I could muster strength to take me back to Taveta.

After a few days' rest in camp—strengthened by good food and spurred to fresh exertion by the barren result of my first effort—I set out again, accompanied by more men and in a different direction.

My faith in myself received a pleasant encouragement the day before my departure. My head man came to me and said trade was at a standstill, and that the natives could not be induced to bring food to sell. On asking him why, I learned that the Taveta people had found three dead hippos in Lake Jipé and one rhino near its shores. Meat—a rare treat to them, even when not quite fresh—filled their minds and bodies, and they were proof even against the most tempting beads and the brightest cloths. I cannot say that I shared my head man's anxiety. The fact that I had not labored altogether in vain, even though others reaped the benefit of my efforts, filled me with a certain satisfaction.

A day's march from Taveta brought me to the banks of an almost stagnant brook, where I made camp. The country round about was a plain studded with low hills, here thinly thatched with short grass, and there shrouded with thick bush, above which every now and then rose a giant acacia. The morning after my arrival, I set out from camp with my 8-bore in my hands and hope in my heart. Not 200 yards from my tent, I was startled by a snort and then by the sight of two rhinos dashing across my path some fifty yards away. This time I did not succumb to my gun's recoil, but had the doubtful satisfaction of seeing, from a standing position, the animals disappear in the bush. I made after them and found, to my delight, a clear trail of fresh blood. Eagerly pressing on, I was somewhat suddenly checked in my career by almost stumbling over a rhino apparently asleep on its side, with its head toward me. Bang! went the 8-bore and down I went. I was the only creature disturbed by the shot, as the rhino had been dead some minutes—slain by my first shot; and my satisfaction was complete when I found the hole made by my bullet. My men shouted and sang over this, the first fruits of my expedition, and even at this late day I forgive myself for the feeling of pride I then experienced. I have a table at home made of a piece of this animal's hide, and supported in part by one of its horns.

The next day I made an early start and worked till 4 o'clock P. M., with no result. Then, being some eight miles from camp, I turned my face toward home. I had not gone far, and had reached the outskirts of an almost treeless savanna, when my gun-bearer brought me to a halt by the word *mbogo*. This I knew meant buffalo. I adjusted my glass and followed the direction of my man's finger. There, 500 yards away, I saw a solitary buffalo feeding slowly along toward two low bushes, but on the further side of them. I did not think what rifle I held (it was a .450), but dashed forward at once. My gun-bearer was more thoughtful and brought with him my 577. We actually ran. When within eighty or ninety yards of the two bushes behind which the beast was now hidden, I slackened pace and approached more cautiously. My heart was beating and my hands trembling with the exertion of running when I reached the nearest bush, and my nerves were not exactly steadied by meeting the vicious gaze of a large buffalo, who stood not thirty feet on the other side. My gun-bearer in an instant forced the .577 into my hands, and I took aim at the shoulder of the brute and fired, without knowing exactly what I was doing. The smoke cleared, and there, almost in his tracks, lay my first buffalo. His ignorance of my noisy and careless approach was apparently accounted for by his great age. His hide was almost hairless and his horns worn blunt with many encounters. He must have been quite deaf and almost blind, or his behavior cannot be accounted for. The noise made by our approach, even with the favorable wind, was sufficient to frighten any animal, or at least put it on its guard.

My men, who were dreadfully afraid of big game of all sorts, when they saw the buffalo lying dead, danced with joy and exultation. They kicked the dead body and shouted curses at it. Camp was distant a good two hours' march, and the day was drawing to a close. The hungry howl of the hyenas warned me that my prize would soon be taken from me were it left unguarded. So piles of firewood were made and the carcass surrounded by a low wall of flames. I left three men in charge and set out for camp. There was but little light and my way lay through bits of forest and much bush. Our progress was slow, and my watch read 10:30 P. M. before I reached my tent and bed.

The following day I set out for a shooting ground distant two days' march from where I had been camped. Several rivers lay in my path and two tribes of natives. These natives inhabit thick forest and are in terror of strangers, as they are continually harassed by their neighbors. When they saw the smallness of my force, however, they endeavored to turn me aside, but without success. Quiet and determination generally win with these people. The rivers gave me more trouble, as they were deep and swift of current, and my friends, the natives, had removed all bridges. But none of the streams exceeded thirty feet in width, and an hour's hard work with our axes always provided us with a bridge.

The second day from my former camp brought me to the outskirts of the forest and the beginning of open country. I had hardly made camp before three Swahili traders came to me, and after the usual greetings began to weep in chorus. Their story was a common one. They had set out from Mombasa with twelve others to trade for slaves and ivory with the natives who inhabit the slopes of Kiliman-jaro. Fortune had favored them, and after four months they were on their way homeward with eighteen slaves and five good sized tusks. The first day's journey was just over when they were attacked by natives, three of their number slain and all their property stolen. In the darkness they could not distinguish what natives attacked them; but their suspicions rested on the very tribe among whom they had spent the four months, and from whom they had purchased the ivory and slaves. I gave them a little cloth and some food, and a note to my people at Taveta to help them on their way. Of course, they were slave traders, and as such ought possibly to have been beaten from my camp. But it is undoubtedly a fact that Mahomedans look on slave trading as a per-fectly legitimate occupation; and if people are not breaking their own laws, I cannot see that a stranger should treat them as brigands and refuse them the least aid when in distress. I know that my point of view in this matter has few supporters in civilization.

The next day, after a short march, I pitched my tent on the banks of a small stream, and then set out to prospect for game. I found nothing, but that night my slumbers were disturbed by the splashing and grunting of a herd of buffalo drinking.

These sounds kept me awake, so that I was enabled to make a very early start—setting out with four men at 4:45. The natives had assured me that the buffalo came to drink about midnight, and then fed slowly back to their favorite sleeping-places in the thick bush, reaching there just about sunrise. By making such an early start I hoped to come up with my quarry in the open places on the edge of the thick bush just before dawn, when the light is sufficiently bright to enable one to see the foresight of a rifle. Dew falls like rain in this part of the world, and we had not gone fifty paces in the long grass before we were soaking wet, and dismally cold to boot. My guide, cheered by the prospect of a good present, led us confidently along the most intricate paths and through the thickest bush. The moon overhead, which was in its fifteenth day, gave excellent light. Every now and then some creature would dash across our path, or stand snorting fearfully till we had passed. These were probably waterbuck and bushbuck. Toward half past five the light of the moon paled before the first glow of dawn, and we found ourselves on the outskirts of a treeless prairie, dotted here and there with bushes and covered with short dry grass. Across this plain lay the bush where my guide assured me the buffalo slept during the day, and according to him at that moment somewhere between me and this bush wandered at least 100 buffalo. There was little wind, and what there was came in gentle puffs against our right cheeks. I made a sharp detour to the left, walking quickly for some twenty minutes. Then, believing ourselves to be below the line of the buffalo, and therefore free to advance in their direction, we did so.

Just as the sun rose we had traversed the plain and stood at the edge of what my men called the *nyumba ya mbogo* (the buffalo's home). We were too late. Fresh signs everywhere showed that my guide had spoken the truth. Now I questioned him as to the bush; how thick it was, etc. At that my men fidgeted uneasily and murmured "Mr. Dawnay." This young Englishman had been killed by buffalo in the bush but four months before. However, two of my men volunteered to follow me, so I set out on the track of the herd.

This bush in which the buffalo live is not more than ten feet high, is composed of a network of branches and is covered with shiny green leaves; it has no thorns. Here and there one will meet with a stunted acacia, which, as if to show its spite against its more attractive neighbors, is clothed with nothing but the sharpest thorns. The buffalo, from constant wandering among the bush, have formed a perfect maze of paths. These trails are wide enough under foot, but meet just over one's shoulders, so that it is impossible to maintain an upright position. The paths run in all directions, and therefore one cannot see far ahead. Were it not for the fact that here and there—often 200 feet apart, however— are small open patches, it would be almost useless to enter such a fastness. These open places lure one on, as from their edges it is often possible to get a good shot. Once started, we took up the path which showed the most and freshest spoor, and, stooping low, pressed on as swiftly and noiselessly as possible. We had not gone far before we came upon a small opening, from the center of which rose an acacia not more than eight inches in thickness of trunk and perhaps eighteen feet high. It was forked at the height of a man's shoulder. I carried the 8-bore, and was glad of an opportunity to rest it in the convenient fork before me. I had just done so, when crash! snort! bellow! came several animals (presumably buffalo) in our direction. One gun-bearer literally flew up the tree against which I rested my rifle; the other, regardless of consequences, hurled his naked skin against another but smaller tree, also thorny; both dropped their rifles. I stood sheltered behind eight inches of acacia wood, with my rifle pointed in front of me and still resting in the fork of the tree. The noise of the herd approached nearer and nearer, and my nerves did not assume that steelly quality I had imagined always resulted from a sudden danger. Fly I could not, and the only tree climbable was already occupied; so I stood still.

Just as I looked for the appearance of the beasts in the little opening in which I stood, the crashing noise separated in two portions— each passing under cover on either side of the opening. I could see nothing, but my ears were filled with the noise. The uproar ceased, and I asked the negro in the tree what had happened. He said, when he first climbed the tree he could see the bushes in our front move like the waves of the sea, and then, *Ham del illah*—praise be to God—the buffalo turned on either side and left our little opening safe. Had they not turned, but charged straight at us, I fancy I should have had a disagreeable moment. As it was, I began to understand why buffalo shooting in the bush has been always considered unsafe, and began to regret that the road back to the open plain was not a shorter one. We reached it in safety, however, and, after a short rest, set out up wind.

I got a hartbeest and an mpallah before noon, and then, satisfied with my day, returned to camp. By 4 P. M. my men had brought in all the meat, and soon the little camp was filled with strips of fresh meat hanging on ropes of twisted bark. The next day we exchanged the meat for flour, beans, pumpkins and Indian corn. I remained in this camp three more days and then returned to Taveta. Each one of these days I attempted to get a shot at buffalo, but never managed it. On one occasion

I caught a glimpse of two of these animals in the open, but they were too wary to allow me to approach them.

When I reached Taveta, I found a capital camp had been built during my absence, and that a food supply had been laid in sufficient for several weeks. Shortly after my arrival I was startled by the reports of many rifles, and soon was delighted to grasp the hands of two compatriots—Dr. Abbott and Mr. Stevens. They had just returned from a shooting journey in Masai land, and reported game plenty and natives not troublesome. My intention was then formed to circumnavigate Mt. Kilimanjaro, pass over the yet untried shooting grounds and then to return to the coast.

I left five men in camp at Taveta in charge of most of my goods, and, taking 118 men with me, set out into Masai land. Even at this late date (1895) the Masai are reckoned dangerous customers. Up to 1889 but five European caravans had entered their territory, and all but the last—that of Dr. Abbott—had reported difficulties with the natives. My head man, a capital fellow, had had no experience with these people, and did not look forward with pleasure to making their acquaintance; but he received orders to prepare for a start with apparent cheerfulness. We carried with us one ton of beans and dried bananas as food supply. This was sufficient for a few weeks, but laid me under the necessity of doing some successful shooting, should I carry out my plan of campaign. Just on the borders of Masai land live the Useri people, who inhabit the northeast slopes of Kilimanjaro. We stopped a day or two with them to increase our food supply, and while the trading was going on I descended to the plain in search of sport.

I left camp at dawn and it was not till noon that I saw game. Then I discovered three rhinos; two together lying down, and one solitary, nearly 500 yards away from the others. The two lying down were nearest me, but were apparently unapproachable, owing to absolute lack of cover. The little plain they had chosen for their nap was as flat as a billiard table and quite bare of grass. The wind blew steadily from them and whispered me to try my luck, so I crawled cautiously toward them. When I got to within 150 yards, one of the beasts rose and sniffed anxiously about and then lay down again. The rhinoceros is nearly blind when in the bright sun—at night it can see like an owl.

I kept on, and when within 100 yards rose to my knees and fired one barrel of my .577. The rhinos leapt to their feet and charged straight at me. "Shall I load the other barrel or trust to only one?" This thought ran through my mind, but the speed of the animals' approach gave me no time to reply to it. My gun-bearer was making excellent time across the plain toward a group of trees, so I could make no use of the 8-bore. The beasts came on side by side, increasing their speed and snorting like steam engines as they ran. They were disagreeably close when I fired my second barrel and rose to my feet to bolt to one side. As I rose they swerved to the left and passed not twenty feet from me, apparently blind to my whereabouts. I must have hit one with my second shot, for they were too close to permit a miss. Perhaps that shot turned them. Be that as it may, I felt that I had had a narrow escape.

When these rhinos had quite disappeared, my faithful gun-bearer returned, and smilingly congratulated me on what he considered my good fortune. He then called my attention to the fact that rhinoceros number three was still in sight, and apparently undisturbed by what had happened to his friends. Between the beast and me, stretched an open plain for some 350 yards, then came three or four small trees, and then from these trees rose a semi-circular hill or rather ridge, on the crest of which stood the rhino. I made for the trees, and, distrusting my gun-bearer, took from him the .577 and placed it near one of them. Then, telling him to retire to a comfortable spot, I advanced with my 8-bore up the hill toward my game. The soil was soft as powder, so my footsteps made no noise. Cover, with the exception of a small skeleton bush, but fifty yards below the rhino, there was none. I reached the bush and knelt down behind it. The rhino was standing broadside on, motionless and apparently asleep. I rose and fired, and saw that I had aimed true, when the animal wheeled round and round in his track. I fired again, and he then stood still, facing me. I had one cartridge in my pocket and slipped it in the gun. As I raised the weapon to my shoulder, down the hill came my enemy. His pace was slow and I could see that he limped. The impetus given him by the descent kept him going, and his speed seemed to increase. I fired straight at him and then dropped behind the bush. He still came on and in my direction; so I leapt to my feet, and, losing my head, ran straight away in front of him. I should have run to one side and then up the hill. What was my horror, when pounding away at a good gait, not more than fifty feet in front of the snorting rhino, to find myself hurled to the ground, having twisted my ankle. I thought all was over, when I had the instinct to roll to one side and then scramble to my feet. The beast passed on. When he reached the bottom of the hill his pace slackened to a walk, and I returned to where I had left my .577 and killed him at my leisure. I found the 8-bore bullet had shattered his off hind leg, and that my second shot had penetrated his lungs. I had left the few men I had brought with me on a neighboring hill when I had first caught sight of the rhinos, and now sent for them. Not liking to waste the meat, I sent to camp for twenty porters to carry it back. I reached camp that night at 12:30 A. M., feeling quite worn out.

After a day's rest we marched to Tok-i-Tok, the frontier of Masai land. This place is at certain seasons of the year the pasture ground of one of the worst bands of Masai. I found it nearly deserted. The Masai I met said their brethren were all gone on a war raid, and that this was the only reason why I was permitted to enter the country. I told them that I had come for the purpose of sport, and hoped to kill much game in their country. This, however, did not appear to interest them, as the Masai never eat the flesh of game. Nor do they hunt any, with the exception of buffalo, whose hide they use for shields. I told them I was their friend and hoped for peace; but, on the other hand, was prepared for war should they attack me.

From Tok-i-Tok we marched in a leisurely manner to a place whose name means in English "guinea fowl camp." In this case it was a misnomer, for we were not so fortunate as to see one of these birds during our stay of several days. At this place we were visited by some fifty Masai warriors, who on the receipt of a small present danced and went away. The water at guinea fowl camp consisted of a spring which rises from the sandy soil and flows a few hundred yards, and then disappears into the earth. This is the only drinking-place for several miles, so it is frequented by large numbers and many varieties of game. At one time I have seen hartbeest, wildbeest, grantii, mpallah, Thomson's oryx, giraffes and rhinoceros.

We supported the caravan on meat. I used only the .450 Express; but my servant, George Galvin, who used the Winchester, did better execution with his weapon than I with mine.

Here, for the first and last time in my African experiences, we had a drive. Our camp was pitched on a low escarpment, at the bottom of which, and some 300 feet away, lay the water. The escarpment ran east and west, and extended beyond the camp some 500 yards, where it ended abruptly in a cliff forty or fifty feet high. Some of my men, who were at the end of the escarpment gathering wood, came running into camp and said that great numbers of game were coming toward the water. I took my servant and we ran to the end of the escarpment, where a sight thrilling indeed to the sportsman met our eyes. First came two or three hundred wildbeest in a solid mass; then four or five smaller herds, numbering perhaps forty each, of hartbeest; then two herds, one of mpallah and one of grantii. There must have been 500 head in the lot. They were approaching in a slow, hesitating manner, as these antelope always do approach water, especially when going down wind.

Our cover was perfect and the wind blowing

steadily in our direction. I decided, knowing that they were making for the water, and to reach it must pass close under where we lay concealed, to allow a certain number of them to pass before we opened fire. This plan worked perfectly. The animals in front slackened pace when they came to within fifty yards of us, and those behind pressed on and mingled with those in front. The effect to the eye was charming. The bright tan-colored skins of the hartbeest shone out in pleasing contrast to the dark gray wildbeest. Had I not been so young, and filled with youth's thirst for blood, I should have been a harmless spectator of this beautiful procession. But this was not to be. On catching sight of the water, the animals quickened their pace, and in a moment nearly half of the mass had passed our hiding-place. A silent signal, and the .450 and the Winchester, fired in quick succession, changed this peaceful scene into one of consternation and slaughter. Startled out of their senses, the beasts at first halted in their tracks, and then wheeling, as if at word of command, they dashed rapidly up wind—those in the rear receiving a second volley as they galloped by. When the dust cleared away, we saw lying on the ground below us four animals—two hartbeest and two wildbeest. I am afraid that many of those who escaped carried away with them proofs of their temerity and our bad marksmanship.

Ngiri, our next camp, is a large swamp, surrounded first by masses of tall cane and then by a beautiful though narrow strip of forest composed of tall acacias. It was at this place, in the thick bush which stretches from the swamp almost to the base of Kilimanjaro, that the Hon. Guy Dawnay, an English sportsman, had met his death by the horns of a buffalo but four months before. My tent was pitched within twenty paces of his grave and just under a large acacia, which serves as his monument, upon whose bark is cut in deep characters the name of the victim and the date of his mishap.

Here we made a strong zariba of thorns, as we had heard we should meet a large force of Masai in this neighborhood. I stopped ten days at Ngiri, and, with the exception of one adventure hardly worth relating, had no difficulty with the Masai. Undoubtedly I was very fortunate in finding the large majority of the Masai warriors, inhabiting the country through which I passed, absent from their homes. But at the same time I venture to think that the ferocity of these people has been much overrated, especially in regard to Europeans; for the force at my disposal was not numerous enough to overawe them had they been evilly disposed.

One morning, after I had been some days at Ngiri, I set out with twenty men to procure meat for the camp. The sun had not yet risen, and I was pursuing my way close to the belt of reeds which surrounds the swamp, when I saw in the dim light a black object standing close to the reeds. My men said it was a hippo, but as I drew nearer I could distinguish the outlines of a gigantic buffalo, broadside on and facing from the swamp. When I got to within what I afterwards found by pacing it off to be 103 paces, I raised my .577 to my shoulder, and, taking careful aim at the brute's shoulder, fired. When the smoke cleared away there was nothing in sight. Knowing the danger of approaching these animals when wounded, I waited until the sun rose, and then cautiously approached the spot. The early rays of the sun witnessed the last breathings of one of the biggest buffaloes ever shot in Africa. Its head is now in the Smithsonian Institute at Washington, and, according to the measurement made by Mr. Rowland Ward, Piccadilly, London, it ranks among the first five heads ever set up by him.

After sending the head, skin and meat back to camp, I continued my way along the shore of the swamp. The day had begun well and I hardly hoped for any further sport, but I was pleasantly disappointed.

Toward 11 o'clock I entered a tall acacia forest, and had not proceeded far in it before my steps were arrested by the sight of three elephants, lying down not 100 yards from me. They got our wind at once, and were up and off before I could get a shot. I left all my men but one gun-bearer on the outskirts of the forest and followed upon the trail of the elephant. I had not gone fifteen minutes before I had traversed the forest, and entered the thick and almost impenetrable bush beyond it. And hardly had I forced my way a few paces into this bush, when a sight met my eyes which made me stop and think. Sixty yards away, his head towering above the surrounding bush, stood a monstrous tusker. His trunk was curled over his back in the act of sprinkling

dust over his shoulders. His tusks gleamed
white and beautiful. He lowered his head,
and I could but just see the outline of his
skull and the tips of his ears. This time my
gun-bearer did not run. The sight of the ivory
stirred in him a feeling, which, in a Swahili,
often conquers fear—cupidity. I raised some
dust in my hand and threw it in the air, to see
which way the wind blew. It was favorable.
Then beckoning my gun-bearer, I moved forward at a slight angle, so as to come opposite
the brute's shoulder. I had gone but a few
steps when the bush opened and I got a good
sight of his head and shoulder. He was apparently unconscious of our presence and was lazily flapping his ears against his sides. Each
time he did this, a cloud of dust arose, and a
sound like the tap of a bass drum broke the
stillness. I fired my .577 at the outer edge of his
ear while it was lying for an instant against his
side. A crash of bush, then silence, and no elephant in sight. I began to think that I had been
successful, but the sharper senses of the negro
enabled him to know the contrary. His teeth
chattered, and for a moment he was motionless
with terror. Then he pointed silently to his
left. I stooped and looked under the bush. Not

twenty feet away was a sight which made me share the feelings of my gun-bearer. The elephant was the picture of rage; his forelegs stretched out in front of him, his trunk curled high in the air, and his ears lying back along his neck. I seized my 8-bore and took aim at his foreward knee, but before I could fire, he was at us. I jumped to one side and gave him a two-ounce ball in the shoulder, which apparently decided him on retreat. The bush was so thick that in a moment he was out of sight. I followed him for some time, but saw no more of him. His trail mingled with that of a large herd, which, after remaining together for some time, apparently separated in several directions. The day was blazing hot, and I was in the midst of a pathless bush, far away from my twenty men.

By 2 P. M., I had come up with them again and turned my face toward camp. On the way thither, I killed two zebras, a waterbuck and a Thomsonii. By the time the meat was cut up and packed on my men's heads the sun had set. The moon was magnificently bright and served to light our road. For one mile our way led across a perfectly level plain. This plain was covered with a kind of salt as white as snow, and with the bright moon every object was as easily distinguished as by day. The fresh meat proved an awkward load for my men, and we frequently were forced to stop while one or the other re-arranged the mass he carried. They were very cheery about it, however, and kept shouting to one another how much they would enjoy the morrow's feast. Their shouts were answered by the mocking wails of many hyenas, who hovered on our flanks and rear like a pursuing enemy. I shot two of these beasts, which kept their friends busy for a while, and enabled us to pursue our way in peace.

This white plain reaches nearly to the shores of Ngiri Swamp on the north, and to the east it is bounded by a wall of densely thick bush. We had approached to within 400 yards of the point where the line of bush joins the swamp, when I noticed a small herd of wildbeest walking slowly toward us, coming from the edge of the swamp. A few moments later, a cry escaped from my gun-bearer, who grasped my arm and whispered eagerly, *simba*. This means lion. He pointed to the wall of bush, and near it, crawling on its belly toward the wildbeest, was the form of a lion. I knelt down and raised the night sight of my .450, and fired at the moving form. The white soil and the bright moon actually enabled me to distinguish the yellow color of its skin. A loud growl answered the report of my rifle, and I could see the white salt of the plain fly as the lion ran round and round in a circle, like a kitten after its tail. I fired my second barrel and the lion disappeared. The wildbeest had made off at the first shot. I tried, in the eagerness of youth, to follow the lion in the bush; but soon common sense came to my rescue, and warned me that in this dark growth the chances were decidedly in favor of the lion's getting me, and so gave up the chase. Now, if I had only waited till the great cat had got one of the wildbeest, I feel pretty sure I should have been able to dispose of it at my leisure. When I returned to camp, I ungratefully lost sight of the good luck I had had, and gnashed my teeth at the thought that I had missed bringing home a lion and an elephant. I was not destined to see a lion again on this journey, but my annoyance at my ill fortune was often whetted by hearing them roar.

However, by good luck and by George's help, I succeeded in securing one elephant.

The story of how this happened shall be the last hunting adventure recorded in this article. We had left Ngiri and were camped at the next water, some ten miles to the west. I had been out after giraffes and had not been unsuccessful, and therefore had reached camp in high good humor, when George came to me and said things were going badly in camp— that the men had decided to desert me should I try to push further on into the country; and that both head men seemed to think further progress was useless with the men in such temper. I was puzzled what to do, but wasted no time about making up my mind to do something. I went into the tent and called the two head men to me. After a little delay, they came, greeted me solemnly and at a motion from me crouched on their hams. There is but little use in allowing a negro to state a grievance, particularly if you know it is an imaginary one. The mere act of putting their fancied wrongs into words magnifies them in their own minds, and renders them less likely to listen to reason. My knowledge of Swahili at this time did not permit me to address them in their own language, so I spoke to them in English, knowing that they understood at least a few words of that tongue. I told them that I was determined to push on; that I knew that porters were like sheep and were perfectly under the control of the head men; consequently, should anything happen, I would know on whom to fix the blame. I repeated this several times, and emphasized it with dreadful threats, then motioned for them to leave the tent. I cannot say that I passed a comfortable night. Instead of songs and laughter, an ominous stillness reigned in the camp, and, though my words had been brave, I knew that I was entirely at the mercy of the men.

Before dawn we were under way, keeping a strict watch for any signs of mutiny. But, though the men were sullen, they showed no signs of turning back. Our road lay over a wide plain, everywhere covered thickly with lava, the aspect of which was arid in the extreme.

No more green buffalo bush, no more acacias, tall and beautiful, but in their place rose columns of dust, whirled hither and thither by the vagrant wind. Two of my men had been over this part of the road before, but they professed to be ignorant of the whereabouts of the next water place. Any hesitation on my part would have been the signal for a general retreat, so there was nothing for it but to assume a look of the utmost indifference, and to assure them calmly that we should find water. At noon the appearance of the country had not changed. My men, who had incautiously neglected to fill their water bottles in the morning, were beginning to show signs of distress.

Suddenly my gun-bearer, pointing to the left, showed me two herds of elephants approaching us. The larger herd, composed principally of bulls, was nearer to us, and probably got our wind; for they at once turned sharply to their right and increased their pace. The other herd moved on undisturbed. I halted the caravan, told the men to sit down and went forward to meet the elephants, with my servant and two gun-bearers. I carried a .577, my servant carried the old 12-bore by Lang, his cartridges crammed to the muzzle with powder. We were careful to avoid giving the elephants our wind, so we advanced parallel to them, but in a direction opposite to that in which they were going. As they passed us we crouched, and they seemed unconscious of our presence. They went about 400 yards past us, and then halted at right angles to the route they had been pursuing. There were five elephants in this herd—four large, and one small one, bringing up the rear. Some 60 yards on their right flank was a small skeleton bush, and, making a slight detour, we directed our course toward that. The leading animal was the largest, so I decided to devote our attention to that one. I told George to fire at the leg and I would try for the heart. We fired simultaneously, George missing and my shot taking effect altogether too high.

Two things resulted from the discharge of our rifles: the gun-bearers bolted with their weapons and the elephants charged toward us in line of battle. As far as I can calculate, an elephant at full speed moves 100 yards in about ten seconds, so my readers can judge how much time elapsed before the elephants were upon us. We fired again. My shot did no execution, but George, who had remained in a kneeling position, broke the off foreleg of the leading animal at the knee. It fell, and the others at once stopped. We then made off, and watched from a little distance a most interesting sight.

The condition of the wounded elephant seemed to be known to the others, for they crowded about her and apparently offered her assistance. She placed her trunk on the back of one standing in front of her and raised herself to her feet, assisted by those standing around. They actually moved her for some distance, but soon got tired of their kindly efforts. We fired several shots at them, which only had the effect of making two of the band charge in our direction and then return to their stricken comrade. Cover there was none, and with our bad marksmanship it would have been (to say the least) brutal to blaze away at the gallant little herd. Besides, cries of "water!" "water!" were heard coming from my thirsty caravan. So there was nothing for it but to leave the elephant, take the people to water, if we could find it, and then return and put the wounded animal out of its misery.

An hour and a half later we reached water, beautiful and clear, welling up from the side of a small hill. This is called Masimani. On reaching the water, all signs of discontent among my people vanished, and those among them who were not Mahomedans, and therefore had no scruples about eating elephant meat, raised a cheerful cry of *tembo tamu*—elephant is sweet. I did not need a second hint, but returned, and, finding the poor elephant deserted by its companions, put it out of its misery. It was a cow with a fine pair of tusks. The sun was setting, and my men, knowing that activity was the only means of saving their beloved elephant meat from hyenas, attacked the body with fury—some with axes, others with knives and one or two with sword bayonets. It was a terrible sight, and I was glad to leave them at it and return to camp, well satisfied with my day's work.

From Masimani, for the next four days, the road had never been trodden by even an Arab caravan. I had no idea of the whereabouts of water, nor had my men; but, having made a success of the first day's march, the men followed me cheerfully, believing me possessed of magic power and certain to lead them over a well-watered path. A kind providence did actually bring us to water each night. The country was so dry that it was absolutely deserted by the inhabitants, the Masai, and great was the surprise of the Kibonoto people when we reached there on the fourth day. They thought that we had dropped from the clouds, and said there could not have been any water over the road we had just come. These Kibonoto people had never been visited by an European, but received us kindly. The people of Kibonoto are the westernmost inhabitants on the slopes of Kilimanjaro.

From there to Taveta our road was an easy one, lying through friendly peoples. After a brief rest at Taveta, I returned to the coast, reaching Zanzibar a little over six months after I had set out from it.

Perhaps a word about the climate of the part of the country through which I passed will not be amiss. Both my servant and myself suffered from fever, but not to any serious extent. If a sedentary life is avoided—and this is an easy matter while on a journey—if one avoids morning dews and evening damps, and protects his head and the back of his neck from the sun, I do not think the climate of East Africa would be hurtful to any ordinarily healthy person. For my part, I do not think either my servant or myself have suffered any permanent ill effects from our venture; and yet the ages of twenty-one and seventeen are not those best suited for travels in the tropics.

W. A. Chanler.

A MOUNTAIN SHEEP.

To the Gulf of Cortez

About a year ago, my brother, who is a
very sagacious physician, advised me to take
the fresh liver of a mountain sheep for certain
nervous symptoms which were troublesome.
None of the local druggists could fill the
prescription, and so it was decided that I
should seek the materials in person. With me
went my friend J. B., the pearl of companions, and we began the campaign by outfit-
ting at San Diego, with a view to exploring
the resources of the sister republic in the peninsula of Lower California. Lower California is very different from Southern California. The latter is—well, a paradise, or
something of that kind, if you believe the inhabitants, of whom I am an humble fraction.
The former is what you may please to think.

At San Diego we got a man, a wagon, four
mules and the needed provisions and kitchen
—all hired at reasonable rates, except the
provisions and kitchen, which we bought.

Then we tried to get a decent map, but were foiled. The Mexican explorer will find the maps of that country a source of curious interest. Many of them are large and elaborately mounted on cloth, spreading to a great distance when unfolded. The political divisions are marked with a tropical profusion of bright colors, which is very fit. A similar sense of fitness and beauty leads the designer to insert mountain ranges, rivers and towns where they best please the eye, and I have had occasion to consult a map which showed purely ideal rivers flowing across a region where nature had put the divide of the highest range in the State.

My furniture contained a hundred cartridges, a belt I always carry, given by a friend, with a bear's head on the buckle (a belt which has held, before I got it, more fatal bullets than any other west of the Rockies), and my usual rifle. J. B. prepared himself in a similar way, except the belt.

Starting south from San Diego, we crossed the line at Tia Juana, and spent an unhappy day waiting on the custom house officials. They, however, did their duty in a courteous manner, and we, with a bundle of stamped papers, went on. The only duties we paid were those levied on our provisions. The team and wagon were entered free under a prospector's license for thirty days, and an obliging stableman signed the necessary bond.

The main difficulty in traveling in Lower California lies in the fact that you can get no feed for your animals. From Tia Juana east to Tecate, where you find half a dozen hovels, there is hardly a house and not a spear of grass for thirty miles. At Tecate there is a little nibbling. Thence south for twenty-five miles we went to the Agua Hechicera, or witching water; thence east twenty-five miles more to Juarez, always without grass; thence south to the ranch house of the Hansen ranch, at El Rayo, twenty-five miles more. There, at last, was a little grass, but after passing that point we camped at Agua Blanca, and were again without grass for thirty miles to the Trinidad Valley, which once had a little grass, now eaten clean. Fortunately we were able to buy hay at Tia Juana, and took some grain. Fortunately, also, we found some corn for sale at Juarez. So, with constant graining, a little hay and a supply of grass, either absent or contemptible, we managed to pull the stock through.

Besides our four hired mules there was another, belonging to our man, Oscar, which we towed behind to pack later. The animal was small in size, but pulled back from 200 pounds to a ton at every step. Its sex was female, but its name was Lazarus, for the overwhelming necessity of naming animals of the ass tribe either Lazarus or Balaam tramples on all distinctions of mere sex. We started, prepared for a possible, though improbable, season of rain; but we did not count on extreme cold, yet the first night out the water in our bucket froze, and almost every night it froze from a mere skin to several inches thick. To give an idea of the country, I will transcribe from a brief diary a few descriptions. Starting from Tia Juana, we drove or packed for nearly 200 miles in a southeasterly direction, until we finally sighted the Gulf and the mountains of Sonora in the distance. At first our road lay through low mountains, in valleys abounding in cholla cactus. From Tecate southward, the country was rolling and clotteotted with brushwood, until you reach Juarez. Juarez is an abandoned, or almost abandoned, placer camp. Here, amid the countless pits of the miners, the piñons begin, and then, after a short distance, the pine barrens stretch for forty miles. Beyond again you pass into hills of low brush, and plains covered with sage and buckweed, until finally you cross a divide into the broad basin of the Trinidad Valley. This is a depression some twenty miles long and perhaps five miles wide on the average, with a hot spring and a house at the southwestern end, walled on the southeast by the grim frowning rampart of the San Pedro Martir range, and on the other sides by mountains of lesser height, but equal desolation.

We had intended at first to strike for the Cocopah range, near the mouth of the Colorado River, and there do our hunting. Several reasons induced us to change our plan and make for the Hansen ranch, where deer were said to be plenty and sheep not distant; so we turned from Tecate southward, made one dry camp and one camp near Juarez, and on the fifth day of our journeying reached a long meadow, called the Bajio Largo, on the Hansen ranch. We turned from the road and followed the narrow park-like opening for four miles, camping in high pines, with water near, and enough remnants of grass to amuse the animals. This region of pine barrens occurs at quite an elevation, and the nights were cold. The granite core of the country crops out all along in low broken hills, the intervening mesas consisting of granite sand and gravel, and bearing beside the pines a good deal of brush. Thickets of manzanita twisted their blood-colored trunks over the ground, and the tawny stems of the red-shank covered the country for miles. The red-shank is a lovely shrub, growing about six or eight feet high, with broom-like foliage of a yellowish green, possessing great fragrance. If you simply smell the uncrushed shoots, they give a faint perfume, somewhat suggestive of violets; and if you crush the leaves you get a more pungent odor, sweet and a little smoky. Also, the gnarled roots of the red-shank make an excellent cooking fire, if you can wait a few hours to have them burn to coals. All things considered, the pine barren country is very attractive, and if there were grass, water and game, it would be a fine place for a hunter.

From our camp at Bajio Largo, J. B. and I went hunting for deer, which were said to be plentiful. We hunted from early morning till noon, seeing only one little fellow, about the size of a jack rabbit, scuttle off in the brush. Then we decided to go home. This, however, turned out to be a large business. The lofty trees prevented our getting any extended view, and the stony gulches resembled each other to an annoying degree. At last even the water seemed to flow the wrong way. So we gave up the attempt to identify landmarks, and, following our sense of direction and taking our course from the sun, we finally came again to the long meadow, and, traveling down that, we came to camp. Here we violated all rules by shooting at a mark—our excuse was that we had decided to leave the vicinity without further hunting; and, at all events, we spoiled a sardine box, to Oscar's great admiration.

In order to get a fair day's journey out of a fair day, we had to rise at 4 or 5 o'clock. Oscar once or twice borrowed my watch to wake by, but the result was only that I had to borrow J. B.'s watch to wake Oscar by; so I afterwards retained the timepiece, and got up early enough to start Oscar well on his duties.

The question of fresh meat had now become important. We left Bajio Largo and drove to Hansen's Laguna, a shallow pond over a mile long, much haunted by ducks. Here we made a bad mistake, driving six or eight miles into the mountains, only to reach nowhere and be forced to retrace our steps. Night, however, found us at El Rayo, the Hansen ranch house, and, as it turned out, the real base of our hunting campaign. The Hansen ranch is an extensive tract, named after an old Swede, who brought a few cattle into the country years ago. The cattle multiplied exceedingly, to the number, indeed, of several thousand, and can be seen at long range by the passer-by. They are very wild and gaunt at present, and will prance off among the rocks at a surprising rate before a man can get within 200 yards of them. Ex-Governor Ryerson now owns these cattle, and his major-domo, Don Manuel Murillo, a fine gray-haired veteran, learning that I had known the Governor, gave me much friendly advice, and sent his son to guide us well on the road to the Trinidad Valley and the sheep land. He also provided us with potatoes and fresh meat, so that we lived fatly thenceforth.

Our track lay past an abandoned saw-mill, built by the International Company. Thence we were to go to Agua Blanca, the last water to be had on the road; for the next thirty miles are dry. The saw-mill was built to supply timber to the mining town of Alamo, some twenty-five miles south. The camp is now in an expiring state and needs no timber, but is said to shelter some rough and violent men. The road from the mill was deep in sand, and our pace was slow. The darkness was coming cold and fast when we finally drove on to the water and halted to camp.

Two men were there before us, with a saddle-horse each, and no other apparent equipment. When we arrived, the men were watering their animals, and at once turned their backs, so as not to be recognized. Then they retired to the brush. We supped and staked out the mules, and then sent Oscar to look up our neighbors. Oscar went and shouted, but got no answer, and could find no men. We thought that our mules were in some danger, and J. B., who is a yachtsman, proposed to keep anchor watch. So Oscar remained awake till midnight, when he awoke me and retired freezing, saying that he had seen the enemy prowling around. I took my gun and visited the mules in rotation till 2:30. Then J. B. awoke, chattering with cold, but determined, and kept faithful guard until 5, when we began our day with a water-bucket frozen solid.

All our property remained safe, and a distant fire twinkling in the brush showed that our neighbors were still there. After breakfast Oscar again sought the hostile camp, and finally found a scared and innocent French-man, who cried out, on recognizing his visitor:

"Holy Mary! I took you for American rob-bers from the line, and I have lain awake all night, watching my horses."

From Agua Blanca we drove across the Santa Catarina ranch, for the most part plain and mesa, covered with greasewood and buck-brush. This latter shrub looks much like sage, except that its leaves are of a yellow-green in-stead of a blue-green. It is said to furnish the chief nutrition for stock on several great ran-ches. Certainly there was no visible grass, but buckbrush can hardly be fattening. Toward night, we crossed the pass into the Trinidad Valley and drove down a grade not steep only, but sidelong, where the wagons both went tobogganing down and slid rapidly toward the gulch. The mules held well, however, and be-fore dark we were camped near the hot spring at the house of Alvarez.

To the Gulf of Cortez

Our friend, Don Manuel Murillo, had recommended us both to Alvarez and to his sister, Señora Paula, but both of these were absent. Don Manuel had also urged us to get the Indian Anastasio for a guide.

"For heaven's sake," he said, "don't venture without a guide. You may perish from thirst, as others have done before you."

We tried at first to hire burros and let our mules rest, but the Indian who owned the burros stated that his terms were "one burro, one day, one dollar"—an impudent attempt at robbery, which we resented.

We interviewed Anastasio, however, who said he would start at any moment; and, leaving Oscar to guard the wagon, we packed two mules, saddled two more for J. B. and myself, and, giving Anastasio the tow-rope of a pack-mule, we started after him. Anastasio was the most interesting figure of the trip, and I must be pardoned if I go into some detail about him. He spoke some Spanish and understood a good deal. When he did not understand, he never stated that fact, but either assumed a stony look or answered at cross-purposes; so that we did not get to know a great deal about each other for some time.

He had, too, a lingering remnant of the distrust of horses and mules that his ancestors must have felt in Spanish times, and when his pack-mule got a stone in her hoof, he observed it with anxiety from a distance, but could not summon resolution to meddle with so serious a matter.

Moreover his measure of distance was primitive. I would ask, for instance, how many miles it was to our next stop. He might say three miles for an all-day journey of six times that length, or he might tell you that we were nine miles from a spot which we reached in half an hour.

I then substituted leagues for miles, thinking that the Mexican usage would be more familiar to him; but at last Anastasio said, rather impatiently, that all this business of leagues and miles was rather confusing and outside of his experience. We would reach the next water shortly before sunset, and that was all the calculation he was accustomed to, and quite close enough.

Aside from his knowledge of Spanish, Anastasio was indeed a fine representative of the best of the stone age, and as we journeyed on, one got an excellent idea of the life of the savage here in early times. About 3 o'clock in the afternoon, we reached the only water spot on the trail. Anastasio parted some withered reeds, and, looking earnestly, said, "Dry." A short distance further up, he repeated the word, and yet again, till, at his fourth attempt, he said, "Very little," and we camped. By scraping away the mud and grass, we got a small gravelly hole, and dipped out the slowly seeping water, a cup at a time. We thus managed to give each of the mules a little in a pan, and to get a canteen full for cooking.

Then I noticed Anastasio gathering wood, which I thought at first was for general use, but I found it was a private pile, to be used, so to speak, for bedding. Anastasio did not take the ax to secure his wood, but smashed off mesquite branches with a rock or pulled out some old root. He quite despised piñon and juniper logs, saying they gave no heat—meaning, probably, that they burned out too soon.

We turned in soon after supper, and the night was cold. Anastasio said he feared snow. The reason for his fear was soon evident. My bed was about twenty feet from Anastasio's, and during the night I would turn and watch him. He carried but one small blanket of about the texture of a gunny sack. He lighted a long smouldering fire, stripped himself naked, except a breech-clout, and, with his back to the coals and his front protected by his gauzy blanket, he slept until the cold roused him, when he put on more wood and slept again. I offered him four pairs of warm horse blankets to sleep in, but that was not the thing. He said that he needed to have the fire strike him in the small of the back, and that he slept in that way always. So throughout the night, in my wakeful moments, I saw the light reflected from his mahogany person. Evidently snow or cold rain would be disastrous to people who need a fire all night; for, with no covering against the cold and with fires extinguished by storm, they might easily freeze to death.

We were packed and marching at 7:30 next morning, and to those who know the inwardness of packing in winter, that statement means a good deal. It means, for instance, that J. B. got up, at my summons, long before dawn and cooked a splendid breakfast, and that the mules were caught and grained and saddled, and the packs made and lashed, by the earliest sun.

To the Gulf of Cortez

J. B. was a wonder. He seemed to enjoy giving his fellow mortals the best breakfasts and suppers—for we never had any midday meals—that our supplies could furnish. Always rising at the first call, in the dark, sometimes with an accompaniment of snow or rain, he managed the commissariat to perfection.

I in my humble way packed and saddled and did other necessary work, and Anastasio regarded us with benevolent curiosity, though always ready to get wood or water or mules when we asked him to do so.

We were now approaching the true desert. This term is not restricted to the broad level sand wastes along the Gulf, but includes the arid and waterless mountains adjacent, and this must be borne in mind when the Mexicans tell you that sheep are to be found in the desert.

We passed the last of the brushy hills, and, crossing a small divide, came over slopes of volcanic cinders to a little water spot with dwarf willows and grass. This was our hunting camp. The country through which our route had lain heretofore was altogether granitic, though one could see hills apparently of stratified material in the distance. Toward the desert, we met beds of conglomerate and trachyte, and mountains covered with slide-rock, ringing flint-like clinkers from some great volcanic furnace. But doubtless some accurate and industrious German has described all this, in a work on the geology of the peninsula, and to that valuable treatise I will refer you for further facts.

The vegetation had somewhat changed. There were more cactuses, particularly the fleshy kind called venaga, though I noticed with surprise the absence of the great fruit-bearing cactuses, the saguarro and pitaya, all along our route. The Spanish daggers were very numerous, as were also mescal plants, both of these forming veritable thickets in places.

The venaga cactus is similar to the bis-naga, found in other parts of Mexico, except in the disposition and curvature of the thorns. They are stumpy plants, growing from a foot to three feet or so in height, and a foot or more in diameter, like a thickset post. Those of us who delighted in Mayne Reid's "Boy Hunters" will remember how the adventurous young men saved themselves from dying of thirst by laying open these succulent cactuses with their long hunting knives and drinking the abundant juices. I have often and faithfully tried to perform the same feat, out of reverence for my heroes, but failed to find anything juicier than, say, a raw turnip—by no means satisfying as a drink. The venagas are found on the mountains where sheep haunt, with their hard prickly rinds broken and the interior hollowed out, and Anastasio said that the sheep do this by knocking holes in the cactus with their horns and then eating the inside.

This cactus country makes the third variety of wilderness encountered in the peninsula. There are four: First, and best, the pine barrens; second, the brushy hills and plains, covered with sage, greasewood and buckweed; third, this spike-bearing volcanic region; and fourth, the appalling desolation of the acknowledged desert.

The moment we had unloaded and watered our animals, Anastasio and I set out to look for deer. Anastasio wore the spotted and tattered remnant of a frock-coat, once green, given him by an Englishman, of whom I shall say more later. He had guarachis, or sandals, on his feet, bare legs, a breech-clout, and on his head a reddish bandanna handkerchief in the last stages of decay; and as he peered over some rock, glaring long and earnestly in search of game, he reminded one of those lean and wolfish Apaches that Remington draws in a way so dramatic and so full of grim significance.

Anastasio was fifty-one years old and had no upper incisors, but the way he flung his gaunt leathern shanks over those mountains of volcanic clinkers, armed with the poisoned bayonets of myriads of mescal, cactus and Spanish dagger, was astonishing.

I told him that I was not racing and that he would scare the game. In fact, he did start one little fellow, but he said he always saw the game first, and for this day I was quite powerless to hold him in; so I decided to return to camp before dark. This disgusted Anastasio greatly. "In this way we shall never kill," said he. "We are going to suffer from hunger." I assured him that we had plentiful supplies, but he had come for meat. Unbounded meat had been the chief incentive for his trip, and hungry he was determined to be.

The next day J. B. set out early with the red

man. I arranged camp, and two or three hours later took what I supposed was a different direction, but soon encountered the pair returning. J. B. had a painful knee, and Anastasio had started his racing tactics and kept them up until J. B. was quite lame.

The Indian reported that he had seen sheep. J. B. had used the glass without finding them, and then Anastasio had captured it and looked through the wrong end, nodding and saying he could count five, very big. This, I am sorry to say, was false and affected on Anastasio's part, and J. B. was skeptical about the sheep altogether; but I knew how hard it was to find distant game, when you don't know exactly how it should appear. To reach the supposed sheep, the mountain must be climbed and the crest turned, for the wind permitted no other course. J. B. did not feel up to the task, and I directed him to camp. Anastasio and I climbed for about four hours, and reached a position whence his sheep would be visible. He was now discontented because J. B. had not lent him his gun. No request had been made for the gun, to be sure, but I confess that a request would have met with my earnest opposition in any event. Evidently Anastasio's expectations of fresh meat were now so dim as to cast serious shadows on my skill as a hunter; but, resigning himself to the inevitable, he crawled to the summit of the ridge for a view. He stared long and said he could make out one ewe lying down under a juniper. I tried the glass. He was right. His unaided sight seemed about equal in definition to my field-glass. On this occasion he declined to use the glass, even with some appearance of disgust. We could get no nearer unseen, and, though the distance was very great, I decided to risk a shot.

I fired, in fact, two or three shots at the ewe, alarming her greatly, when from beneath a cliff which lay below us a band streamed out. Two big rams started off to the right. Anastasio and I ran down a bit, and I tried a long shot at the leading ram. The distance was great, and the run had pumped me a little. I missed. The second ram was still larger. He stopped a moment at 150 yards and I dropped him. Anastasio grunted satisfaction. I swung to the left, where the rest of the band was journeying, sighted at the shoulder of a young ram and fired. The ball passed through my intended victim, dropping him, and entered

ROCKY MOUNTAIN AND POLO'S SHEEP, DRAWN TO SAME SCALE.

the eye of a yearling ram who stood behind, thus killing two rams at one shot—a most unusual accident.

The rest of the band were now quite distant, and, though I fired several shots, at Anastasio's desire—he said he wanted a fat ewe—none took effect.

I cleaned the sheep and skinned out the big head. Anastasio took one small ram entire on his back, supporting it by a rope passed over the top of his head, and started down with it, while I followed after with the big horns. It was 1 o'clock. The head might have weighed thirty-five pounds fresh. It grew to weigh 1,500 pounds before dark. Stumbling down through the slide-rock, with legs full of venomous prickers, I passed below camp without noticing it, and was well on the other side, when I thought I had gone about far enough, and shouted. J. B.'s voice answered across a small hill, and I discovered that he had never reached camp at all, but had found a water spot, and wisely decided not to leave it without good reason.

I scouted a bit to the west, but found unfamiliar country, and, as the sun had set, we were seemingly about to stay by that water all night, when I turned around and saw a pale column of smoke rising above the crest of the ridge against the evening sky.

At once we marched around the ridge, and, as we rose over the divide, we saw the whole hillside flaming with signal fires. Our dear old Anastasio had become alarmed and set fire to fifteen or twenty dead mescals in different places to guide us home. God bless a good Indian!

With vast content we prepared and ate a luxurious supper. Anastasio, however, fearing that he might be hungry in the night, impaled all the ribs of one side of the ram on a pole and planted it in a slanting position over the fire. Thus he was enabled to put in his time during his wakeful moments, and face the prospect of a remote breakfast without discouragement.

The next day, I spent the morning in washing, resting, and cutting spikes out of my legs. Anastasio packed in the second small ram, and ate ribs and slept. Then, in the afternoon, we got the rest of the big fellow down. Anastasio, to make his load lighter, smashed off the shanks with a stone, although he carried a knife in his belt—a striking trick of heredity.

And then we talked. "The Trinidad Valley is not my country," said Anastasio; "this is my country. Yonder, under that red rock on the mountain side, about five miles away, there is a spring in the gulch on the edge of the desert. I was born there, and lived there twenty years with my father's family. Here where your camp is"—about twenty feet square of slide-rock level enough to stand on—"we sowed crops. We scraped a hole between the stones with our hands, put in squash seeds, watered them by carrying water from the spring in our hands and raised several hills."

So he went on, not in so connected a way, but showing, bit by bit, his manner of life. His tribe, which he called the Kil-ee-ou, must have been very restricted in numbers at best. His territory was a few leagues of desert, or almost desert, mountains, every yard of which he knew by heart, while just over the ridge dwelt the Cocopahs, his mortal enemies. Sometimes a score of men armed with bows would start a tribal hunt for deer, though the sheep were beyond their means of attack. Sometimes they journeyed a few leagues to the Gulf to eat mussels. We could see the great blue sheet and the leagues of salt incrustations glimmering white on the hither side, and at one spot on the horizon the blue peak of some Sonora mountain rose out of the seeming ocean.

But a few deer and mussels and a half dozen hills of squashes could not fill the abyss of the Indian appetite. The stand-by was roasted mescal. These plants grow in great numbers in the country adjoining the desert, and at every season there are some just right for roasting. The Indians selected these and cooked them for two or three days in a hole in the ground, by a process called tatema, similar in principle to a clam-bake. This roasting converts the starchy leaves and heart into a sugary mass, so that the resulting food is something like a sweet fibrous beet. The Indian's life really lay in gathering and roasting mescal. And when a storm prevented the necessary fires, the tribe passed days, often many days, without food.

So much for Anastasio's early life. A year ago, he told us, he went hunting with two Americans. One of them came from under the earth, where there were six months of night, and had passed two seas and been a month on the train. We supposed, from this, that Anastasio had served as guide to an Englishman, whose home he described at the Antipodes. The six months of night were, perhaps, represented by the London fogs, and, if he passed a month on the train, he must have come by the Southern Pacific. The Englishman had presented Anastasio with the very undesirable gaberdine I have before described. Anastasio said that the Englishman shot quail in the head every time with his rifle, but on meeting a band of eleven sheep he fired nine shots without hitting. Anastasio said he trembled, but I incline to think that the Indian had run him out of breath. Finally the Englishman secured two ewes and a lamb, after three weeks of hunting.

Look at my fortune! A single day on the mountain, and three rams to show for it; one with horns that are an abiding splendor—sixteen inches around the base and forty-two inches on the outer sweep.

I thought at first that the horns made more than one complete spiral, but, on leveling them carefully, I saw that the entire curve would not be complete without the points, which were smashed off. In this connection it is only fair to consider that I carried my lucky bear's head belt, and invariably sacrificed to the Sun, as several ragged garments, hung on spikes and branches, may still testify.

The weather threatened storm. J. B.'s leg would not permit him to hunt. Anastasio was full of meat, eating roasted ribs night and day, beside his regular meals, and we decided to retreat.

I noticed that the sheep hides had little of the under wool that the Northern sheep have in December, nor were the animals fat, though the flesh was sweet and tender, and the livers had their desired medicinal effect.

Anastasio said it was customary to hunt in summer, when the sheep were fat, and were compelled to resort to the water holes. Aside from the meanness of taking advantage of the animals' necessities, the summer is a bad season for hunting, both because the flesh is rank and spoils quickly, and the heat and insects are intolerable.

We packed our mules in a gentle rain, and Anastasio made a great bundle of rejected meat for his own use. To get rope, he slightly roasted the leaves of the Spanish dagger, tore the hot spikes in shreds with his tough fingers and knotted the fragments into a strong, pliable cord.

In two days we were again in the Trinidad Valley, and in two days more—one of them passed in facing a cold, driving storm, of great violence—we had reached our old friend, Don Manuel Murillo, at El Rayo. Here we lay over a day to rest the animals, and Don Manuel again played the part of a good angel in letting us have some hay.

I tried a shot at a duck on a little pond. The shot was a costly success. The duck died, but I had to wade for his remains through many yards of frozen mud and dirty water. The duck, though lean, was tender. My last hunt was for deer at El Rayo, with a boy of Don Manuel's for guide. Toward noon I saw two deer and shot them. I do not at present know just how to class them. The tail is that of the ordinary mule-deer, or black-tail, of Colorado and Montana, but there is no white patch on the rump.

The most of the deer in Lower, as well as in Southern, California have little white on their rumps, as in these specimens, but the upper surface of the tail is generally dark. The majority of the animals also are smaller than the typical mule-deer of our Northern States, but whether the differences between the two are great enough and constant enough to form a defined variety, some more competent naturalist must decide. Pending authoritative decision, I will submit, as a working theory of a purely amateur kind, this suggestion: that the Mexicans are right in saying that the northern zone of their country contains two varieties of deer—one a large animal, called "buro," identical with our Northern mule-deer; the other called "venado," a mule-deer too, but only a cousin of the "buro," much smaller, and with the white parts of the mask, throat, rump and tail either absent or much diminished in extent.

Our journey home was accomplished in the worst weather. Snow, cold rain, gales of surprising fury, made life a struggle; but we jumped at every chance for progress, and finally crossed the line twenty-five days after we had left it—tired, ragged, dirty, but with our mules alive and our hearts contented.

Our experience of the peninsula indicated that there were few inhabitants of any kind, brute or human. We saw hardly a dozen rabbits on the trip. There were some quail and many ducks, but the latter were visitors only. Deer were very scarce, and there were but a few half-wild cattle visible.

As for human beings, there was not an inhabited house on our road from Alvarez Place, in the Trinidad Valley, to El Rayo, a distance of fifty-five miles; nor from El Rayo to Juarez, twenty-five miles more. Indeed, except for the few hovels at Tecate, the houses for the rest of the way were hardly more numerous. And yet we had a strong impression that the country had nearly all the population it could support. Given a moderately dry year, and the part of Lower California which we visited can be thought fit only for bogus land companies and goose-egg mines; or, yes, it might be an ideal spot for a health resort or a penal colony.

George H. Gould.

A Canadian Moose Hunt

In October, 1893, I made an extended trip with my brother into the country around the head waters of the Ottawa. Our original plan, to push northward toward the "Height of Land" after caribou, was frustrated by high winds, which made travel on the large lakes slow and dangerous. The crossing of a ten-mile lake, which could be accomplished in a morning if calm, would consume several days with a high wind blowing, necessitating a tedious coasting on the windward shore. After much delay from this cause and from heavy rains, which made hunting difficult in the extreme, we at length abandoned the hope of caribou on this trip, and turned southward from Birch Lake into Lake Kwingwishe—the Indian name for meat bird. This was about the northern limit of moose, although a few are found beyond it.

Our repeated failures to see this great deer would not form interesting reading, although, if recorded, they would, no doubt, bring to the

A MOOSE OF THE UPPER OTTAWA.

mind of many a moose hunter memories of times when the hunt was hard and the result —a blank. It is my purpose in this article to merely sketch one or two instances of this sort, which, in contrast to days of unrewarded watching, were red-lettered with excitement. I only give the episodes because too often we relate our victories alone, and missed shots and barren tramps are consigned to ill-merited oblivion, however real they were.

After hunting the country around Lake Kwingwishe, we at length camped on a small pond near the east shore. Here we watched and called every night and morning; then we visited neighboring swamps and ponds, carrying a canoe through the forest by compass. It was always the same—wet and hungry, tired out with tramping through tamarack swamps, we would call half the night, sometimes startled with false alarms from hoot owl or loon, and then lie down in a rain-soaked tent without a fire, for smoke always scares a moose. The first streaks of dawn came, and again we were up and anxiously watching the shore for the appearance of the monster we were after. There were his tracks a few hours old but we could never catch him making them. It was too early in the season to trail them down, as the bulls were traveling continuously in impenetrable swamps, and our best chance was to run across them on the waterways.

One morning, on a pond we had named "Little Trout Pond," because it looked as though it should have trout in it, but did not; we awoke, after some specially exhausting and disappointing "back pond" expeditions, and found Chabot, one of our two Indian guides, gone. Late in the afternoon he returned. He had been seeing the country, and had found a swamp about three miles off full of fresh tracks, "so big moose," and he described tracks such as must have belonged to the Irish elk. Soon after sunrise on the following day we were there. Cold lunch, no dinner and lots of beautiful fresh tracks, one the largest I ever saw.

We watched motionless all day, saw the sun cross the zenith and sink out of sight, saw the twilight fade away and the moon come up. About midnight we went back to camp, through the woods. Night travel in a forest that you can scarcely get through in the daytime is beyond description.

"So good swamp," said Chabot sadly that night as he crawled into his tent.

The next day we pitched a rough camp on a hogback between two barren plains, about five miles from our main camp. It rained hard as soon as we got the tent up, and we watched a runway at the foot of the hill until dark and then turned in.

The next morning it rained so heavily that we lay in our tent, four of us, until about 11 A. M., when it slacked up a little. My diary says, "No fire and little breakfast." Before this "little breakfast" was finished we heard a moose call close by. Seizing our rifles, we started with Chabot to stalk him. The brevity of a diary is sometimes eloquent. Mine says, "Walked from 12 M. to 4.30 P. M. through the bush. Didn't hear that moose again."

The latter hour found us back in camp to get breakfast, when our other guide, Jocko, who had gone to the main camp for food, came back in great excitement, having found some fresh signs close at hand. Breakfast was dropped and again we started. We got back just after dark from that trip and ate—for the first time that day—some cold partridge and pork.

This was a fair sample of our hunting day, but did not equal the following one. It rained all that night, and the tent, not having been properly stretched, leaked. We were awakened by the crackling of a fire the guides had made. It was direct disobedience of orders, and contrary to the most elementary rules of moose hunting; but, cold and faint for want of food, we yielded to the innate perversity of the Indian. We made a wild-eyed, starved group, warming our fingers around the little blaze as it snapped up through the still, wet morning air. The teapot was just beginning to boil, the pork was just sizzling, when we sprang to our feet. A crash of antlers, as though two bulls were fighting, sounded not a hundred yards away. The noise was perfectly clear, having a metallic ring to it, and was caused by moose horns striking a hard substance.

Again. Without a word, we seized our rifles, and left our breakfast and fire, and I never saw that spot afterward. Again came the sound, still distinct, but further off, this time like a birch canoe dragged through alders. The animal had been on the runway which crossed at the foot of the hill we were camped on when he scented the fresh-lit fire. Well, to make a long story short, we followed that trail three weary hours of running and creeping through frightful swamps and thickets, hearing every few minutes the sound just ahead of us, but with never a sight of the game. His huge tracks, which we crossed now and again, showed he was not even trotting. Nearly exhausted, we kept following the sound directly, and so cutting across and gaining on him. Once he seemed just ahead, and we expected to see him each second; but we had to pay for the luxury of that fire, as for other good things in life, so we never saw a hair of him. When, at last, completely used up, we burst out on a lake and saw the muddy tracks and the water still "riled up" where he had crossed, Jocko swore he heard him crash up the opposite bank; but we were at the end of our strength and could go no further. A man must eat sometimes, even on a moose hunt.

Now comes the really tragical part of this episode; our canoe was not twenty feet from where this perverse animal had entered the water, and we were on the little pond where our permanent camp stood. Still we felt encouraged, for, as Chabot said that night, "Hear him now, see him pretty soon." But not for many days.

One more sample to encourage would-be moose hunters, and then we will kill a moose just to show how easy it is. Two nights after the above adventure we changed our camp and the weather at the same time. It was clear now, but it grew very cold, and made night work in the canoe a horror.

It was my brother's turn to call, and I was just dropping off to sleep in my tent, within a few feet of the lake shore, when from the other side of the water, about a quarter of a mile distant, a bull moose called. On the cold, still air it rang out like a trumpet—a long call, very different from the call made by Indian hunters. Jocko, who was with me in camp, was frantic with excitement, especially as my brother, who must have heard it, did not answer. Again the call sounded. The bull must be on the shore. I thought he might swim over. Then came the answering call, close at hand, of a cow. Jocko laughed and whispered, "Chabot call him." Then there was silence for a few minutes, followed by a final bellow, evidently further off. The mock cow bawled and screamed and bleated frantically, but no sound came back. My brother and his man kept it up until late that night, and then came to the camp almost frozen. That incident ruined my faith in calling, for every condition of wind and weather was perfect, and Chabot's calling apparently most enticing.

After this and similar episodes, we left the Kwingwishe country, after hunting it carefully as far north as Sassanega Lake. We passed Sair's Lake and the Bois Franc, and finally reached the Little Beauchene. Near the last lake my brother killed a young bull moose, whose meat was the first fresh food, except partridge, we had had for over three weeks. It was delicious, and we felt the change of diet at once in increased strength and energy. For continuous use moose meat is much superior to other venison, as it is of a rich flavor which does not readily pall on the taste. The myth about moose muffle being such a hunters' delicacy has never allured me to actually eat it, but I suppose a starving man might, after consuming his boots, manage to swallow it.

There were many fresh signs in the neighborhood of the Little Beauchene Lake, but some lumbermen had arrived a few days before us and had scared the game away. This starting the quarry is the real difficulty in moose hunting; for, when once disturbed, the bull leaves with all his kith and kin, so the only chance in these regions is to find him immediately on arrival in a new district and before he comes across your tracks.

Still working slowly southward, we hunted more back ponds, until at last my turn came on the twenty-seventh hunting day. Let no man say that moose hunting is a picnic.

We had camped on a little strip of land, between a pond and a long narrow swamp, about 4 o'clock on a beautiful afternoon. Leaving my brother and Jocko to eat dinner in comfort, I started to the head of the swamp. The water was so low that we could barely force the light canoe through the lily-pads. Old moose signs were plenty. A family of moose had evidently been there all summer, but until we reached the upper end we saw no fresh tracks. The sluggish stream we were on drained a shallow lake, and, after a few hard plunges, our canoe floated clear of the mud into the silent waters of a circular pond. It was a basin about a half mile across, surrounded by low hardwood hills, and so shallow that a moose, I think, could have waded across the deepest part. The shores were marked up with some very large tracks, but fresh signs had long since ceased to excite in me anything more than a passing interest. We made the tour of the lake slowly and quietly. Nothing was in sight except four wood ducks. This was "last chance" pond, and if I got no moose here, we must return to Mattawa for another outfit, which I had about made up my mind to do. The night settled still and cold—oh, so cold!—and the stars came out with wonderful distinctness.

What was that?

Chabot had started up, listened, and a second later was driving the birch across the lake noiselessly. As we neared the shore, it was inky black—a mammoth would not have been visible ten yards away. Twigs breaking at long intervals told that something was on shore just in cover of the bushes. We waited some time and at last I whispered to Chabot, "Muckwa?" (bear).

"Not muckwa—cow," answered the guide.

As he spoke, the short call of a bull

floated out on the cold air from the side of the pond that we had just left. I think Chabot was right about the cow being in the bushes, but he may have been mistaken—one's hearing becomes unnaturally sensitive after a few weeks' continuous straining to catch and distinguish the most distant sounds. But there was no mistake about that bull's call. He was well back from the shore on the hillside. The wind was wrong, and, although he grunted at intervals for an hour, he paid no attention to Chabot's most seductive pleadings. We imitated with paddles the splashings of a cow walking in the shallow water, but this and other devices had no effect. When at last even my Indian could no longer bear the bitter cold of the wind which had sprung up, we started for camp. Long past midnight we crawled into our blankets, and I dropped asleep cursing the day I had first gone after moose.

We were on that pond again before daylight. Not a sound to be heard, not a living thing to be seen, when the sun rose. We took our stand on a small point opposite the outlet and watched. I sat on a fallen tree motionless, hour after hour. Chabot dozed beside me.

A Canadian Moose Hunt

Those four ducks played and fed within thirty feet, and a muskrat worked at house-building a few yards away. The silence was intense. There was not a breath of wind. I knew my brother was doing the same thing on a neighboring pond, and I fell to thinking whether there was some special Nemesis about this hunt, or it was the fault of the guides. I glanced at the outlet in front of me, about a half mile distant.

There was a moose, stalking with the utmost deliberation along the edge of the woods and then into the shallow water.

Chabot was roused by a hasty shake, and a second later the canoe was flying across the lake. As we crossed, I inspected the moose closely. He was walking slowly, nibbling the long reed-like grass that stuck up from the water. His neck seemed very stiff, and he swung his legs from his hips and shoulders. The hump was extremely conspicuous, perhaps because his head was carried low to get at the grass. He was a young bull, nearly full grown, and with small antlers. He looked occasionally at the canoe, now fast nearing him; but we had the advantage of the wind, and the sun was going down behind us. It was just 5 o'clock. He walked, now out toward us, now back to shore, as though about to bolt for the bush, but working slowly toward the north, where we afterwards found a much-used runway, leading to the marsh my brother was watching, two miles away. I opened fire about fifty yards off, when the moose was standing in about a foot of water, looking suspiciously at us. The shot was too high, but struck him in the shoulder. He started in a lumbering gallop along the shore. I fired again. This turned him into the woods at an old lumber road. We heard the twigs snap sharply for a minute, and then a heavy crash and silence. I thought we had lost him, but Chabot declared that he was down. I sprang ashore the moment the canoe grounded, and dashed in on his trail, which was perfectly clear on the soft moss. Looking ahead through the open woods for the animal, which I thought had turned, I almost fell over his prostrate body.

His head rested against a small windfall, which he had tried to clear—an effort which appeared to have cost him his life. Moss hung from some small spruce trees close by, which had been kicked up in the death struggle. The shoulder shot had been the fatal one, but he had been hard hit in the side too.

He was not full grown, and measured only 5 feet 6½ inches in height, and 8 feet 3¼ inches in length, from the nose to root of tail. His girth at the shoulder was 5 feet 11¼ inches. His nose showed none of the Jewish characteristics which taxidermists are fond of giving their mounted moose heads. The forehead and shoulders were brownish instead of black, like the rest of the body. The hindlegs were wholly white, as were the forelegs below the knee. I am inclined to think he was a ranger moose, but could not tell with certainty, as his horns were too undeveloped. The velvet was still hanging in places, but very dry. This was unusual, as it was the 10th of October.

Ordering Chabot to dress the moose, I went back to the canoe, having decided to watch until dark, although there seemed no possibility of seeing another moose after the firing. My lazy guide, instead of obeying my order, merely cut the skin, with the result that all the meat spoiled—probably just what he wanted, fearing he would have to portage it out of the bush. We returned to our point and dozed again. At a quarter of 7 it was getting dark fast, and in the north a black, ugly-looking cloud was gathering. We might as well go back to camp if it was going to blow and rain, so I told Chabot to shove off and to give one last toot of his horn, just for luck.

The air was still as death with the dread of the impending storm. Chabot took up the coiled birch, and the echoes rang out with a short grunting call, which so much resembles a man chopping wood. Before they died away, there came from behind us, just to our right, the unmistakable answering grunt of a bull moose. He was probably on his way to the lake, and our call merely hastened him and brought him out into the open before it was too dark to shoot. He was very near and came steadily forward, stopping now and then to listen. We could hear him plainly as his horns broke the twigs at every step—once or twice he lashed the bushes with them. He repeated his grunts, ungh! ungh! every few steps. He was so evidently reckless that, to take no chance, I allowed Chabot to answer only once —with the short call. I say short call, in distinction to the long modulated call which is used to good purpose in Maine and New Brunswick, but which I have never known to succeed in this part of Canada. The moose paused for a moment in the alders that formed a close thicket at the water's edge, and I feared he had seen or scented us; then suddenly and noiselessly he stepped out from a cove a short hundred yards away. He had taken less than ten minutes from the first call to his appearance.

At the first alarm we had pushed off and were floating quietly just by the shore. The water was so shallow that the birch made, to my ears at least, a frightful scraping as it pushed over the dead sticks that lay in the water, and the wind was unfavorable. I never shall forget the appearance that bull made as he stepped fiercely and proudly out, with his head up, swinging a splendid set of antlers as lightly as straws. He did not see us, but strode about ten yards into the shallow lake, where the water scarcely covered his hoofs, and, first glancing away for a second, turned like a flash and faced us full, looking down on us in surprised disgust. He was greatly excited and the mane on his hump was erect, increasing his natural height, and there was nothing timid or deer-like in his appearance. I have seen in the arena a bull step out from the darkened stall into the glare of sunlight, and gaze for a moment at the picadors with a sort of indignant surprise; so this great bull moose looked.

We gazed motionless at each other, I knowing that it was one of the grandest and rarest sights on the American continent, and he thinking, no doubt, what a disgraceful imitation of a cow the motionless canoe made. Chabot's breath was coming hard behind me, and I felt the birch bark quiver.

As I raised my rifle, I realized that it had suddenly grown very dark under this western bank, and the bull precisely resembled in color the background, and, large as he was, made a very poor mark. The tall grass, which I had looked over in watching him, now sticking up in front of the sights, bothered me. I fired at the root of his neck, and the rifle gave a suppressed roar in the heavy air and the smoke hung like a pall. The bull ran straight forward, hesitated as though about to charge, then turned and made wonderful speed along the lake shore. The moment I could see him I fired again. In the dim twilight he was almost out of sight. When the smoke cleared he was gone.

Neither of us moved. It was too frightful to miss such an immense creature at that range. We heard him crash up the hillside and then stop a short distance back in the wood. Then I knew he either was down or had turned, unless he had found an open lumber road, where his horns would make no sound; for a moose can go in the most mysterious manner when he chooses to be quiet—but there was nothing quiet about this bull.

Chabot declared that he had heard him cough, but I did not believe it. I pointed to the spot where he had entered the bush, and a moment later the canoe grated on the beach. There were the huge tracks with the hoofs wide spread, and the trail entering an old lumber road.

All this took less time to happen than to read, and yet it was now dark, so quickly had night fallen. By straining my eyes I saw it was 7 o'clock—just two hours after the first bull was killed. Chabot wanted to go back to camp, which was the roper thing to do, especially as I had now just one cartridge left. I had only taken a handful with me that morning.

We entered the forest foot by foot, Chabot following the trail where I could scarcely see to step. A few yards in and the track turned from the old road into the thick bush, and we knew the moose was near. A little further, and we scarcely moved—stepping like cats from tree to tree, expecting every second to hear an angry grunt and have the bull emerge from the impenetrable veil of night that hung around us.

At last we came to a windfall, and we were for some time at a loss to find whether he had gone across or around it. In lighting a match with extreme caution, the light fell on a tall moose wood stem about as large as one's finger. Four feet from the ground it was dripping with bright red blood. The coughing Chabot had heard was now, we thought, explained, and the game hard hit. We decided to go back to camp; for, as my guide put it very clearly, the wounded bull would either fight or run. I wasn't anxious for the first alternative in the dark and tangled wood, with one cartridge; and the second meant a long chase on the morrow. If we left him until the morning, he would be either dead or too stiff from his wound to go far.

A Canadian Moose Hunt

So back we went to camp, amply repaid by the events of two hours for weeks of hardship and exposure. Just at daylight the next morning, as we were leaving camp, prepared to take and keep the trail of that bull if it led to Hudson Bay, my brother appeared with Jocko. He had had no breakfast, and had come a long distance through a frightful bush in order to be in at the death, as he had heard the firing, and shrewdly suspected that in the dusk a wounded moose was the result.

"From the tracks at my lake," said he, as he strode up to the fire, "there are two bull moose around here—a large and a small one; which did you get?"

"Both," replied Chabot.

We took the trail at the water's edge, and found it smeared with blood. The bull could not have gone far. A short walk brought us to the windfall where we had turned back the night before, and which had seemed so deep in the woods.

A hundred yards beyond it lay the bull on his right side. The second shot had struck him in the center of the left ham and ranged through him. The meat was spoiled, as was the hide—that is, the hair came out so badly that it was not worth while to prepare it; but the neck and scalp were perfect, except a bad scar on the forehead, received in fighting.

He was a grand sight as he lay dead in that silent autumn forest—for I never can get over the impression that somehow or other the moose is a survival of a long past order of nature, a fit comrade for the mammoth and the cave bear. He was short and thickset, with immense chest power—probably a swamp moose. The neck was short and stout, and he had a Jewish cast of nose. No bell—merely the common dewlap. He measured at the shoulder 6 feet 6 inches; 9 feet 8½ inches from nose to tip of tail; girth at shoulders, 6 feet 2½ inches. We skinned and decapitated the moose, one after the other. The meat of both was completely spoiled, and it seemed wicked to leave those two huge carcasses to the bears and wolves; but there was no help for it, so we started for Mattawa. I doubt if we could have carried out any of the meat if we had tried, for we had to throw away everything not absolutely necessary on the long portages that followed. At last we reached Rosiceau's, on Snake Lake, and, with the welcome the old man gave us, felt quite at home once more. Then passing by the scenes of a former hunt, we reached Fort Eddy, an old Hudson Bay post, and then the Ottawa River. We ran the Cave rapids, and at sundown on a beautiful day the town of Mattawa swung in sight, and the hunt was over.

The country we had traversed contained little except bears and moose. We saw a few caribou tracks, and brought home with us a curious caribou antler, which we found in the woods.

The fur animals have, within the last five years, been exterminated, and the very few beaver that survive have abandoned their old habits, and live in holes in the banks of the larger streams. We found traces of one of these bank beaver, but he was probably traveling and we could not catch him. A few mink were shot, but the country is completely stripped of everything else of value. If the present law, prohibiting the trapping of otter and beaver, can be enforced, perhaps the land may be restocked, but it will take years. It is fit for nothing except fur and timber, and, with efficient game wardens, could be made to produce a large return from these sources. Partridges and loons abounded, but ducks were seldom seen.

The lakes form a complete system of communication by means of easy portages, but there are no streams that contain trout and no springs to supply drinking water. This lack of fresh water caused us considerable suffering, as the lake water is supposed to be dangerous, and a pail of spring water, which we got at the start, was carried for days over portages as our most precious baggage. We did not see a sign of a brook trout during the entire trip, and I do not believe that there were any in the waters we traversed. There may have been lake trout, but our trolling produced only pike and pickerel.

This absence of small game and fish makes the country very uninteresting, and the long monotony between most exciting events is the greatest drawback to hunting on the Upper Ottawa.

Madison Grant.

A Hunting Trip in India

Early in 1881 I landed at Bombay, intending to get as many varieties of big game shooting as possible during the course of the year. I was well armed with introductions, including many from the Department of State, and during my stay in India was treated by the English military officers, civil officials, planters and merchants with a hearty hospitality which I cordially appreciated. Thanks to this hospitality, and to the readiness with which all to whom I was introduced fell into my plans, I was able to get a rather unusually varied quantity of sport.

My first trip was in March, after tigers. On the 1st of March I started from Hyderabad with Colonels Fraser and Watson, and traveled by palanquin that day and night, and most of the next day, striking the foot of the Gāt at a place called Rungapore, and then going on over a great plain, beyond which we camped. The scenery was magnificent, and we heard much news of the devastation of tigers among the large herds of miserable-looking cattle belonging to the poor villagers roundabout. The thermometer went up to 96 degrees in the shade during the day, but the nights were lovely and cool. Thanks to Colonel Fraser, we were fitted out as comfortably as we could be, and the luxury of the camp life offered the strongest possible contrast to my experiences in roughing it on the buffalo range in northwestern Texas.

For the first two days we accomplished nothing, though several of the cattle we had put out for baits were killed, and though we started and beat the jungles with our elephants whenever we received khubber, or news. Our camp equipage included twenty elephants, forty camels and bullocks, thirty horses for the troopers, and fifty baggage horses. We had seventeen private servants, twenty-six police, fifty-two bearers, and an indefinite number of attendants for the elephants and camels, and of camp followers. An Indian of high position, Sir Salar Jung, was along also; so our total retinue comprised 350 men, in addition to which we employed each day of beaters 150 or 200 more.

A Hunting Trip in India

On March 5th, one of the shikaris brought word that he had seen and heard a tigress and two cubs at a nullah about six miles away. Immediately we started up the valley, Col. Fraser, Col. Watson and myself, each on his own elephant. The jungle was on fire and the first beat was not successful, for we had to fight the fire, and in the excitement the brute got off. However, some of the watchers saw her, and marked her down in another small ravine. Through this we again beat, the excitement being at fever heat. I was, of course, new to the work, and the strangeness of the scene, the cries of the beaters and watchers, the occasional explosion of native fireworks, together with the quantity of other game that we saw, impressed me much. In this ravine I was favored by good luck. The tigress broke right in front of me, and I hit her with a ball from a No. 12 smooth-bore. She sickened at once and crawled back into the jungle. In we went on the elephants, tracking her up. She made no attempt to charge, and I finished her off with another barrel of the smooth-bore and two express bullets. The crowd of natives ran up, abusing the tigress and praising me, while the two colonels drank my health. We then padded the tigress and rode back to camp, having been gone from half past 9 in the morning till 7 in the evening. This tigress weighed, when we brought her in, 280 pounds; her living weight must have been much more.

Next day we again got news of a tigress, with one cub, but we failed to find her. The following day, for a change, I tried still-hunting through the woods. There was not much game, but what we did see was far from shy, and the shooting was easy. The camp was on a terrace, and from it we went up a range of hills to the stalking ground. It was a stony country and the trees were scrubby. I shot two cheetul, or spotted deer, and also two of the little jungle cocks. The next day again was a blank, but on the 9th we got another tiger. Thanks to the courtesy of my friends, I was given the first shot, again hitting it with one barrel of the smooth-bore. The heat was very great on this day. It was not possible to touch the gun barrels without a glove, and the thirst was awful. In the evening the cool bath was a luxury indeed. By moonlight the camp was very fine. The next morning I was off at daybreak, snipe shooting around a big tank, seven miles away. On my return I found that my companions had gone out for a beat, and so, after a hurried breakfast, I jumped on my horse and rode after them. That afternoon we beat two ravines and got a tiger. This was the last tiger that we killed. The weather was getting very warm, and, though we stayed a week longer out, we failed to get on terms with Mr. Stripes again. However, I shot three sambur stags. Two of them were weighed in camp, their weight being, respectively, 450 and 438 pounds.

It was now getting hot, and I determined to start northward for my summer's hunting in the Himalayas and Cashmere, although it was rather early to try to get through the mountains. I left Lahore on April 6th for the Pir Pinjal. My transportation consisted of eight pack ponies and three native single-horse carts. I was shown every courtesy by Mr. McKay, a member of the Forest Department, at Gujarat. I intended to make a hunt for gorals and bears in the mountains around the Pir Pinjal before striking through to Cashmere. The goral is a little mountain antelope, much like the chamois, only with straight horns. The bear in the region in which I was hunting was the black bear, which is very much like our own black bear. Further on in the Himalayas is found the red or snow bear, which is a good deal like the great brown bear of Europe, or a small and inoffensive grizzly. After leaving Gujarat, I traveled for several days before coming to my hunting ground proper, although on the way I killed some peacocks, partridges, and finally some very handsome pheasants of different kinds. The country offered the greatest possible contrast to that in which I had been hunting tigers. Everything was green and lovely, and the scenery was magnificent beyond description—the huge steep mountains rising ahead of me, while the streams were crystal-clear, noisy torrents. The roads were very rough, and the wild flowers formed great carpets everywhere.

On the 16th of April I began my shooting, having by this time left my heavy baggage behind, and having with me only what the coolies could carry. I had two shikaris, four servants and twelve coolies, besides myself. On April 16th I killed my first goral. I had hunted in vain all day, but about 5 o'clock one of the shikaris advised my starting out again and climbing around the neighboring cliffs. I did this for two and one-half hours, and then got a close shot and killed the little beast. This was my first trial of grass-shoes, and my first experience in climbing over the stupendous mountain masses; for stupendous they were, though they were only the foothills of the Himalayas proper. Without grass-shoes it is impossible to climb on these smooth, grassy slopes; but I found that they hurt my feet a great deal. The next day I again went off with my two shikaris over the mountains. Each of them carried a gun. I had all I could do to take care of myself without one, for a mis-step would have meant a fall of a thousand or two feet. In the morning we saw five gorals and I got one. At 10 I stopped and a coolie came up with a lunch, and I lay reading, sleeping and idly watching the grand mountains until the afternoon, when we began again to examine the nullahs for game, being all the time much amused by the monkeys. At 4 we started again, and in a jagged mass of precipices I got another goral. The next day I repeated my experience, and had one of the characteristic bits of bad luck, offset by good luck, that come to every hunter—missing a beautiful shot at fifty yards, and then, by a fluke, killing a goral at 300 yards. The animal, however, fell over 1,000 feet and was ruined. I myself had a slip this day and went down about fifty feet. The following day I again went off to climb, and the first ascent was so steep that at the top I was completely blown, and missed a beautiful shot at a goral at fifty yards. I then arranged a beat, but nothing came from it, and the morning was a blank. In the afternoon I gave up beating and tried still-hunting again. It was hard work, but I was very successful, and killed two gorals and a bear.

At this time I was passed by two English officers, also going in to shoot—one of them, Captain S. D. Turnbull, a very jolly fellow and a good sportsman, with whom I got on excellent terms; the other, a Captain C., was a very bad walker and a poor shot, and was also a disagreeable companion, as he would persist in trying to hang around my hunting grounds, thus forcing me continually to shift.

On April 21st I tried driving for gorals, and got four, and on the next two days I got three gorals and two bears. So far I had had great luck and great sport. The work was putting me in fine trim, except my feet, which were getting very sore. It was very hard work going after the gorals. The bears offered easier stalking, and, like our American black bear but unlike our grizzly, they didn't show fight. The climbing was awful work. The stones and grass-shoes combined bruised and skinned the soles of my feet, so that I could not get relief without putting them in clarified butter and then keeping them up in the air. Accordingly I tried resting for a day, and meant to rest the following day too; but could not forbear taking a four hours' stroll along the banks of the brawling, snow-fed river, and was rewarded by shooting a surow —a queer, squatty, black antelope, about the size of a Rocky Mountain white goat and with similar horns. The next day I rested again, hoping my feet would get better. Instead they got worse, and I made up my mind that, as they were so bad, I might as well get some hunting anyhow, so off I tramped on the 27th for another all-day job. It would be difficult to describe the pain that my feet gave me all day long. However, it was a real sporting day. I suffered the tortures of the damned, but I got two gorals and one tahr—a big species of goat with rather small horns—and then hobbled back to camp. Next day I stayed quietly in camp, and then started back to the camp where I had left my heavy baggage. On the way I picked up another black bear. My feet were in a frightful condition, but I had had a fortnight's excellent sport.

I then went on to Cashmere, and on May 6th reached Siringur. The scenery was beautiful beyond description, and the whole life of the natives very attractive to look at. However, something did not agree with me, for I was very sick and had to go to bed for several days. There were one or two American friends there, and these and the Englishmen, to whom I had letters of introduction, treated me with extreme courtesy. As soon as I got well, I started off for the real mountains, hoping especially to get ibex and markhoor. The ibex is almost exactly the same as the European animal of that name. The markhoor is a magnificent goat, with long whitish hair and great spiral horns. They also have in these Cashmere valleys a big stag called the barramigh, which is a good deal like our wapiti, only not half so large. On May 21st I started off, first by boat, but I was bothered from the beginning by chills and fever. I was weak, and glad I didn't have to march. At first, all I did in shooting was to have my coolies beat some brush patches near camp. Out of one of them they started a little musk-deer, which I shot. Soon I began to get very much better and we took up our march. I was going toward Astor, but encountered much snow, as it was still early in the season for these high mountains. I saw some grand barramigh, but their horns were, of course, only just growing, and I didn't molest them.

Very soon I got into a country where the red bears literally swarmed. From May 26th to June 5th, during which time I was traveling and hunting all the time, I shot no less than sixteen, together with two musk-deer, but saw nothing else. The marching was very hard, and some of the passes dangerous. I met a British officer, Lieutenant Carey, on the 30th, who treated me very well indeed. The scenery was very beautiful, although rather bleak. I did not pick up strength as much as I had hoped. On June 3d I christened my camp Camp Good Luck, because of the phenomenal success I had with the bears. That morning we left by 4 to cross the river before the snow had melted. The thermometer would go down to 30 degrees, even in the valleys, at night, so that everything would freeze, and then would go up to 110 in the day, and when the snow melted the streams would come down in a perfect torrent. Not two miles beyond the river I saw three bears on the side of a hill, a she and two two-year-old cubs. My shikari made a splendid stalk and brought me within forty yards, and I got all three with a shot apiece. The delight of my camp followers was amusing. I then left the tents, and, taking only my blankets and a lunch basket with me, started off again. At midday I slept, and at 2 o'clock started up the nullah, seeing a number of bears. One of them I got within fifty yards, and two others, right and left, at 100 yards. The skinning took a long time, and the stream which I had to cross was up with the evening flood, so that I didn't get back to camp until 10 o'clock. I had shot unusually well, I had been happy and was all tired out, and it is needless to say how I slept.

Soon after this I began to suffer from fever, and I had to work very hard indeed, as I was now on the ibex ground. For several days, though I saw ibex, I was unable to get near them. Finally, on June 9th, I got my first one, a young buck with small horns. I had to hunt way up the mountain, even beyond bush vegetation, and the hot sun at midday was awful. Nevertheless, by very hard climbing, I managed on this day to get within shot first of a herd of nine females, which I did not touch, and then of the young buck, which I killed. On June 13th, by another heart-breaking climb, very high up, I got a second small buck. I did not get back to camp that night till half past 9 —tired out, feet badly cut with the stones and bruised all over; but in spite of the fever I enjoyed every day—the scenery was so grand and the life so exhilarating. Four days afterwards came a red-letter day. I started early in the morning, clambering up among the high mountains. Until noon I saw nothing; then several flocks of ibex came in sight, one of them of eleven big bucks. I had to wait four hours to get into a position to stalk; then by quick work and awful climbing I came within close range and killed three. It was half past 10 in the evening before I got back to camp, very nearly done up, but exultant over my good luck.

The traveling now became very severe and I had a great deal of difficulty even with the coolies, and though I hunted hard I got little game until July 8th. I had been shifting, trying to get on markhoor ground, and on this day I killed my first markhoor. The shikaris and I left the coolies to go around the path while we went over the mountain, a five hours' climb, keeping a sharp lookout for game. Just at the beginning of the ascent we saw three fine-looking markhoor grazing in a nullah, and after a stalk of about a mile, during which time it began to rain, the beasts went into a jungle on the steep side of the mountain. Through this we still-hunted and I got a shot through the bushes at 100 yards. By good luck I hit and great was the rejoicing. Five days later I got two ibex, which at a distance we had mistaken for markhoor. Then I was attacked by a terrible dysentery and was within an ace of dying. For a fortnight I was unable to leave camp, excepting when I was carried slowly along by the coolies in the effort to get me out of the mountains. On August 1st I shot a second markhoor. We were journeying at the time. In the very rough places I had to walk, though awfully weak; elsewhere the coolies carried me. The markhoor was just below us, round a turn in the Indus Valley. I was in advance with one of the shikaris and got a quiet shot, and more by good luck than anything else—for I was very weak—I killed. I now began gradually to pick up strength, and when near Astor I got a urial, a kind of wild sheep.

I had no other experience of note till I got back to Siringur, where I stayed to recuperate, and at the end of August went off once more into the foothills, this time after barramigh. In a week's work I killed three, but again became sick, and had to give up and come in.

I forthwith returned to India, the hot weather being by this time pretty well over. As I was very anxious to kill an elephant, I went down to Ceylon, reaching that island the end of October and going out to Kandy. I met a number of Englishmen, who were very kind to me, as were some Eurasian gentlemen. On November 16th I left Minerva for a regular hunt. It was very interesting shooting through the tropical jungle and I had good luck. There were plenty of elephants, but at first I didn't get any, though I shot five spotted deer and a boar. Finally, however, I got two of the big brutes I was mainly after. One of them, which I killed on the 20th of the month, was said to be a rogue that had killed two villagers and done at intervals a good deal of damage to the crops. An old native tracker had guaranteed to show me this elephant. He kept his word. For three or four miles we had a very exciting track, and then came on him standing in the jungle, occasionally flapping his ears, and crept up to within thirty yards. I think he was asleep and I got a perfectly good shot, but, extraordinary to say, I missed. However, when he ran I went after him, and, getting very close, I shot him in the hip, so injuring his leg that he could not get away. He could still get round after us, and we passed a most lively half-hour, he trumpeting and charging incessantly, until, after expending a great quantity of cartridges, I finally put a bullet behind his eye, and down he went.

Soon after this I went back to Kandy, and early in December left India for good.

Elliott Roosevelt.

HOW OUR OUTFIT WAS CARRIED.

Dog Sledging in the North

A good many years ago, my friends, Boies Penrose, Granville Keller, and I concluded that it would be a fitting termination to a very successful summer and fall hunting trip in the Rocky Mountains to endeavor to kill some moose and caribou in the Lake Winnipeg country, Manitoba. Thus we should combine very different kinds of sport amid surroundings more dissimilar than we imagined at the time. The whole of this rather memorable trip occupied nearly six months.

Our adventures during the latter part of the hunt, that is, during our sojourn in the far north—while a part of the every-day experience of those familiar with the winter life in the woods of that country—were of a character totally unknown to the majority of sportsmen in the United States, and for this reason it has been thought worth while to give a short account of them.

If my recollection serves me correctly, we

arrived at Selkirk, at the lower end of Lake Winnipeg, in the latter part of October, to find navigation already closed. We had hoped to reach the upper part of the lake by means of a steamer, but found this impossible, and were therefore obliged to go on sleds to our first hunting ground—a moose country to the south of the head waters of the Fisher River, between Lake Winnipeg and Lake Winnipegosis.

At Selkirk we were joined by a Mr. Phillips, and we had there employed an Indian boy to look after the dogs. This Indian was a magnificent specimen physically, and certainly the best walker that I have ever known. With the exception of a pardonable fondness for our whisky, he behaved very well at first, but afterward became so insufferably lazy that he was scarcely fit for the simple work of driving one of the dog teams—a change which was to be attributed entirely to our kind treatment of him. He was, however, a good trailer, but the worst shot that I remember to have met. He seemed to have no difficulty in finding moose, but could not hit them, which was the exact reverse of our experience.

Portions of the country between Lakes Winnipeg and Winnipegosis, visited by our party, are as flat as the flattest portions of New Jersey, and for great distances nothing could be more level except possibly a billiard table. It is traversed by very few rivers or even creeks, there being immense stretches of territory where the only guide back to camp is the sun when it shines, or when it does not your compass, or the dog-sled trail through the snow leading to the camp. The different portions of this region are so much alike that it is almost impossible to tell one from another.

Owing to the fact that it is very dangerous to be caught out over night, with the thermometer ranging anywhere from zero to 50 degrees below, we took the precaution to mount a big red flag in the top of the highest spruce we could find near our camp, so that, by climbing a high tree anywhere within a radius of a mile or so, one could easily see this flag. To still further reduce the chance of getting lost, we blazed the trees in a straight line for four miles due south of the camp, and, as the dog-sled trail came into our camp (which was in the heavy timber) from the north, it was not difficult to find one's way home in the evening. These precautions—needless elsewhere, but wise in this country—were taken principally because each of us had always been in the habit for years of hunting alone—a practice which I would recommend to anyone who desires to be really successful in killing big game.

This vast expanse of flat country is quite heavily wooded over large areas, the timber being spruce, tamarack, poplar, birch, etc., with a great abundance of red and gray willow. The underbrush is sometimes very thick. There are, however, innumerable open places, which bear the local name of muskets. These are, of course, marshes in summer, and covered with a heavy growth of grass; in winter they are frozen hard, and traveling over them is comparatively easy.

The moose seem to be fond of remaining close to the edges of these muskegs, which are usually fringed with a heavy growth of willows. It would appear, however, that they venture out into these open places either during the night, early in the morning, or late in the afternoon; and, as these were the times when we were very glad either to be in camp or to be returning to it, we had more success in finding the moose in the timber, or on the little so-called ridges, which sometimes attain the remarkable height of four or five feet.

Up to the time of leaving this camp we had very little opportunity to use snowshoes, as the snow was not yet—about the last of November—deep enough to make these necessary. We hunted all of the time in moccasins, boots of any description being simply out of the question, as they would soon freeze as hard as iron. After the cold weather set in, one day's experience with boots was quite sufficient for me, and I came to the conclusion, as I had often before in other regions, that it is very difficult to improve, in the matter of clothing, upon the customs of the country. The sudden change to moccasins was very tiring at first, but after one gets used to walking in them he will find that he can walk further and hunt better in them than any other style of foot-gear. We used, as I remember, first one or two pairs of heavy woolen socks, then a very heavy so-called "German" sock, coming up to the knee, over which we wore the high laced moccasin of the country.

Before we had very long been engaged in moose hunting we all learned that we were not so expert in the art of killing big game as we

previously imagined ourselves. In all my experience I have never met with any animal
which is so difficult to get a shot at, even when
quite numerous, as the moose in this region. It
must always be borne in mind that to kill a
moose—especially in a country where they
have been hutned for generations by the Indians—by the thoroughly sportsmanlike method
of following the trail of one until you finally
get a shot at it and kill it, is a totally different
thing from killing the same moose either by
calling him at night in the autumn or by pad-
dling on him in a canoe in the summer. In
fact, of all the difficult things I have ever un-
dertaken in the way of sport, I regard this as
the most difficult; and before I got my first
shot I began to think that there was a great
deal of truth in the Indian's sneering remark,
"White man no kill moose." Finally one day
my luck turned, but that it did so was due
more to the realization of my own inferiority,
and lack of the proper kind of knowledge, than
to anything else.

It happened in this way: having thoroughly
convinced myself that the moose either smelt
me or in some other way found out that I was
in their neighborhood before I could be made

aware of the same fact, I concluded that there was something radically wrong in my manner of hunting them, although I employed every method known to me—methods which had been acquired in an experience during which I had killed considerably over one hundred head of big game, throughout the Rockies and the Alleghanies. In short, I was exceedingly painstaking and careful. Notwithstanding all my precautions, however, I remember that I had the satisfaction one night of knowing that I had started during the day eight different moose, each separately, without hearing or seeing a single one of them. This sort of thing lasted for twenty-two consecutive days, or until I finally concluded that, as our Indian seemed to have no trouble in seeing moose, I would follow his tactics. Waiting, therefore, one morning until I was sure that the Indian had left camp, I changed my course so as to intersect his trail, followed this for some distance, and watched carefully his foot-prints, so as to read the record of his hunt.

Pretty soon it became apparent that he had come across a moose trail. He tried it first with the toe of his moccasin, then with the butt of his gun, and satisfied himself that it was too old to follow. He went on until he came across another trail, and evidently had spent considerable time in making up his mind whether it was worth while to follow this trail or not. He then followed it for a few yards, and, to my surprise, suddenly left it, and went off almost at right angles to the leeward. I supposed that he had given up the moose trail, but nevertheless I followed further on his track. Again to my surprise, I presently found him gradually coming around in a circuitous fashion to the trail again, until he finally reached it. He then immediately retraced his steps, making another semi-circle, bearing generally, however, in the direction the moose had gone, and again came to the trail. This occurred four or five times, until finally the explanation of his conduct flashed upon me, for there lay his cartridge. I saw— as he afterward described it to me—where he had shot at the moose, which had just arisen out of its bed a short distance away, but, as usual, he had missed it. Now I had noticed, in my three weeks' experience, that I had come upon the moose either lying down or standing in some thicket, but that they had been able to wind me considerably before my arrival at the spot marked by their beds in the snow. Not until then had occurred to me what is well known to many who still-hunt moose, namely, that before lying down they generally make a long loop to the leeward, returning close to their trail, so that they can readily get the wind of anyone following upon it long before he reaches them, when, of course, they quietly get up and sneak away. In fact, they do not seem to have an atom of curiosity in their composition, and in this are different from most other wild animals that I have known. By making these long loops to the leeward the hunter reduces to a minimum the likelihood of being smelt or heard by the moose; and in these animals the senses of smell and hearing are very acute, although their eyesight seems to be bad.

Having quite satisfied myself as to what it was necessary to do, I waited until the next day to put it into execution, because by the time I had made my discovery it was about half past 2 o'clock, and the sun was near the horizon.

The following day I went out bright and early, and, after varying success in finding a good trail, I ran across a trail made by five bull moose, a photograph of one of which is shown. After satisfying myself that the trail had been made during the previous night, I began making the long loops to the leeward which I had found to be so necessary. I finally came to the place where the moose had lain down—a bed showing one of them to have unusually large horns—but they had gone on again, in a manner, however, that showed that they were merely feeding, and not alarmed. I redoubled my precautions, stepping as if on eggs, so as not to break the twigs underneath my feet. In a short time I heard the significant chattering of one of the little red pine squirrels so abundant in that region. I at once knew that the squirrel had seen something, but had not seen me. It did not take me long to make up my mind that the only other living things in that vicinity which would be likely to cause him to chatter were these moose, and that they were probably startled, although I had not been conscious of making any noise. At any rate, I ran quite rapidly toward the end of a small narrow muskeg on my left, but some distance away, to which chance conclusion and prompt action I owe probably one of the most fortunate and exciting pieces of shooting that has occurred in my experience. I was shooting at that time a little double rifle (.450-120-375 solid bullet), which had been made for me by Holland & Holland, and which was fitted with one of my conical sights.

Before I was within fifty yards of the end of the muskeg, I saw one of the moose dash across it, about 150 yards away. I fired quickly, and in much the same way that I would shoot at a jacksnipe which had been flushed in some thicket; but had the satisfaction of seeing the animal lurch heavily forward as he went out of sight into the timber. Almost immediately, and before I had time to reload, the second moose followed. I gave him the other barrel, but I did not know until afterward that he was hit. In fact, it was hard to get a bullet through the timber. I reloaded quickly, and ran forward to get to the opening; but before I reached it, the third moose passed in immediately behind the others. I again, shot quickly, and felt that I had probably hit him. By running on rapidly I reached the edge of the opening in time to intercept the fourth moose. As he came into the opening I got a good shot at him, not over eighty yards distant, and felt very sure of this one at least. I then reloaded, when, to my amazement, the fifth, in a very deliberate manner, walked, not trotted, into the muskeg, which at the point where the moose crossed it was not over sixty or seventy feet wide. He first looked up and down, as if undetermined what to do, and then, probably seeing one of the other moose on the ground, commenced walking up toward me. As luck would have it, I got a cartridge jammed in my rifle, and could not pull it out or knock it in, although I nearly ruined my fingers in my attempt to do so. Of course, this was the biggest bull of all, and I had the supreme satisfaction of seeing him deliberately walk out of my sight into the woods, and he was lost to me forever. His horns were much larger than those which I got. Up to that time I had no idea that I had killed any except the last moose that I shot at, but thought that perhaps I had wounded one or two of the others, feeling that I would be very lucky if I should ever come up with them.

Going down to the place where the moose had disappeared, after I had got my rifle fixed —that is, had extracted the cartridge and put in another—I found one of the moose dead;

another, a big one, on his knees, and the third a short distance away, looking very dejected and uncomfortable. I did not know then that the largest bull of all had stopped on the other side of a little thicket; and when I commenced to give the finishing touches to the wounded moose in sight, he, accompanied by another wounded one, got away. As I shot the big one on his knees, I was surprised by a noise, and upon turning around found the dejected looking small bull coming full drive toward me. I had only time to turn around and shoot him in the breast before he was on me. I do not think that he intended to charge; his coming toward me was probably entirely accidental. Still it had the effect of sending my heart in my mouth. I then started out after the wounded one, but when I saw that he was not bleeding much concluded that, as it was growing late, and I was seven or eight miles from camp, I would not have more than time to cover up the three moose with snow so that I could skin them the next morning. Before doing so, however, I sat down on top of my biggest moose, and, as these were the first moose that I had ever seen, I surveyed them with a great deal of satisfaction.

About this time Phillips, who had been attracted by the shooting, appeared in the distance, and I hailed him by a shot, when he came to me. We then carefully covered up the moose with snow and pulled out for camp. When we arrived there and told our story, a more disconsolate looking Indian you could not have found in the whole region, and he doubtless came to the conclusion that his sweeping assertion as to the inability of a white man to kill a moose in that country was perhaps a little too broad.

Our luck seemed to turn from this time and we got several very good moose, but unfortunately no other large heads. After telling this story I do not wish to go upon record as a game slaughterer, for those who know anything of my hunting know that I am strongly opposed to anything of the kind. We usually have killed only enough game for meat in camp, but at this time we had to feed beside ourselves ten dogs. Moreover, I have never thought that the killing of bulls made very much difference in the amount of the game, although in shooting them we have usually made it a rule to kill only such heads as we wished to take home. I should add, moreover, that all the meat that we did not use of the moose that we killed in this country was distributed among some Indians whom we met on our return, and who, hearing of our luck, followed our dog trail to the hunting grounds after our departure.

Having had enough moose hunting, and anxious to kill caribou, we concluded to cross Lake Winnipeg, which by this time—early in December—was frozen hard with nearly six feet of ice, the cracking of which, especially at night, produces a very curious and never-to-be-forgotten sound, which can be heard for miles. We soon reached the lake, but were detained a day or two waiting for a favorable day to cross—that is to say, one when the wind did not blow, as when it does the exposure in crossing on the ice is terrific. After finally venturing upon the ice, we made some forty or fifty miles the first day, and reached the edge of an island, in the middle of which there were a few houses occupied principally by Icelandic immigrants. These earn a precarious livelihood by fishing for whitefish and jackfish principally in the summer. They keep up this fishing all through the winter, however, to supply their own needs, by setting their nets

underneath the ice, employing a very simple
method, which, if De Long and his party had
known and provided for, they would never
have perished so miserably in the Lena delta.
Here we were witnesses to the fact which enti-
tles us to claim that the common domestic cow
is not, strictly speaking, properly to be classed
among the *herbivora*. We distinctly saw a very
ordinary looking cow devour with evident relish, while she was being milked, a large
jackfish, which had been taken from a frozen
pile stacked up outside of the house and
thawed for her evening meal.

These Icelanders live as a rule in a primitive but very comfortable way. They are
much more neat and cleanly than many of the
immigrants who come to the United States,
and it is a pity that we do not have them in
this country, for they seem to be very industrious and would make good citizens. However, it is probable that they were in search of
cold weather, and would not be happy unless
they had it. If this is the case, they most certainly have chosen the best spot on this continent which is at all accessible; for the region
around Lake Winnipeg is, I am told, one of
the coldest places where any reliable record

of the temperature is kept. During our trip, and especially while we were on the east side of the lake, the temperatures recorded were very low, often 45 degrees below zero. In fact, during our absence there was a record of 50 degrees below zero at Selkirk and Winnipeg; and, as we were over a hundred miles to the north, it is not unreasonable to suppose that the temperature was quite as low, if not lower, with us. It must not be forgotten, however, that, except for the cracking of the frozen trees, it is deathly still and quiet in these regions when the temperature drops to 10 degrees below zero. Indeed, when the temperature is below that point, it is usually much more comfortable for one who is out in such weather than a temperature of zero, or even 20 degrees above, with a heavy wind. Under these conditions, however, an ordinary man when out hunting cannot occasionally sit down on a log and smoke his pipe, for any length of time, with a great amount of pleasure. Like the persecuted boy in the play, although there are no policemen about, he is compelled, and indeed is usually perfectly willing, to keep "movin' on."

After leaving Big Island, as I remember the

name, we made our way across to the mouth of the Bad Throat River, where there was an old lumber camp, which a great many years ago was the scene of an important conflict between the Hudson Bay Company's men and the men of the Northwest Fur Company, in which quite a number were killed. Here we got another team of dogs, and picked up another member for our party in the person of an Englishman, who by choice had drifted into this country and lived there, marrying an Indian squaw shortly after our return. Unfortunately, the good old-fashioned plan of performing the marriage ceremony by running together under a blanket had been abolished, so he had to wait until the yearly visit of the priest. This marrying of squaws is of course common among the white men of this region.

As we had only a few things to get before starting out for the famous caribou country between the head waters of the Hole, the Askandoga and the Blood Vein rivers, we were not delayed long at this place. The snow was now quite heavy, at least enough so for comfortable snowshoe traveling, and we made rapid time after leaving the Bad Throat River. In this connection it is to be remarked that comparatively little snow falls in this region. This seems singular, and I do not know the meteorological explanation of the fact. There is certainly very much less, for instance, than in Minnesota, hundreds of miles to the south. The snow, however, is usually a dry powder all through winter, and very rarely becomes crusted.

In traveling over broken timbered country with dog-sleds, very much the same routes are followed that one takes with a canoe in summer—that is to say, you avoid the rough country by traveling on the rivers, which are usually covered with thick ice, or over the same portages that are used in summer. It was necessary for either Penrose, Keller or myself to lead the way with our snowshoes, while the others took care of the dog-sleds behind. The dogs followed accurately in the trail beaten out by our snowshoes for them.

The country on this side of the lake, unlike that of the west, is very rough, rocky and rugged, and especially so near the lake shore. It is quite thickly timbered. As one advances into the interior, however, this aspect changes, so that the country near the height of land is more open, and there are long stretches of nearly level country traversed by rocky, moss-covered and roughly parallel ridges. There is more or less timber on these ridges, and in the so-called muskegs between them. This is the country which the caribou seem to prefer.

After about two weeks' hard traveling, we reached the country which had been recommended to us and came upon great abundance of caribou sign. In fact, there were millions of tracks, but, curiously enough, no caribou were to be seen. We afterward found that they had been driven out by a lot of wolves, which probably had followed them down from the north. While this explanation was interesting, it was not productive of any great amount of satisfaction to the party, for we had been counting definitely upon fresh meat, and so had our dogs. At least, after doing the terrific work necessary to make this journey, it is fair to presume that they had counted upon being fed, and not being left to starve miserably while tied to a tree.

To add to our hardships, our Indian te-pee, made of canvas, began to smoke so excessively as to cause us the greatest discomfort, and we all thought we had pneumonia; but afterward concluded it was nothing but irritation of the lungs, due to breathing pine smoke a good many hours each day. In fact, it was almost unbearable. An Indian tepee of this kind, properly made by a squaw, is beyond doubt the most comfortable of all hunting tents in any respectable climate; but in a climate of 40 degrees below zero it is an abomination. We used frequently to crawl into our sheep-skin sleeping bags, wrap several blankets around the bags and put the fire out, merely to get relief from the annoyance of the smoke. In the morning the steam which arose from our bodies, and from the meal which we might be cooking, got mixed up with the smoke, so that it was impossible to distinguish each other when four feet apart. In fact, we were sometimes inclined to think that the dogs on the outside were better off than ourselves, though the appearance they presented in the morning was not such as to cause us to wish to change places with them. They were each tied by a short chain to the pine trees about the camp, and after a night of low temperature there were to be seen in the morning only twelve white mounds of snow; not that any snow had fallen during the night, or that the dogs had crawled underneath that already on the ground. Their white appearance was simply due to the dense coating of frost which had been produced from the condensation caused by the heat of their bodies. It must not be forgotten, however, that they are as hardy and as well able to withstand this rigorous climate as the wolves, from which many of them are directly descended. All of the so-called "huskies" are of this type.

Altogether things were not very pleasant about this time. Our Christmas Day rations consisted of one small roll each with a little coffee for breakfast, and in the evening each man was given a small piece of rabbit.

The rabbits in this country were unfortunately not as abundant as they were on the opposite side of the lake, where the Indian boy one day went out with one of our rifles to visit his rabbit snares and to shoot rabbits for the dogs. Before long we heard him shoot four times. He came back to camp with eight rabbits, which had certainly been killed with the rifle, none of them having been snared.

Those of us who were able to hunt at all hunted with the greatest perseverance, but with little success, until finally some one brought in the report that caribou had been seen, and in a very few days the country again contained numbers of them.

One morning, shortly after the first caribou had been seen, Keller, who had been quite sick, was unable longer to tolerate the smoke of the tepee, and took a little walk with his rifle close around our camp. He soon came upon the fresh trail of a bunch of caribou. He had followed it only a few hundred yards when he saw one of the caribou lying down. He is a dead shot, the best I have ever known in my life. He carefully steadied himself, raised his .45-90 Winchester, aimed at the caribou lying down and fired. When he went up to look at it, to his amazement, he came across another dead caribou, between the spot where he had fired and the one at which he had aimed. It had been shot straight through the temples. On going further, he found the other caribou shot exactly where he had aimed at it, some twenty yards distant from the first one. The only possible way in which he could explain this remarkable occurrence is that the caribou which had been shot through the head, and which he had not seen, had risen out of its bed just as he was in the act of firing and interposed his head directly in the line of fire. The fact of having fresh meat in camp, of course, brought great joy to us all, and especially to the semi-starved dogs. As in the case of killing the first moose, it seemed to have the effect of changing our luck, for we afterward killed a number of caribou, although we were not successful in getting good heads.

These caribou are totally different from the moose in the kind of food they live upon and in their general habits. They prefer a different sort of a country, the two rarely being found together. They spend much of their time in the muskegs, which seem to be characteristic of all of that region of the country; but these muskegs are not open, like those on the west side of the lake, being more or less covered with a growth of stubby jack pine, from which usually hangs an abundance of long gray moss. The caribou feed upon this moss, while the moose, on the other hand, are fond of the tender sprouts of the red and gray willow. The caribou, however, are often found on the rocky ridges, where they find good feed on the moss growing upon the rocks. Indeed, they seem to have no settled place of abode, like moose, being probably one of the most restless animals on the face of the earth. They seem to be always on the move. Unlike the moose, they are very inquisitive, in this respect being more like the antelope than any other animal. They are found singly, or in twos or threes, or in small bunches of ten to twenty, but often in great herds of a hundred or perhaps a thousand. They spend a great deal of their time on the lakes in the winter, where they play with each other like kittens. They are wonderfully quick in their actions. They are also very sure of their footing, and we saw a number of places in the snow where they had slid down quite steep rocks for some distance, probably by putting their four feet close together. Great herds often come down from the region on the western shore of Hudson Bay and return the following summer.

Very few people have any idea of the immense numbers of caribou which are found in the great tract of country to the west of Hudson Bay. By many who are familiar with this country they are believed to be as numerous as the buffaloes ever were in the early days. When more or less scarce, as they were during the greater portion of our hunt, they afford excellent hunting; but I should imagine that when they are very numerous there would be little sport in killing them, for as a rule they are not at all shy or difficult to approach. In general it may be said that the caribou of this region, known as the woodland caribou, live in the wooded districts during the summer and autumn, but in the winter time go to the higher land. Wind and cold seem to have no terror for them, and I doubt very much whether there is an animal in the world, with the exception perhaps of the musk-ox or the polar bear, that is so well fitted by nature to withstand the intense cold of the region in which they live. When one sees a caribou's track for the first time, he is amazed at its size, and its difference from the long, narrow, sharp-toed track of the moose, and naturally comes to the conclusion that the animal must be much larger than it really is. As a matter of fact, they are not much larger than the black-tailed deer, and considerably smaller than the elk of the Rocky Mountains. Until he has seen them, one is likely to imagine that the caribou is an ungainly, misshapen animal. This is a great mistake. Not only are they as a rule well proportioned, but they are extremely graceful. Their curious horns give them, of course, rather an odd appearance. The meat we found to be delicious, and rather better than moose meat.

After having remained as long as we desired in this country, and as long as we could stand the infernal smoke of the tepee, and after having secured a good supply of meat for our return journey, we loaded our toboggans, and retraced our steps without especial incident to the mouth of the Bad Throat River. From there we took a sleigh to Selkirk, driving over the lake on the ice, and arriving at Selkirk the latter part of January or the 1st of February.

To those who may contemplate taking a similar trip to the Canadian woods in winter, I would say that it will prove a very interesting and never-to-be-forgotten experience, and that the hardships of such a trip are not necessarily severe if one will be guided entirely by the advice of the inhabitants of the region, especially as to his clothing and general outfit. I feel certain that, if one goes to the right locality, not only will he get good sport, but he will get it under very pleasant and novel conditions, and return home more benefited in every way than if he had taken a trip of the same duration to some warm climate. Under no circumstances, however, let him imagine that he knows more than the people of the country as to what he should do and wear.

D. M. Barringer.

OUTESHAI, RUSSIAN BARZOI.

Wolf-Hunting in Russia

The enormous extent and diversified conditions of the various localities of this empire would naturally suggest a variety of sport in hunting and shooting, including perhaps something characteristic. In the use of dogs of the chase especially is this suggestion borne out by the facts, and it has been said that in no other country has the systematic working together of fox-hounds and greyhounds been successfully carried out.

Unfortunately, this sort of hunting is not now so general as prior to the emancipation of the serfs in 1861. A modest kennel for such sports consists of six to ten fox-hounds and four to six pairs of barzois,* and naturally demands considerable attention. Moreover, to use it requires the presence of at least one man with the fox-hounds and one man for each pair or each three greyhounds. To have a sufficient number of good huntsmen at his service was

*Barzoi—long-haired greyhound, wolf-hound, Russian greyhound.

formerly a much less expensive luxury to a proprietor than now, and to this fact is due the decline of the combined kennel in Russia.

This hunt is more or less practised throughout the entire extent of the Russian Empire. In the south, where the soil is not boggy, it is far better sport than in Northern Russia, where there are such enormous stretches of marshy woods and tundra. Curiously enough, nearly all the game of these northern latitudes, including moose, wolves, hares, and nearly all kinds of grouse and other birds, seem to be found in the marshiest places—those almost impracticable to mounted hunters.

Though the distances covered in hunting, and also in making neighborly visits in Russia, are vast, often recalling our own broad Western life, yet in few other respects are any similarities to be traced. This is especially true of Russia north of the Moscow parallel; for in the south the steppes have much in common with the prairies, though more extensive, and the semi-nomadic Cossacks, in their mounted peregrinations and in their pastoral life, have many traits in common with real Americans. Nor is it true of the Caucasus, where it would seem that the Creator, dissatisfied with the ex-

cess of the great plain,* extending from the
Finnish Gulf to the Black Sea, resolved to establish a counterpoise, and so heaved up the
gigantic Caucasus. There too are to be found
fine hunting and shooting, which merit description and which offer good sport to mountain amateurs.

The annual hunt in the fall of 1893 in the
governments of Tver and Yaroslav, with the
Gatchino kennels, will give a good idea of the
special sport of which I have spoken. It is im-
perative that these hounds go to the hunt once
a year for about a month, although for the
most part without their owner. The master of
the hunt and his assistant, with three or four
guests, and oftentimes the proprietors of the
lands where the hounds happen to hunt, usually constitute the party. The hunt changes locality nearly every year, but rarely does it go
further from home than on this occasion, about
450 versts from Gatchino. As a rule it is not
difficult to obtain from proprietors permission
to hunt upon their estates, and this is somewhat surprising to one who has seen the free-
dom with which the fences are torn down and

*The Waldeir hills, extending east and west half-way between St. Peters-
burg and Moscow, are the only exception.

left unrepaired. It is true that they are not of the strongest and best type, and that peasant labor is still very cheap; yet such concessions to sport would rarely be made in America.

It was at Gatchino, on the 10th day of September, that the hunting train was loaded with men, horses, dogs, provisions and wagons. The hunt called for twenty-two cars in all, including one second-class passenger car, in one end of which four of us made ourselves comfortable, while in the other end servants found places. The weather was cold and rainy, and, as our train traveled as a freight, we had two nights before us. It was truly a picturesque and rare sight to see a train of twenty-two cars loaded with the *personnel,* material and live stock of a huge kennel. The fox-hounds, seventy in number, were driven down in perfect, close order by the beaters to the cracks of the Russian hunting whip and installed in their car, which barely offered them sufficient accommodation. The greyhounds, three sorts, sixty-seven in number, were brought down on leashes by threes, fours or fives, and loaded in two cars. Sixty saddle and draft horses, with saddles, wagons and hunting paraphernalia, were also loaded. Finally the forty-four gray and green uniformed huntsmen, beaters, drivers and ourselves were ready, and the motley train moved away amid the uttered and unuttered benedictions of the families and relatives of the parting hunt.

Our first destination was Peschalkino, in the government of Tver, near the River Leet, a tributary of the Volga, not far from the site of the first considerable check of the Mongolian advance about 1230. I mention this fact in passing to give some idea of the *terrain*, because I think that it is evident to anyone who has visited this region that the difficulty of provisioning and of transportation in these marshes must have offered a greater obstacle to an invading army than did the then defenders of their country.

We passed our time most agreeably in playing vint* and talking of hunting incidents along the route. Many interesting things were told about the habits of wolves and other game, and, as they were vouched for by two thorough gentlemen and superb sportsmen, and were verified as far as a month's experience in the field would permit, I feel authorized to cite them as facts.

*Vint—game of cards resembling whist, boaston and *préférence.*

The bear has been called in folk-lore the moujik's brother, and it must be conceded that there are outward points of resemblance, especially when each is clad in winter attire; moreover the moujik, when all is snow and ice, fast approximates the hibernating qualities of the bear. One strong point of difference is the accentuated segregative character of the former, who always live in long cabin villages.*

But it is rather of the wolf's habits and domestic economy that I wish to speak—of him who has always been the dreaded and accursed enemy of the Russian peasant. In the question of government the wolf follows very closely the system of the country, which is pre-eminently patriarchal—the fundamental principle of the *mir.* A family of wolves may vary in number from six to twenty, and contain two to four generations, usually two or three, yet there is always one chief and one wife—in other words, never more than one female with young ones. When larger packs have been seen together it was probably the temporary marshaling of their forces for some desperate raid

---

*The bear is caricatured in Russian publications as a humorous, light-hearted, joking creature, conversing and making common sport with the golden-hearted moujik, his so-called brother.

or the preliminaries of an anarchistic strike. The choruses of wolves and the special training of the young for them are interesting characteristics. Upon these choruses depends the decision of the hunter whether or not to make his final attack upon the stronghold of the wolves; by them he can tell with great precision the number in the family and the ages of the different members. They are to wolf-hunters what tracks are to moose- and bear-hunters —they serve to locate the game. When the family is at home they occur with great regularity at twilight, midnight and dawn.

In camp near Billings, Montana, in the fall of 1882, we heard nightly about 12 o'clock the howling of a small pack of coyotes; but we supposed that it was simply a "howling protest" against the railway train, passing our camp at midnight, that had just reached that part of the world. Possibly our coyotes have also howling choruses at regular intervals, like the Russian wolves.

There was such a fascination in listening to the wolves that we went out several times solely for that purpose. The weirdness of the sound and the desolateness of the surroundings produced peculiar sensations upon the listener.

To an enthusiastic lover of sport and nature these pleasurable sensations might be well compared with the effect of the Niebelungen songs upon an ardent Wagnerite. The old professional huntsmen could tell just what members of the family and how many were howling; they scarcely disagreed upon these points.

These old hunters pretended to interpret the noisy assemblies of the wolves as regards content or discontent, satisfaction or dissatisfaction.

Owing to the difficulty of securing wolves under most favorable circumstances, especially old ones, it would be considered folly to make a drive if the matinal howl had not been heard. But to make a successful drive in a large marshy forest many beaters must be employed, and, as they are gathered from far and near, considerable time is necessary to collect them; therefore it is almost essential to know that the wolves were "at home" at midnight as well as dawn.

While in the vicinity of a certain wolf family whose habitat was an enormous marshy wood, entirely impossible to mounted men, we were compelled to await for forty-eight hours the return of the old ones, father and mother. At times during this wait only the young ones, at other times the young and the intermediate ones, would sing. Not hearing the old ones, we inferred they were absent, and so they were—off on a raid, during which they killed two peasant horses ten miles from their stronghold. It was supposed that the wolves of intermediate age also made excursions during this time, as indicated by the howlings, but not to such great distances as the old ones. It was perfectly apparent, as we listened one evening, that the old ones had placed the young ones about a verst away and were making them answer independently. This seemed too human for wolves.

After one day and two nights of travel we arrived at the little station of Peschalkino, on the Bologoe-Rybinsk Railway, not far from the frontier between the two governments, Tver and Yaroslav, where we were met by two officers of the guard, a Yellow Cuirassier and a Preobiajensky, on leave of absence on their estates (Koy), sixteen versts from the rail. They were brothers-in-law and keen sportsmen, who became members of our party and who indicated the best localities for game on their property, as well as on the adjoining estates.

Peschalkino boasts a painted country tavern of two stories, the upper of which, with side entrance, we occupied, using our own beds and bed linen, table and table linen, cooking and kitchen utensils; in fact, it was a hotel where we engaged the walled-in space and the brick cooking stove. As to the huntsmen and the dogs, they were quartered in the adjacent unpainted log-house peasant village—just such villages as are seen all over Russia, in which a mud road, with plenty of mud, comprises all there is of streets and avenues. After having arranged our temporary domicile, and having carefully examined horses and dogs to see how they had endured the journey, we made ready to accept a dinner invitation at the country place of our new members. Horses were put to the brake, called by the Russians *Amerikanka* (American), and we set out for a drive of sixteen versts over a mud road to enjoy the well-known Slav hospitality so deeply engrafted in the Ponamaroff family.

I said road, but in reality it scarcely merits the name, as it is neither fenced nor limited in width other than by the sweet will of the trav-

eler. Special mention is made of this road because its counterparts exist all over the empire.
It is the usual road, and not the exception, which is worse, as many persons have
ample reasons for knowing. This condition
is easily explained by the scarcity of stone,
the inherent disregard of comfort, the poverty
of the peasants, the absence of a yeoman
class, and the great expense that would be
entailed upon the landed proprietors, who live
at enormous distances from each other. The
country in these and many other governments
has been civilized many generations, but so
unfinished and primitive does it all seem that
it recalls many localities of our West, where
civilization appeared but yesterday, and where
to-morrow it will be well in advance of these
provinces. The hand-flail, the wooden plow-
share, the log cabin with stable under the
same roof, could have been seen here in the
twelfth century as they are at present. Thanks
to the Moscow factories, the gala attire of the
peasant of to-day may possibly surpass in brilliancy of color that of his remote ancestry,
which was clad entirely from the home loom.
With the exception of the white brick churches, whose tall green and white spires in the

distance appear at intervals of eight to ten versts, and of occasional painted window casings, there is nothing to indicate that the colorings of time and nature are not preferable to those of art. The predominating features of the landscape are the windmills and the evenness of the grain-producing country, dotted here and there by clumps of woods, called islands. The churches, too, are conspicuous by their number, size, and beauty of architecture; school-houses, by their absence. Prior to 1861 there must have been a veritable mania here for church-building. The large and beautiful church at Koy, as well as two other pretentious brick ones, were constructed on his estates by the grandfather of our host.

Arrived at Koy, we found a splendid country place, with brick buildings, beautiful gardens, several hot-houses and other luxuries, all of which appeared the more impressive by contrast. The reception and hospitality accorded us at Koy—where we were highly entertained with singing, dancing and cards until midnight —was as bounteous as the darkness and rainfall which awaited us on the sixteen versts' drive over roadless roads back to our quarter bivouac at Peschalkino.

Wolf-Hunting in Russia

The following morning marked the beginning of our hunting. About 10 o'clock all was in readiness. Every hunter* had been provided with a leash, a knife and a whip; and, naturally, every huntsman with the two latter. In order to increase the number of posts, some of the huntsmen were also charged with leashes of greyhounds. I shall in the future use the word greyhound to describe all the sight hounds, in contradistinction to foxhound; it includes barzois (Russian greyhounds), greyhounds (English) and crosses between the two. The barzois numbered about 75 per cent. of all the greyhounds, and were for the most part somewhat less speedy than the real greyhounds, but better adapted for wolf-hunting. They also have greater skill in taking hold, and this, even in hare coursing, sometimes gives them advantage over faster dogs. One of the most interesting features of the coursing was the matching of Russian and English greyhounds. The leash system used in the field offers practically the same fairness as is shown by dogs at regular coursing matches. The leash is a black nar-

*Hunter-gentleman, huntsman, man of the hunt—conventional terms.

row leather thong about fifteen feet long, with
a loop at one end that passes over the right
shoulder and under the left arm. The long
thong with a slit at the end, forming the hand
loop, is, when not in use, folded up like a lariat
or a driving rein, and is stuck under the knife
belt. To use it, the end is put through the
loop-ring collars, which the greyhounds continually wear, and is then held fast in the left
hand until ready to slip the hounds. Where
the country is at all brushy, three dogs are the
practical limit of one leash, still for the most
part only two are employed. It is surprising
to see how quickly the dogs learn the leash
with mounted huntsmen; two or three days
are sufficient to teach them to remain at the
side of the horse and at a safe distance from
his feet. Upon seeing this use of the leash
with two dogs each, I was curious to know
why it should be so; why it would not be
more exciting to see half a dozen or more
hounds in hot pursuit racing against each
other and having a common goal, just as it
is more exciting to see a horse race with a
numerous entry than merely with two com-
petitors. This could have been remedied, so
I thought, by having horsemen go in pairs,

or having several dogs when possible on one leash. Practice showed the wisdom of the methods actually employed. In the first place, it is fairer for the game; in the second, it saves the dogs; and finally, it allows a greater territory to be hunted over with the same number of dogs.

There are two ways of hunting foxes and hares, and, with certain variations, wolves also. These are, by beating and driving with fox-hounds, and by open driving with greyhounds alone. In the first case a particular wood (island) is selected, and the fox-hounds with their mounted huntsmen are sent to drive it in a certain direction. The various leashes of greyhounds (barzois alone if wolves be expected) are posted on the opposite side, at the edge of the wood or in the field, and are loosed the second the game has shown its intention of clearing the open space expressly selected for the leash. The mounted beaters with the fox-hounds approach the thick woods of evergreens, cottonwood, birch and undergrowth, and wait on its outskirts until a bugle signal informs them that all the greyhound posts are ready. The fox-hounds recognize the signal, and would start immediately were they not terrorized by the black *nagaika*—a product of a country that has from remotest times preferred the knout* to the gallows, and so is skilled in its manufacture and use. At the word *go* from the chief beater the seventy fox-hounds, which have been huddled up as closely as the encircling beaters could make them, rush into the woods. In a few minutes, sometimes seconds, the music begins—and what music! I really think there are too many musicians, for the voices not being classified, there is no individuality, but simply a prolonged howl. For my part, I prefer fewer hounds, where the individual voices may be distinguished. It seemed to be a needless use of so many good dogs, for half the number would drive as well; but they were out for exercise and training, and they must have it. Subsequently the pack was divided into two, but this was not necessitated by fatigue of the

*Though not pertinent to the subject, I cannot refrain from relating a curious comparison made to me by a very intelligent Russian, aide-de-camp general of the late Emperor: "Just as the scarcity of women in early American times caused them to be highly appreciated and tenderly cared for, so the relative scarcity of men in early Russia caused the Government to appreciate them and to preserve them at all hazards. Logically follows the exalted position of woman to-day in the United States and the absence of capital punishment in Russia."

hounds, for we hunted on alternate days with greyhounds alone.

One could well believe that foxes might remain a long time in the woods, even when pursued by such noise; but it seemed to me that the hares* would have passed the line of posts more quickly than they did. At the suitable moment, when the game was seen, the nearest leash was slipped, and when they seemed to be on the point of losing another and sometimes a third was slipped. The poor fox-hounds were not allowed to leave the woods; the moment the game appeared in the open space they were driven back by the stiff riders with their cruel whips. The true foxhound blood showed itself, and to succeed in beating some of them off the trail, especially the young ones, required most rigorous action on the part of all. This seemed to me a prostitution of the good qualities of a race carefully bred for centuries, and, while realizing the necessity of the practice for that

*There are two varieties: the so-called white hare and the so-called red hare. The former becomes white in winter, and weighs, when full grown, ten pounds; the latter has a reddish gray coat which does not change, and weighs about one and a half pounds less than the other variety. The red hare frequents the fields less than does the white. The foxes are the ordinary red ones.

variety of hunt, I could never look upon it with complaisance.

It is just this sort of hunt* for which the barzoi has been specially bred, and which has developed in him a tremendous spring; at the same time it has given him less endurance than the English greyhound. It was highly interesting to follow the hounds with the beaters; but, owing to the thickness of the woods and the absence of trails, it was far from being an easy task either for horse or rider. To remain at a post with a leash of hounds was hardly active or exciting enough for me—except when driving wolves—especially when the hounds could be followed, or when the open hunt could be enjoyed. In the second case the hunters and huntsmen with leashes form a line with intervals of 100 to 150 yards and march for versts straight across the country, cracking the terrible *nagaika* and uttering peculiar exciting yells that would start game on a parade ground.

---

*In Northern Russia, owing to the extensive forest, brush and marsh lands, every effort was made to utilize the small open spaces or clearings for the greyhounds, and this was the usual way of hunting; while in Southern Russia, where steppes predominate, the open hunt—*chasse à courre*—prevailed. This explains why the Crimean barzoi also has more endurance than the now recognized type from the north.

Wolf-Hunting in Russia

After a few days I flattered myself that I could manage my leash fairly and slip them passably well. To two or three of the party leashes were not intrusted, either because they did not desire them or for their want of experience in general with dogs and horses. To handle a leash well requires experience and considerable care. To prevent tangling in the horse's legs, especially at the moment the game is sighted, requires that the hounds be held well in hand, and that they be not slipped until both have sighted the game. I much prefer the open hunt to the post system. There is more action, and in fact more sport, whether it happens that one or several leashes be slipped for the same animal. When it is not possible to know whose dogs have taken the game, it belongs to him who arrived first, providing that he has slipped his leash.

So much for the foxes and hares, but the more interesting hunting of wolves remains. Few people except wolf-hunters—and they are reluctant to admit it—know how rarely old wolves are caught with hounds. All admit the danger of taking an old one either by a dagger thrust or alive from under* barzois,

*This is the Russian phrasing, and correctly describes the idea.

however good they be. There is always a possibility that the dogs may loosen their hold or be thrown off just at the critical moment. But the greatest difficulty consists in the inability of the hounds to hold the wolf even when they have overtaken him. When it is remembered that a full-grown wolf is nearly twice as heavy as the average barzoi, and that pound for pound he is stronger, it is clear that to overtake and hold him requires great speed and grit on the part of a pair of hounds.

A famous kennel,*which two years since caught forty-six wolves by the combined system of hunting, took in that number but one old wolf—that is, three years or more old. The same kennel last year caught twenty-six without having a single old one in the number. We likewise failed to include in our captures a single old wolf. I mention these facts to correct the false impression that exists with us concerning the barzois, as evidenced by the great disappointment when two years since a pair, in one of the Western States, failed to kill outright a full-grown timber wolf. At the field trials on wolves, which take place twice a year at Colomiaghi, near Petersburg, im-

*That of the Grand Duke Nicolas Nicolaievitch.

mediately after the regular field trials on hares, I have seen as many as five leashes slipped before an old wolf could be taken, and then it was done only with the greatest difficulty. In fact, as much skill depends upon the *borzatnik* (huntsman) as the dogs. Almost the very second the dogs take hold he simply falls from his horse upon the wolf and endeavors to thrust the unbreakable handle of his *nagaika* between the jaws of the animal; he then wraps the lash around the wolf's nose and head. If the hounds are able to hold even a few seconds, the skilled *borzatnik* has had sufficient time, but there is danger even to the best. I saw an experienced man get a thumb terribly lacerated while muzzling a wolf, yet he succeeded, and in an incredibly short time. On another occasion, even before the brace of hounds had taken firm neck or ear holds, I saw a bold devil of a huntsman swing from his horse and in a twinkling lie prone upon an old wolf's head. How this man, whose pluck I shall always admire, was able to muzzle the brute without injury to himself, and with inefficient support from his hounds, it is not easy to understand, though I was within a few yards of the struggle. Such skill comes from long experience, indifference to pain and, of course, pride in his profession.

Having hunted foxes and hares, and having been shooting as often as the environs of Peschalkino and our time allowed, we changed our base to a village twenty-two versts distant over the border in the government of Yaroslav. It was a village like all others of this grain and flax district, where the live stock and poultry shared the same roof with their owners. A family of eleven wolves had been located about three versts from it by a pair of huntsmen sent some days in advance; this explained our arrival. In making this change, I do not now recall that we saw a single house other than those of the peasant villages and the churches. I fancy that in the course of time these peasants may have more enlightenment, a greater ownership in the land, and may possibly form a yeoman class. At the present the change, slow as it is, seems to point in that direction. With their limited possessions, they are happy and devoted subjects. The total of the interior decorations of every house consists of icons, of cheap colored pictures of the imperial family and of samoovars. In our lodgings, the house of the village

starost, the three icons consumed a great part
of the wall surface, and were burdened with
decorations of various colored papers. No
one has ever touched upon peasant life in Russia without mentioning the enormous brick
stove (*lezanka**); and having on various hunts
profited by them, I mean to say a word in behalf of their advantages. Even as early as
the middle of September the cold continuous
rains cause the gentle warmth of the *lezanka*
to be cordially appreciated. On it and in its
vicinity all temperatures may be found. Its
top offers a fine place for keeping guns, ammunition and various articles free from mois-
ture, and for drying boots;† while the horizontal abutments constitute benches well adapted
to thawing out a chilled marrow, or a sleeping
place for those that like that sort of thing. A
generous space is also allowed for cooking purposes. In point of architecture there is nothing that can be claimed for it but stability; excepting the interior upper surface of the oven,
there is not a single curve to break its right
lines. It harmonizes with the surroundings,
and in a word answers all the requirements of

Lezanka means something used for lying on.

†Hot oats poured into the boots were also used for drying them.

the owner as well as of the hunter, who always preserves a warm remembrance of it.

The wolves were located in a large marshy wood and, from information of the scouts based on the midnight and dawn choruses, they were reported "at home." Accordingly we prepared for our visit with the greatest precautions. When within a verst of the proposed curved line upon which we were to take our stands with barzois, all dismounted and proceeded through the marsh on foot, making as little noise as possible. The silence was occasionally broken by the efforts of the barzois to slip themselves after a cur belonging to one of the peasant beaters, that insisted upon seeing the sport at the most aggravating distance for a sight hound. It was finally decided to slip one good barzoi that, it was supposed, could send the vexatious animal to another hunting ground; but the cur, fortunately for himself, suddenly disappeared and did not show himself again.

After wading a mile in the marshy bog, we were at the beginning of the line of combat— if there was to be any. The posts along this line had been indicated by the chief huntsman by blazing the small pine trees or by hanging a heap of moss on them. The nine posts were established in silence along the arc of a circle at distances from each other of about 150 yards. My post was number four from the beginning. In rear of it and of the adjoining numbers a strong high cord fence was put up, because it was supposed that near this part of the line the old wolves would pass, and that the barzois might not be able to stop them. The existence of such fencing material as part of the outfit of a wolf-hunter is strong evidence of his estimate of a wolf's strength—it speaks pages. The fence was concealed as much as possible, so that the wolf with barzois at his heels might not see it. The huntsmen stationed there to welcome him on his arrival were provided with fork-ended poles, intended to hold him by the neck to the ground until he was gagged and muzzled, or until he had received a fatal dagger thrust.

While we were forming the ambuscade—defensive line—the regular beaters, with 200 peasant men and women, and the fox-hounds, were forming the attack.

Everything seemed favorable except the incessant cold rain and wind. In our zeal to guard the usual crossings of the wolves, we ignored the direction of the wind, which the wolves, however, cleverly profited by. It could not have been very long after the hounds were let go before they fell upon the entire family of wolves, which they at once separated. The shouts and screams of the peasants, mingled with the noises of the several packs of hounds, held us in excited attention. Now and then this or that part of the pack would approach the line, and, returning, pass out of hearing in the extensive woods. The game had approached within scenting distance, and, in spite of the howling in the rear, had returned to depart by the right or left flank of the beaters. As the barking of the hounds came near the line, the holders of the barzois, momentarily hoping to see a wolf or wolves, waited in almost breathless expectancy. Each one was prepared with a knife to rush upon an old wolf to support his pair; but unfortunately only two wolves came to our line, and they were not two years old. They were taken at the extreme left flank, so far away that I could not even see the killing. I was disappointed, and felt that a great mistake had been made in not paying sufficient attention to the direction of the wind. Where is the hunter who

FOXHOUNDS OF THE IMPERIAL KENNELS.

has not had his full share of disappointments when all prospects seemed favorable? As often happens, it was the persons occupying the least favorable places who had bagged the game. They said that in one case the barzois had held the wolf splendidly until the fatal thrust; but that in the other case it had been necessary to slip a second pair before it could be taken. These young wolves were considerably larger than old coyotes.

So great was the forest hunted that for nearly two hours we had occupied our posts listening to the spasmodic trailing of the hounds and the yelling of the peasants. Finally all the beaters and peasants reached our line, and the drive was over, with only two wolves taken from the family of eleven. Shivering with cold and thoroughly drenched, we returned in haste to shelter and dry clothes.

The following morning we set out on our return to Peschalkino, mounted, with the barzois, while the fox-hounds were driven along the road. We marched straight across the country in a very thin skirmish line, regardless of fences, which were broken down and left to the owners to be repaired. By the time we had reached our destination, we had enjoyed some good sport and had taken several hares. The following morning the master of the imperial hunt, who had been kept at his estates near Moscow by illness in his family, arrived, fetching with him his horses and a number of his own hounds. We continued our hunting a number of days longer in that vicinity, both with and without foxhounds, with varying success. Every day or two we also indulged in shooting for ptarmigan, black cocks, partridges, woodcocks and two kinds of snipe—all of which prefer the most fatiguing marshes.

One day our scouts arrived from Philipovo, twenty-six versts off, to report that another family of wolves, numbering about sixteen, had been located. The *Amerikanka* was sent in advance to Orodinatovo, whither we went by rail at a very early hour. This same rainy and cold autumnal landscape would be intolerable were it not brightened here and there by the red shirts and brilliant headkerchiefs of the peasants, the noise of the flail on the dirt-floor sheds and the ever-alluring attractions of the hunt.

During this short railway journey, and on the ride to Philipovo, I could not restrain certain reflections upon the life of the people and of the proprietors of this country. It seemed on this morning that three conditions were necessary to render a permanent habitation here endurable: neighbors, roads and a change of latitude; of the first two there are almost none, of latitude there is far too much. To be born in a country excuses its defects, and that alone is sufficient to account for the continuance of people under even worse conditions than those of these governments. It is true that the soil here does not produce fruit and vegetables like the Crimean coast, and that it does not, like the black belt, "laugh with a harvest when tickled with a hoe"; yet it produces, under the present system of cultivation, rye and flax sufficient to feed, clothe and pay taxes. What more could a peasant desire? With these provided his happiness is secured; how can he be called poor? Without questioning this defense, which has been made many times in his behalf, I would simply say that he is not poor as long as a famine or plague of some sort does not arrive—and then proceed with our journey.

From Orodinatovo to Philipovo is only ten versts, but over roads still less worthy of the name than the others already traveled. The *Amerikanka* was drawn by four horses abreast. The road in places follows the River Leet, on which Philipovo is situated. We had expected to proceed immediately to hunt the wolves, and nearly 300 peasant men and women had been engaged to aid the fox-hounds as beaters. They had been assembled from far and near, and were congregated in the only street of Philipovo, in front of our future quarters, to await our arrival. What a motley assembly, what brilliancy of coloring! All were armed with sticks, and carried bags or cloths containing their rations of rye bread swung from the shoulders, or around the neck and over the back. How many pairs of boots were hung over the shoulders? Was it really the custom to wear boots on the shoulders? In any case it was *de rigueur* that each one show that he or she possessed such a luxury as a good pair of high top boots; but it was not a luxury to be abused or recklessly worn out. Their system of foot-gear has its advantages in that the same pair may be used by several members of a family, male and female alike.

It was not a pleasure for us to hear that the wolves had been at home at twilight and midnight, but were not there at dawn; much less comforting was this news to those peasants living at great distances who had no place near to pass the night. The same information was imparted the following day and the day following, until it began to appear doubtful whether we could longer delay in order to try for this very migratory pack.

Our chances of killing old wolves depended largely upon this drive, for it was doubtful whether we would make an attack upon the third family, two days distant from our quarters. Every possible precaution was taken to make it a success. I was, however, impressed with the fact that the most experienced members of the hunting party were the least sanguine about the old wolves.

Some one remarked that my hunting knife, with a six-inch blade, was rather short, and asked if I meant to try and take an old wolf. My reply was in the affirmative, for my intentions at that stage were to try anything in the form of a wolf. At this moment one of the land proprietors, who had joined our party, offered to exchange knives with me, saying that he had not the slightest intention of attacking a wolf older than two years, and that my knife was sufficient for that. I accepted his offer.

At a very early hour on this cold rainy autumnal morning we set out on our way to the marshy haunts of the game. Our party had just been reinforced by the arrival of the commander of the Empress's Chevalier Guard regiment, an ardent sportsman, with his dogs. All the available fox-hounds, sixty in number, were brought out, and the 300 peasants counted off. The latter were keen, not only because a certain part of them had sportsmanlike inclinations, but also because each one received thirty copecks for participation in the drive. Besides this, they were interested in the extermination of beasts that were living upon their live stock.

The picture at the start was more than worthy of the results of the day, and it remains fresh in my mind. The greater portion of the peasants were taken in charge by the chief beater, with the hounds, while the others followed along with us and the barzois. Silence was enforced upon all. The line of posts was established as before, except that more care was exercised. Each principal post, where three barzois were held on leash, was strengthened by a man with a gun loaded with buckshot. The latter had instructions not to fire upon a wolf younger than two years, and not even upon an older one, until it was manifest that the barzois and their holder were unequal to the task.

My post was a good one, and my three dogs were apparently keen for anything. At the slightest noise they were ready to drag me off my feet through the marsh. Thanks to the *nagaika*, I was able to keep them in hand. One of the trio was well known for his grit in attacking wolves, the second was considered fair, while the third, a most promising two-year-old, was on his first wolf-hunt. Supported by these three dogs, the long knife of the gentleman looking for young wolves and the yellow cuirassier officer with his shotgun, I longed for some beast that would give a struggle. The peasants accompanying us were posted out on each flank of our line, extending it until the extremities must have been separated by nearly two miles.

The signal was given, and hunters, peasants and hounds rushed into the woods. Almost instantly we heard the screams and yells of the nearest peasants, and in a short time the faint barking of the fox-hounds. As the sounds became more audible, it was evident that the hounds had split into three packs—conclusive that there were at least three wolves. My chances were improving, and I was arranging my dogs most carefully, that they might be slipped evenly. My knife, too, was within convenient grasp, and the fox-hounds were pointing directly to me. Beastly luck! I saw my neighbor, the hunter of young wolves, slip his barzois, and like a flash they shot through the small pine trees, splashing as they went. From my point of view they had fallen upon an animal that strongly resembled one of themselves. In reality it was a yearling wolf, but he was making it interesting for the barzois as well as for all who witnessed the sight. The struggle did not last long, for soon two of the barzois had fastened their long teeth in him—one at the base of the ear, the other in the throat. Their holder hastened to the struggle, about 100 yards from his post, and with my knife gave the wolf the *coup de grace*. His dogs had first sighted the game, and therefore had the priority of right to the chase. So long as the game was in no danger of escaping no neighboring dogs should be slipped. His third barzoi, on trial for qualifications as a wolf-hound, did not render the least aid.

Part of the fox-hounds were still running, and there was yet chance that my excited dogs might have their turn. We waited impatiently until all sounds had died away and until the beaters had reached our line, when further indulgence of hope was useless. Besides the above, the fox-hounds had caught and killed a yearling in the woods; and Colonel Dietz had taken with his celebrated Malodiets, aided by another dog, a two-year-old. What had become of the other wolves and where were most of the hounds? Without waiting to solve these problems, we collected what we could of our outfit and returned to Philipovo, leaving the task of finding the dogs to the whippers-in. The whys and wherefores of the hunt were thoroughly discussed at dinner, and it was agreed that most of the wolves had passed to the rear between the beaters. It was found out that the peasants, when a short distance in the woods, had through fear formed into squads instead of going singly or in pairs. This did not, however, diminish the disappointment at not taking at least one of the old ones.

The result of this drive logically brought up

the question of the best way to drive game. In certain districts of Poland deer are driven from the line of posts, and the same can be said of successful moose-hunts of Northern Russia. Perhaps that way may also be better for wolves.

After careful consideration of the hunting situation, we were unanimous in preferring hare and fox coursing with both fox-hounds and barzois, or with the latter alone, at discretion, to the uncertainty of wolf-hunting; so we decided to change our locality. Accordingly the following day we proceeded in the *Amerikanka* to the town of Koy, twenty-five versts distant. We arrived about noon, and were quartered in a vacant house in the large yard of Madam Ponamaroff. Our retinue of huntsmen, dogs, horses, ambulance and wagons arrived an hour later.

There was no more wolf-hunting.

Henry T. Allen.

A Bear-Hunt in the Sierras

A few years ago, a friend and I were cruising for our amusement in California, with outfit of our own, consisting of three pack horses, two saddle animals, tent and camp furnishings. We had started from Los Angeles; had explored various out-of-the-way passes and valleys in the San Bernardino and San Rafael Mountains, taking care the while to keep our camp supplied with game; had killed deer and exceptionally fine antelope in the hills adjoining the Mojave Desert; had crossed the San Joaquin Valley and visited the Yosemite, where the good fortune of finding the Half Dome, with the Anderson rope, carried away by ice, gave us the opportunity for one delicious climb in replacing it.

Returning to Fresno, we had sold our ponies and ended our five months' jaunt. My friend had gone East, and I had accepted the invitation of a member of the Union Club in San Francisco, to whom I bore a letter of introduction, to accompany him upon a bear-hunt in the Sierras. He explained to me that the limited extent of his ranch in the San Joaquin Valley—a meager and restricted demesne of only 7,000 acres, consisting of splendid pasturage and arable land—made it necessary for the sheep to look elsewhere than at home for sustenance during the summer months.

Many of the great ranches in the valley possessed prescriptive rights to pasturage over vast tracts in the high Sierras. These, although not recognized by the law, were at least ignored, and were sanctioned by custom. The land belonged to nobody—that is, it belonged to Uncle Sam, which, so far as a Texas or California stockman was concerned, amounted to exactly the same thing. The owner of such a right to pasturage zealously maintained his claim; and if, for any reason, he could not use it himself during a particular season, he formally gave his consent to some one else to enjoy the privilege in his stead. It was considered a gross violation of etiquette for a stockman to trespass upon that portion of the forest habitually used by other sheep. Such intrusions did occur, particularly upon the part of Mexicans with small flocks—"tramp sheep" they were called; but when the intruder was shot, small sympathy accompanied him to the grave, and the deep damnation of his taking off, in more senses than one, served as a salutary reminder to other gentlemen with discourteous tendencies to maraud. The consequence of all this was that a big ranchman spoke of his summer range with the same sense of proprietorship and security of possession as of his alfalfa field or pits of ensilage.

We arrived at my friend's ranch in the evening, and the next morning but one were in the saddle and on our way—it having been arranged that the younger brother of my host was to take his place upon the hunt. As we were to arrive at the sheep-herders' camps on the fourth day from the ranch, no elaborate preparations were necessary; we took but a single animal for the pack, besides the horses we rode. A Mexican herder, Leonard, was the third member of the party—cook, packer, guide, general storehouse of information and jest. The first night we camped in the foot hills, in a grove of big-cone pines, curiously enough in the exact place where, a fortnight before, my friend Proctor and I had pitched our tent on the way from the Yosemite to Fresno, and which we had left without the slightest expectation, on the part of either, of ever seeing again.

Little of the journey to the mountains remains in my memory. We passed a great timber chute of astonishing length—twenty or forty miles, or something of the sort—down which timber is floated from the great pine and spruce forests to the railroad, with little trouble and at slight expense; the water being of commercial value for purposes of irrigation during the summer, and bringing a good price after it has fulfilled its special function as carrier. The drinking water for my friend's ranch was taken from this, a supply being drawn in the cool of the morning sufficient to last throughout the day, and most grateful we found it during sultry August days in a part of the country where ice is not to be procured.

Each of the four days of our journey we were climbing higher among the mountains, into a thinner and more invigorating atmosphere. The days were hot so long as one remained exposed to the sun, but the shadows were cool and the nights most refreshing. Upon the last morning of our journey, crossing a mountain creek, my attention was called to a rude bridge, where had occurred a battle of the ranchmen upon the occasion of an attempted entry by a "tramp" owner with his flock into somebody's "summer range." The intruder was killed, and I believe in this particular instance the possessor of the unwritten right of exclusive pasturage upon Government land found the laws of California awkward to deal with; not so deadly, it may be, as a six-shooter, but expensive and discouraging to quiet pastoral methods.

Another point of interest was Rattlesnake Rock, which we rounded upon the trail. This was a spot peculiarly sheltered and favored by the winds, the warmest corner that snakes wot of, and here they assemble for their winter's sleep. In the mild days of early spring, when the rest of the world is still frozen and forbidden, this one little nook, catching all the sun, is thawed and genial. From beneath the ledge crawl forth into the warmth great store of rattlers, big and little. Coming out from the Yosemite Valley, I had killed one quite four feet in length and of exactly the same girth as my wrist, which I was assured was not at all an extraordinary size for them "in these parts." Near this rock, in an unfeeling manner, I shot the head off another big one, and he will no longer attend the yearly meeting of his kind at Rattlesnake Rock.

Upon this stage of our journey we met no one, yet the noble forest of spruce through which we were traveling bore only too plainly the signs of man's presence in the past, and of his injurious disregard of the future. Everywhere were the traces of fire. The trees of the Sierras, at the elevation at which we were, an altitude of 8,000 or 10,000 feet, grow more sparsely than in any forest to which we are accustomed in the East. Their dry and unimpeded spaces seem like heaven to the hunter familiar only with the tangled and perplexing undergrowth of the "North Woods," where the midday shadow, the thick underbrush, the uneven and wet, mossy surface, except upon some remote hardwood ridge, are the unvarying characteristics. In the Rocky Mountains, and that part of the Sierras with which I am familiar, it is quite different. In California the trees do not crowd and jostle one another, but have regard for the sacredness of the person so far as the mutual relation of one and all are concerned. Broad patches of sunshine beneath the trees encourage the growth of rich grasses, none so sweet as those which are found at a great altitude; and, although the prevailing tint under foot is that of the reddish earth, tufts of succulent feed abound sufficient to repay the sheep for cruising everywhere, while occasional glades furnish the most delicious and abundant pasturage. As in every forest, the processes of nature are slow—it takes a long time for the dead past to bury its dead. On every side lie fallen trees; and a generation of rain and snow, sunshine and wind and tempest, must elapse before these are rotted away, and by the enrichment of the soil can furnish nourishment and life to their progeny and successors. Naturally these trees are a hindrance and annoyance to the sheep herder; they separate his flock and greatly increase his labors. The land is not even his master's, whose one idea is temporary gain, hence there is no restraining influence whatever for their preservation. "So long as it lasts my lifetime, what matter?" is the prevailing sentiment.

As there is no rain during the summer months, the fallen trees become perfectly dry; a handful of lighted twigs is all that is required to set fire to them, when they blaze or smoulder until consumed. Owing to the absence of underbrush, forest fires are far less common than would be expected; but, of course, the soil is impoverished by the deprivation of its natural enrichment, the decaying wood, and the centuries to come will there, as well nigh everywhere in our country, point the finger of scorn at our spendthrift forestry.

Although this is the chief economic injury, the beauty of the woods is sadly marred; all large game is frightened away, except the bear, which is half human and half hog in his methods, and minds it not at all—in fact, finds the presence of man perfectly intelligible, and his fat flocks a substantial addition to his own bill of fare. Leonard pointed out to us a certain mountain shrub, a rank poison to sheep. Every cluster of it in his range is known to the herder, who keeps the sheep in his charge at a safe distance. This is one of his important duties; for, if a sheep eats of this plant, he is a "goner."

In one particular the pasturage of the high Sierras has greatly suffered. The ranchmen naturally wish to get their sheep off the home range as early in the spring as possible—in fact, the last month there is one of starvation.

A Bear-Hunt in the Sierras

The new crops have not yet grown, nothing remains standing of the old but a few dead stalks of weeds, the supply of alfalfa cut the year before has long since been exhausted, and, metaphorically speaking, the sheep and cattle have to dine, as the hungry Indian is said to do, by tightening his belt half a dozen holes and thinking of what he had to eat week before last. Only the weaklings die, however; the others become lean and restless, and as eager as their masters to start for the mountains. The journey supplies them with scant pickings, just enough to keep body and soul together, but morally it is a relief from the monotony of starvation at home, and they work their way stubbornly and expectantly up the mountains and into the forest as soon as the sun permits and anything has grown for them to eat. The consequence of this close grazing is that certain species of the grasses upon which they feed are never allowed to come to flower and mature their seed; hence those with a delicate root, the more strictly annual varieties, which rely upon seed for perpetuation of the plant, have a hard time of it. Where the sheep range, the wild timothy, for example—a dwarf variety and an excellent, sweet grass—has almost disappeared, although formerly it grew in abundance.

The forest glades through which we passed had the appearance of a closely-cropped pasture, as different as possible from the profusion of tall grasses and beautiful flowering plants which grow in similar openings untroubled by sheep. So far as the grasses are concerned—or "grass," by which, I take it, is ordinarily designated the foliage of the plant— I doubt if it is molested to any great extent by deer. Their diet is mainly the tender leaves of plants—"weeds" to the unscientific person. The heads of wild oats and of a few of the grasses might prove sufficiently sweet and tempting to arrest their fancy; but as for grazing, as sheep or cattle do, it is not their habit. When deer shall have come to trudge up hill in the plodding gait of the domestic beasts, and shall have abandoned their present method of ascending by a series of splendid springing leaps and bounds, the very embodiment of vigor and of wild activity, time enough then for them to take to munching grass, the sustenance of the harmless, necessary cow. At present they are most fastidious in their food, and select only the choicest, tenderest tips and sweetest tufts of herbage, picking them here and there, wandering and meditating as they eat. I will not say that they never touch grass, for I have seen deer feeding among cattle in the open, but it is not by any means the chief article of their diet, and when they partake of it under such circumstances, it is more as a gratification of their social instincts, I think, than from any particular love of the food itself.

A little before noon upon the fourth day, we arrived at one of the sheep camps, to which we had been directed by a stray herd, and where we were to find the foreman of the sheep gang. At that hour of the day there were naturally in camp but a few men. The cook was there, of course. His functions were simple enough—to make bread, tea, and boil mutton, or bake it in a Mexican oven beneath the coals. With him was the chief herder and a half-witted Portuguese, who, upon the day following, in the plenitude of his zeal and mental deficiency, insisted upon offering himself as live bait for a grizzly, as will be narrated.

During the afternoon I strolled further up the mountain with my rifle, in the hope of a shot at a stray deer, and to have a look at the lay of the land. Bear tracks I saw and a little deer sign also, but it was too early in the day regularly to hunt. All nature nodded in the dozy glare of the August afternoon, and after the hot journey in the saddle I found a siesta under the clean spruce trees refreshing. Toward sunset I awoke to find a pine martin in a tree across the gulch reconnoitering, and evidently turning over in his mind the probabilities whether the big creature curled up on the hillside "forninst" him were of the cast of hunter or hunted. I soon brought him out of that, and upon my return to camp the hide was graciously accepted by the chief herder, who converted the head of it into a tobacco pouch with neatness and dispatch. At the evening meal there were good-natured references to *chile con oso*—bear's meat cooked with red peppers—regret expressed that the camp's larder could at present afford none, and expressions of confidence that this delicacy would soon be set before us—all most politely and comfortably insinuated. They had the gratification of their desire; it was on the next day but one.

That night there was a great jabbering of

bad Spanish around the camp-fire. Had this been the rendezvous of Sicilian brigands, it doubtless would have had a slightly more picturesque appearance, but the difference would have been only of degree, not at all of kind. The absence of rain made tents unnecessary. Piles of bedding, of cooking and riding equipment, defined the encampment. Around the fire a dozen Mexican clustered, of whom, except the chief herder and Leonard, not one spoke English. They wore the broad hats of their race, and were arrayed for protection against the cool night winds of the Sierras in old and shabby cloaks, some of which had been originally bright in color, but now were subdued by age and dirt into comfortable harmony with the quiet tones of the mountain and the forest. Old quilts and sheepskins carpeted a small space where we had been invited to seat ourselves upon our arrival. Then, as throughout our stay, every possible mark of hospitality was shown us—a delicious, faint survival of Castilian courtesy.

Long after I had turned in, somewhere in the dead vast and middle of the night, I was aroused by the sound of scurry and scampering among the bunch of sheep which was rounded up near the camp. Experience has taught these creatures to efface themselves at night, and they are only too glad to sleep quietly, as near as possible to humans, with no disposition to wander after dark. They realize their danger from bears, yet the protection which a Mexican affords is a purely imaginary thing, as unsubstantial as the baseless fabric of a vision, of as little real substance for the protection of the flock as the dream of mutton stew and fat bear, by no means a baseless fabric, which engrosses the sleeping shepherd, body and mind. The disturbance upon this occasion soon subsided. One and another of the shepherds sleepily moved in his blankets—perhaps swore to himself a hurried prayer or two—but not one of them spoke aloud or indicated the slightest intention of investigating the cause of the commotion. Only too well they and the sheep knew what it signified. Quiet reigned again, and, attaching no importance to the incident, I was promptly asleep.

In the morning I learned that the disturbing cause had been the charge of a grizzly into the flock within a stone's throw of us, a sound too familiar to occasion comment at the time. There were the tracks, to leeward of the sheep, of a she grizzly and two cubs. Their approach had been without a sound; not the snap of a twig, or the faintest footfall, had given any signal of their presence. The mother had critically overhauled the flock in her mind from a slight rise of ground, on a level with their backs or slightly higher, and made deliberate choice of a fat wether, having a discriminating eye, and being too good a judge of sheep flesh to take any but such as are in prime condition. A single quick rush and she has secured her victim, in an instant, before the rest are fairly upon their feet, and is off, carrying the sheep in her mouth as easily as a cat would her kitten, her delighted cubs trotting behind. Every two or three nights this occurrence was repeated, with no interference upon the part of the Mexicans. "What recks it them?" "The hungry sheep look up and are not fed." On the contrary, the bears are. As for the Mexicans, they have "lost no bear!" To have seen the intruder would have been only a gratuitous anxiety, since nothing in the world would have tempted them to fire at it. Should they risk life and limb for a sheep? and that the *patron's,* who had so many! It was not their quarrel! The charge of the grizzly was a thing as much to be accepted as an incident of the Sierras as the thunderbolt—equally dangerous to him who should interfere as the lightning stroke to one daring to interpose his rifle between the angry heavens and the fore-doomed tree.

We may feel sure that the lesson is not lost upon the cubs. They are taught energy, sagacity, craft in maturing their plans, courage and promptness in their execution. They are taught reverence for the ursine genius, unbounded admiration for their mother's leadership and steadiness of nerve, at the same time that they are taught contempt for the stupidity of sheep and the pusillanimity of humans. It may be that an apologist for the latter might find a word to mitigate their too severe sentence. A she grizzly of the Sierras, at night, with hungry cubs to feed, is not an altogether pleasant thing to face when infuriated by wounds, none of which may be bad enough to cripple her, yet combined are amply sufficient to make her pretty cross and dangerous. The Mexican is a poor shot, but what can you expect? His vocation is a humble one. Were he of more positive and deter-

mined temperament, he would be a *vaquero* of
the plains, or *boyero* (*Anglicè* "bull-whacker")
of the Sant Fé trail or down in old Mexico;
and not the dry nurse of these "woolly idiots,"
in whose race, for innumerable centuries, man
has elaborately cultivated stupidity, and, by
systematic process of artificial selection, has
faithfully eliminated every sign of insubordi-
nation and the last trace of individuality of
temperament, and that which in our race is
called character. No native-born white man
in this country can be induced to follow, for
any length of time, the vocation of shepherd.
The deadly monotony of the occupation drives
him either to imbecility or desperation. It is
well known that men who habitually care for
any animal come in time to resemble him.
Stable boys, bred to the vocation of groom,
become horse-faced and equine of disposition,
eventually they wheeze and whistle like a
curry-comb. Cowboys partake of the scatter-
brained recklessness of the Texas steer which
they tend. No one can admit dogs to be daily
and familiar companions without absorbing
into his system somewhat of their sense of humor and of their faithfulness. The lion-tamer,
who enters unscathed the den of his charge,

must share the robustious courage and determination of the beast with which he associates. The rat-catcher, whether he be ferret or man, partakes of the fierce slyness of the game he follows; and I remember that, years ago, before I ever heard mention of this peculiarity of re-semblance, I could detect, plainly writ in the face of the attendant of "Mr. Crowley," when he was kept in the old arsenal building in Central Park, the reflected temperament and animalism of the poor, indolent, captive chimpanzee, whose fellow and all too sympathetic friend he had made himself. Naturalists are well aware of this phenomenon.

If this be so, and stupidity catching, what more potent influence of fatty degeneration of the intellect could there be than the uninterrupted society of sheep, with nothing in the world to think of except their care—without even the stimulating influence of gain to redeem the paralyzing service. The sheep are not their own, and if the bears eat them up the keepers do not feel the stimulating ache in their money-pocket that might tempt them, however feebly, to resist aggression. Moreover, as a rule, they are wretchedly armed. Each of these men carried an old six-shooter of an outlandish and forgotten pattern, good enough to try a chance shot at another Mexican with, but only a source of more or less pleasurable titillation to a bear, were one ever to be discharged at him, and about as effective as pelting an alligator with strawberries. If the last stage of misery for a horse be to drag, along its rigid road of stone and iron, the city horse-car with its thankless freight of fares, the corresponding degradation of the "gun" is to rest upon the hip of a degenerate sheep-herder, half Spaniard, half Indian and half coyote. Any self-respecting weapon reduced to such straits would be conscious of its low estate; its magazine would revolve in a creaky, half-hearted, reluctant fashion; it would doubtless fire an apologetic bullet; its report would be something between "scat" and "beg your pardon," to which a bear would pay but slight heed. Others of the Mexicans were armed with old muskets, somewhat rusty and ramshackly, but with a furry longitudinal perforation throughout their length, along which—it could not creditably be called a bore—a ball could after a fashion, if you gave it time enough, be propelled. Leonard was exceptionally fortunate in this respect; he carried an old rim-fire .44-40 Winchester, the action of which occasionally worked and occasionally did not. Comparatively speaking, he was rather a swell in the matter of firearms; but if one should put his trust in him in case of emergency as a sheet anchor to windward, there was always the remote possibility, were the strain too intense, that he might not be a dependence of absolute security.

The afternoon of this day, much against my real inclination, but in accordance with the prevailing desire, we started out, the whole rabble of us, to follow the she grizzly's trail. It could not be called a "still-hunt," for the reason that six men hunting in a pack are never still; however, it did not matter. We found in a neighboring gulch bits of the fleece, bones and hides of three sheep, and the sufficiently plain evidence, upon the trampled and bloody ground, of recent feasts. Yet this was the banqueting hall and not the children's nursery. A bear thinks nothing of a little stroll of ten miles or so before or after eating. It aids digestion, and in case of a female, as this was, wards off an attack of the nerves. Particularly a bear with cubs would put at least that distance between herself and hunt-

ers. Moreover they are so clever that I doubt
not this one knew already by scent and subtle
process of ratiocination how many of us there
were in camp, where we were from, the color
of our hair, what sort of rifles we carried, their
caliber, how heavy a bullet and how many
grains of powder they fired. This is said in the
light of after events and of further experience.

That afternoon, in our unjustifiably sanguine forecast, we had hopes of finding this
particular bear. The half-witted "Portugee,"
of whom I have spoken, showed especial
zeal in the presence of the *patron*, and insisted, in spite of mild and repeated caution,
in going ahead and scrupulously investigating
every possible ambuscade where there was the
remotest chance of finding the bear, or, what
was much more likely, of the bear finding him.
In consideration of the fact that this was a she
one which we were after, that she was proud
and well fed, and on the lookout for pursuit,
had the "Portugee" found her, she would in
all probability have received his visit with cordial warmth. Not speaking his tongue fluent-
ly, I was unable to express my solicitude except
by signs and admonitory gestures. The rest
of the party apparently seemed to think that,

while the bear was interested and occupied with him, a good opportunity would be offered for getting in a shot; and as Portuguese were a drug in the market in that part of California, and grizzly bears, dead, a great rarity, he was suffered to contribute his mite to the success of *la chasse*, and all went merrily. Not a thicket or a den did he leave unprobed.

An hour or two were spent in beating up the gulch to its head. Then a barren mountain side presented itself, three or four miles of it, with no shelter. Leonard ran the trail here like a dog, literally ran it, and the pack of hunters tailed behind him for a half or three-quarters of a mile. A bit before sundown we were at the edge of the chaparral —a tangle of bushes and quaking asp—rather a baddish place in which to stumble upon her serene highness. However, my companions did me the honor to promote me to the "Portugee's" place and function. With rifle across the crook of arm, we stole as silently as might be—the United States army would have made more noise—into the jungle. Sunset overtook us up on the far edge, with a stretch of open forest in sight, and, I doubt not, with Madam Bruin and her cubs miles ahead in some inaccessible snarl of bushes, where the crackling underbrush would warn her of approach as fully as could the most complete system of burglar alarms.

That night, leaving word that whoever might be the first to stir in the morning should call me, I unrolled my blankets under a spruce somewhat apart from the crowd, and was soon asleep. Before daylight I was astir, had a cup of coffee and a bite, and was off. Upon the previous afternoon I had picked the direction I would take, which was to skirt certain openings in the forest below. Fresh sign I saw that assured me of the excellence of the range for bear, but I encountered nothing alive worth powder and ball, and returned to camp about 9 o'clock. I was greeted by Leonard with the joyful news that during my absence he had seen from camp a big bear across the side of the mountain only a mile or so away, and disappear over the ridge. This happened about 7 o'clock. The chief herder and my companion received the information somewhat in a spirit of respectful incredulity, but Leonard assured me that it was so, and we made preparations to follow the trail toward night. Meanwhile I breakfasted and slept.

We left camp about 3 o'clock in the afternoon, and without the slightest difficulty found
the beast's trail exactly where the Mexican
had said we should. Before this time I had
killed an odd bear or so in Colorado, and had
had some little experience in unraveling the
trail of game. It may be rather priding myself upon the accomplishment, but let me here
acknowledge the superiority of professional
talent. Leonard, to all intents and purposes,
had been born and raised on a sheep range.
His earliest recollections had been of the
sheep camps of the Sierras, of the reputation
of the arch-enemy of the flock and of the
havoc which he works. From infancy he, like
all the herders, had been constantly upon the
lookout for bear sign; it was his one keen-
est intellectual accomplishment and diversion.
The result of this special training was such
an acuteness of vision and nice discrimination
of eye that he could clearly distinguish a bear's
footprints upon the naked sand and gravel
where at a quick glance I was unable to see
any indication whatever. A single grain of
sand displaced was sufficient to arrest his eye;
he detected it instantly. To him the minutest
particle had its weather-beaten side as well as

a boulder. A bear could not put his foot upon the ground without leaving an impress which he could detect. His talent was so quick and unerring that we soon organized a division of labor. He was to concentrate his energies and attention upon the trail, while I, by his side or a step in advance, when the trail read itself and permitted such a course, was to watch ahead and around for both of us. Fortunately this arrangement was satisfactory to him. The hardest of the trail to decipher was where it was written in condensed short-hand across a mountain slide or *coulisse* of naked granite boulders. Here not one trace was to be found in a dozen yards. Fortunately we could trust in the genius of the bear; he was aware, as well as La Place, that a straight line is the shortest distance between two points. He undoubtedly knew exactly where he was heading. We had his general direction, and by beating about for a tuft of grass here with a blade displaced, a stray gooseberry bush there with a leaf awry, and yonder a patch of thicker vegetation, betraying inter-ference, we soon succeeded, owing mainly to Leonard's genius as a pathfinder, in getting through a couple of acres of this most vague and illegible pedography. At last we had the trail upon the mountain side once more, where, after such difficulties surmounted, following it was a comparative luxury.

After having proceeded in this manner for perhaps two hours, we entered timber, and were obliged to advance with greater caution to avoid the slightest sound which might betray our presence and give the alarm. With two men the risk of doing this is increased in geometrical ratio. One person alone, traveling through the woods, may, and almost certainly will, break an occasional twig under foot. If game is within hearing, the sound will inevitably be detected; the deer, if it be a deer, will lift his head and listen; but if the hunter stops and waits for a time, the chances are that the animal will, after due interval of silence, resume his feeding if so engaged, or his rumination, be it physical or moral, and the alarm may not prove fatal. Not so when companions are hunting together. It would seem as if the second man, with dreadful promptness, never failed to snap his twig also, which sounds as loud as a pistol coming upon the strained attention of the listening beast, who is off like a streak, leaving the disappointed hunter, as he hears him crashing away, to moralize that company in the chase halves the pleasure and doubles the sorrow. The only safety where union is necessary is to proceed with exaggerated and fantastic caution.

Leonard was a treasure in this. He had dreamt of grizzlies all his life, yet had never been in at the death. His heart was in the hunt—he fairly sighed for gore. We crept into the woods as silent as panthers and as "purry" in the ardor of the chase. After a mile or so our bear had come to an immense fallen spruce, lying across the trail, with the big butt, five or six feet in diameter, to our right, the top pointing up the hill. Over the middle of this, at right angles, lay another large tree, with the point toward us. I felt that behind the first of these, if I had been the original and unmolested settler in these parts, as the bear was, with all the world before me where to choose, I should have made the bed for my morning nap. It was long after daylight when he had reached this covert. He had doubtless been stirring soon after sunset the evening before; he had, it is not unlikely, been traveling all night; had feasted heartily

upon a sheep during that interval, and by the
time he reached this place, which may have
been in his mind from the start, was feeling
comfortably lazy and inclined to the refresh-
ment of sleep. Behind that tree, so admirably
suited for the purpose, I trusted that he might
still remain. The big end would protect a
cool space from the heat of the morning sun,
and we might yet be so lucky as to find him in
his lair beneath its shelter. A signal to Leonard was enough, and we proceeded to circle
the fallen timber, which fortunately the wind
permitted, with all the caution of which we
were capable. Had the gentleman we were
after been our dearest friend at the crisis of a
fever, we could not have tiptoed about his bed
with more solicitude lest we disturb sweet
slumber. The big tree lay in front of us; by
this we crept at a respectful distance, and then
approached the further end of the tree lying
across it. With great care I sneaked up
until I could look over its trunk at the desired
point. Alas! no bear had made his nest
there.

Sorrowfully, but without a sound, I crawled
upon the intervening log and slowly stood
erect. There, directly beneath me, where I

could have jumped into it most comfortably, was the deserted form of the bear, which he had dug in the morning within an hour after Leonard had seen him, and in which the greater part of the day had been spent, until he had stirred abroad for water, with which to wash down the recollection of his muttons. Although ardently hoping that he was behind the tree, I had not in the least expected to find his bed in this particular place. Had he stayed quietly there until our arrival, he would have given one of us a delicious surprise, and the mutual agitation of the moment might have induced a shot with unpremeditated haste, and possibly have caused me to get off that fallen spruce tree in somewhat quicker time than I had climbed it. One naturally would not feel any keen desire to display his acrobatic skill in walking a log for the entertainment of an infuriated grizzly. A few hairs proclaimed him a cinnamon, who is either a variety of the grizzly or his first cousin—authorities differ; at all events, he closely resembles him except in color, which, although of a uniform light, fady brown, might be an extreme type of the "sorrel top" of the Rockies. In size the cinnamon fully holds his own with the grizzly; I should say that his head was rather longer. The generous excavation which this one had made showed that he was no mean representative of his species.

Not twenty yards away, and near the end of the big tree where I had expected to find him, was a little spring. To this, still without a word, we proceeded, saw where he had stood to drink more than once, doubtless long and deep. To our left, in the soft earth, lay his retreating footsteps—a continuation of the general direction of his previous course. A moment's pause for closer scrutiny, a smile and a whispered word exchanged—just to show that we were not bored; then, respectful of the silence of the darkening woods, we were again upon the trail. It was now easy to see why he had left his lair; it faced the west, and the heat of the afternoon sun had annoyed him, warmly clad and irritable with high living.

We had proceeded only about a stone's throw further when I caught a glimpse of our bear. Within twenty paces, under the shadow of a tree at the edge of a cool, umbrageous thicket, between him and the setting sun, lay the beast we were after; or, as I for a moment thought, judging from the great inchoate mass of brown fur, a pair, perhaps male and female, or one, it might be, a yearling cub. With finger lifted I signaled Leonard to stop. A great head was slowly raised and turned my way. A bullet between the eyes and down it went again, and I threw another cartridge into the chamber, expecting to see the second bear spring to his feet, ready to do whatever, in his judgment, the occasion required, either to fight or to run. Whichever he might elect to do, it was well to be prepared. "Give him another shot," said the prudent Leonard, and I fired a second time, sending this ball quartering and, like the first, through the brain; then I realized that there was but one, and he of creditable size. We soon had him out in the open, for nothing is easier to roll about than a bear just killed. He is like a great jelly-fish, and I have seen a little terrier no larger than a rabbit worry and shake a great carcass four times as large as the most commodious kennel he could desire, provided he were a sensible pup and had the comfortable instinct of wild things for snugness rather than ostentatious display. Enough of daylight remained for us to get his pelt off, with head and claws unskinned and attached, and to hurry over the mountain by moonlight with our trophy, a junk of rank meat for such as might desire it not forgotten.

We were cordially welcomed back to camp, and, after the usual pow-wow, the cook, with due formality, with Mexican *chile* and Spanish politeness, proceeded to concoct the boasted *chile con oso*—a much overrated dish when made of a tough old cinnamon he bear. After I had turned in I heard much laughter, and subsequently learned that it was at an incident of the day. As we were starting out in the afternoon, and before we had struck the bear's trail, in order to avoid any possibility of a premature shot I had casually inquired of Leonard if he wished to earn five dollars.

"Certainly, Señor, I am always glad to get the chance."

"Well, don't shoot then until I give the word, and you shall have it."

This circumstance Leonard had innocently narrated to the group around the camp-fire in the fuller elaboration of the hunt, and the story had an immediate success, the idea seeming to prevail that nothing in the world could have tempted him to fire before he was compelled to—which, as a matter of fact, I think was only prudent on his part, considering the arms he bore.

The next morning, to the infinite chagrin of some of us, the younger *patron* discovered that his presence was required at home, where, if he was mildly chid by my friend, his elder brother, who in generosity to his junior had yielded his own place and the leadership of this expedition, I should not greatly grieve.

Upon the third day thereafter we regained the ranch.

Alden Sampson.

The Ascent of Chief Mountain

In the most northern corner of the Piegans'
country, in northwestern Montana, almost
grazing the Canadian border with its abrupt
side, stands a turret-shaped mountain. Behind
it the great range of the Rockies, which for
hundreds of miles has been trending steadily
northwood, bends sharply away toward the
west, leaving the corner on which the mountain stands a huge protruding pedestal for its
weird shape. Ninety years ago Lewis and
Clarke saw it from far to southward as they
passed along the dwindling Missouri and called it Tower Mountain; but to the Indians it
has always been The Chief Mountain. Even
those prosaic German geographers to whom
we owe so much for information about our
own and other lands have either seen it and
fallen under the spell of its strange power, or
have taken their nomenclature directly from
the Piegans, for they have crowned it Kaiser
Peak.

The Ascent of Chief Mountain

For more than a year we had been numbered with the Chief's subjects. During the
previous summer we had been seeking the
acquaintance of the mountain goat; not the
shorn degenerate which throngs the slopes of
the Cascades and straggles among the southern
peaks of Montana, but the true snowy buffalo
of the northern Rockies; and from the ledges
of the St. Mary Mountains, where we had
sought him, could be seen still further to the
northward the Piegans' Chief. Of the range,
yet not in it, like a captain well to the front of
his battle-line, he pressed out into the broad
prairie, as if leading a charge of Titans toward
the far distant lakes. And through the long
months of an Eastern winter, and the still
longer months of an Eastern summer, above
all the memories of that wondrous land where
every butte and mountain peak teems with
legend, and where every bison skull on the
prairie tells its story, had towered the clear-cut
image of that Northern mountain, a worthy
sovereign of any man's allegiance. Now, as
inevitably as an antelope returns to its lure, we
had returned for a closer look at our mountain. Down deep in our hearts, battling with
the awe which we felt for him, was the almost

unspoken hope that perhaps in some way we might struggle up his sheer sides and make him, in a way he was to no one else, our king.

We were a party of three, the Doctor and I, and our faithful packer, Fox. A cold storm was blowing spitefully across the open foothills and out on to the prairie as we broke camp under the high banks of Kennedy Creek on the morning of the last stage of our journey. The clouds, driving over the range from the northwest, swung so low that they hid the peaks, and the great pedestal of the Chief met them all uncrowned, indistinguishable from the others about him. It was one of those doubtful mornings with which the mountains love to warn off strangers, or to greet their friends—one which might presage a week of storm or usher in a fortnight of surpassing beauty.

We had camped for the night at the last of those ranches which stretch along the bottom lands of the St. Mary River, and just as we started, its owner, Indian Billy, decided to go with us.

Even he had never been to the foot of his tribe's famous peak, and the dark-skinned idlers of the ranch who gathered about us as we flung the lash ropes over our horses could tell us little more than legends of it. Several Bloods from across the Canadian border declared that the boundary line ran, not where the white men had marked it on the prairie with their insignificant piles of stones, but through the deep cleft in the Chief's wall, where the Great Spirit himself had placed it; thus giving to the Bloods, who knew it best, their proper share of the mountain. And, getting warmer in their enthusiasm, they reminded Billy of their standing challenge to his tribe, the Piegans—fifty horses to anyone who should run around that wall, small as it seemed, in half a day.

For our part it was hard to realize even on that cold September morning that the long dreaming was over and the reality before us. It took all the straining of the pack ponies on the wet lead-ropes to remind us that we were at last climbing the foothills of the great peak. Our presence there, far from breaking the long enchantment, surrendered us bodily to it, and Billy, riding over the successive slopes before us, swaying in the saddle with the hawk-like motion of the prairie Indian, seemed a fit ambassador to lead us to his king. As the day passed, the clouds gradually lightened; and finally, just as we surmounted one of the higher foothills, at the summit of the long, sloping, forest-clad pedestal before us broke through the crown of the Chief. Toward us, on the east, it showed a black rectangular wall 2,-000 feet in length, 1,500 in height, and from its sharp corners the broken mists streamed away southward like tattered garments.

A few hasty pictures, taken while Fox mended a broken pack cinch, and we pressed on toward the foot of the mountain. Some benign influence was with us even thus early, and we were guided into the easiest way. Streaks of burned forest, bristling with windfalls, were slowly but successfully threaded, long rock slides luckily avoided, while we mounted steadily slope after slope; until finally, late in the afternoon, we pulled our panting horses out, just above timber line, upon the comparatively level summit of the pedestal. The foot of the great crown wall was still a mile away and 1,000 feet above us, but we were near enough and high enough for our purpose; and in a deep basin, sheltered from the wind and carpeted with softest mountain grass, and with the only water in the neighborhood sparkling up from a spring in the bottom, we found a perfect camp. As soon as the tents were pitched, Fox set about preparing dinner, while the seven horses, freed from their loads, buried their noses in the grass in perfect contentment.

As he sat in the door of the tent, the Doctor's eyes seemed glued to his field glass, while the object lenses ever pointed in the one direction, westward; under the brim of the Indian's broad hat, as he lay apparently dozing before the fire, I could see his black eyes fixed on the same point; and even Fox, constantly shifting his position about the fire, rarely took one which placed his back toward that black wall behind which the sun was now gradually sinking. For myself, all the longing of the past year had concentrated itself into a desire to rush over this last remaining distance; to get to that magic crown, to feel it with hand and foot, and to see whether, as the Piegans aver, it denied even a single foothold for a mortal man.

After dinner the Doctor and I did go to it. We clambered out of our little basin on to the higher portion of the domelike pedestal, and from this platform, on which rests the great crown, looked past its two edges at the vast mountain range behind it, stretching north and south. Then we picked our way toward it, through the loose boulders and broken rock; saw the summit hang further and further over us as we advanced into the gloom at its foot, and after finally reaching it and pressing ourselves against it where it rose sheer from its pedestal, we hurried back to camp through the twilight, thoroughly awed by the solemnity of the place.

The storm of the morning had cleared into a most perfect night; and, as we lay about the fire, Billy told us all that the old men had told him of the Chief. A full-blooded Piegan, in his new life as a ranchman he had not lost touch with the traditions of his tribe. Only one Piegan, he said, had ever attempted to climb the mountain. Years ago a hunting party of their young men had been encamped on the opposite side, where the cliffs do not overhang so much, and ledges run temptingly up for a distance; and one of them, the youngest and most ambitious of the band, declared that he would go to the summit. He started, and his companions watched him from below until he passed along one of the very highest ledges, out of sight. Then the spirit of the mountain must have met him; for, though they waited many days, and searched for him all around the base, he never came back. And the Piegans, being a prairie tribe and not over fond of the mountains at best, thereafter avoided any close acquaintance with their king.

A story had come to them, however, from the Flatheads across the range—a tribe whose prowess they always respected in war, as they believed in their truthfulness in peace—and as the story related to their mountain, they had treasured it among their own legends. Still earlier, many years before even the oldest Piegan was a boy, there had lived a great Flathead warrior, a man watched over by a spirit so mighty that no peril of battle or of the hunt could overcome him. When at last in his old age he came to die, he told the young men his long-kept secret. Many years before, as the time approached for him to go off into the forest and sleep his warrior sleep, in which he hoped to see the vision which should be his guide and protection through life, he had decided to seek a spot and a spirit which had never before been tried. So, carrying the usual sacred bison skull for his pillow, he had crossed the mountains eastward into the far-off Piegan country. Then, with none to aid him save the steady power of his own courage, he had ventured upon the ledges of the Chief of the Mountains, and, choking down each gasp of panic when at overhanging corners the black walls seemed striving to thrust him off and down, he had finally forced his way to the very summit. For four days and nights he had fasted there, sleeping in the great cleft which one can see from far out on the prairie. On each of the first three nights, with ever increasing violence, the spirit of the mountain had come to him and threatened to hurl him off the face of the cliff if he did not go down on the following day. Each time he had refused to go, and had spent the day pacing the summit, chanting his warrior song and waving his peace pipe in the air as an offering, until finally, on the fourth night, the spirit had yielded, had smoked the pipe, and had given him the token of his life. None of the young Flatheads, however, said Billy, had dared to follow their great warrior's example; so that to this day he was the only man who had braved the spirit of the Chief and made it his friend.

After we were rolled in our blankets, and

THE CHIEF'S CROWN, FROM THE EAST.

the late moon, rising from the prairie ocean behind us, had turned the dark, threatening wall to cheering silver, we thought again of the old warrior's steadfastness and longed to make his example ours.

The Doctor's thermometer marked 20 degrees Fahrenheit when Fox called us, and the morning bucket which he dashed over us was flavored with more of the spirit of duty than usual. But otherwise the weather had been made for us. Yesterday's storm had beaten down the smoke from Washington forest fires, which had clouded everything for the past month, and the Sweet Grass Hills twinkled across one hundred miles of prairie as if at our feet; and yet there was hardly a breath of wind. Under the lee of the wall itself absolute stillness brooded over ledges which even a moderate breeze could have made dangerous. We did not make an early start. The thing could be done quickly if it could be done at all, for there was only 1,500 feet of cliff.

Our men did not give the attempt to reach the summit from this, the eastern side, even the scant compliment of a doubt; in their minds its failure was certain, but they were

willing to see how far we could get up. The
Doctor, too, had at first suggested, and with
perfect correctness, that to try a difficult side
of a mountain before reconnoitering the other
was bad mountaineering, to say the least. But,
on the other hand, this east side was the famous side of the Chief—the side which every
passer-by on the prairie saw and wondered at.
With our glasses we had mapped a course
which seemed not impossible; was it not better
to meet our king face to face than to steal on
him from behind? Besides, this wonderful
weather might not last long enough for us to
reach the other side. And so our final conclusion was to try the east face.

Half way up the sheer face of the cliff was
divided horizontally by a broad, steep shelf
which ran nearly the length of the mountain.
That shelf could clearly be crossed at any
place; the difficulty would lie with the walls
below and above it. The lower one was bad
enough at best, but it was easy to recognize as
least bad a place where a slope of shale abutted
against it, shortening it some 300 feet. The
upper wall in general seemed even worse, but
it was furrowed by two deep chimneys, side by
side, one of which led into the mountain's

well-known cleft. The other chimney seemed to lead directly to the summit, but its lower mouth was inaccessible—cut off by overhanging cliff. Our plan, therefore, if we could ever reach the halfway shelf, was to use the first chimney in the beginning, then try to find a way around the dividing shoulder into the second, then follow that to the top. And at 9 o'clock we began on the lower wall.

Of course, the work which followed was not so difficult as it had promised from below— rock work rarely is—but it thoroughly taxed our slender experience, and, for a single man without a rope, must have been far worse. The Doctor and I took turns in leading, carrying up or having thrown to us from below a rope, on which the others then ascended. Most of the difficulty was thus confined to one man, and he could often be assisted from beneath. We were not skilled enough in the use of the rope to risk tying ourselves together.

Two hundred feet up came our first trouble, perhaps the worst of the day. We were sidling along a narrow shelf, with arms outstretched against the wall above, when we reached a spot where the shelf was broken by a round protruding shoulder. Beyond it the ledge com-

menced again and seemed to offer our only
way upward. I was leading at the time, and,
after examining it, turned back to a wider portion of the shelf for consultation. It was not a
place one would care to try if there was an
alternative.

We braced the Indian against the wall, and
his skillful hand sent the lariat whirling up at
a sharp rock above our heads. Time after time
the noose settled fairly around it, but found no
neck to hold it, and came sliding down. Then,
almost before we knew it, the Doctor had run
out along the ledge to the shoulder and had
started around. For a moment he hung, griping
the rounded surface with arms and knees; then
a dangerous wriggle and he was on the other
side.

Under his coaching the Indian and I followed; but Fox, when half way, lost his head,
and barely succeeded in getting back to the
starting point. He would not try again. The
poor fellow's moccasins had lost some of their
nails and he had slipped once or twice that
morning, thus destroying the nerve of one who
had at other times shown himself a good
climber. But of the Indian's companionship for
the rest of the day we were now sure.

Again, when near the top of that first wall, and when the halfway ledge seemed almost within our grasp, the shallow cleft—up which we were scrambling—ended in a deep pocket in the cliff's face, with no outlet above. The Doctor tried it at one corner, but the treacherous crumbling rock warned him back. I tried it at another, but was stopped by an overhang in the cliff. No help for it but to go back and try to find a way around.

Fifty feet below we landed on a small shelf running horizontally along the mountain's face, and, after following it northward a few moments, we found another channel leading up. The Doctor started to investigate it, while Billy and I continued on slowly looking for a better. Almost immediately, however, we heard the Doctor shout "All right," and, following him, came out at last upon the great halfway shelf of the mountain.

This was a steep slope of shale, which seemed in places quite ready to slide in an avalanche of loose rock over the edge of the cliff below; but the relief of being out upon it, and able once more to stand upright without the sensation of a wall against your face, apparently trying to shove you outward

from your slender foothold, was simply inde-
scribable.

After crossing the shelf and eating our
lunch in the mouth of the first or left-hand
chimney, we attacked the upper wall. Following up the chimney a short distance, we
found at last a narrow ledge leading to the
right, and, creeping around on it, I looked
into the right-hand chimney above its forbidding mouth. It led as a broad, almost easy,
staircase clear to the top of the wall above,
and for the first time we felt as if our king
were really ours.

Six or seven hundred feet more of steady
work, and we could feel the summit breeze beginning to blow down the narrow mouth of
the chimney. Billy was then sent to the front,
and at half past one the first Piegan stepped
out on the summit of the Chief Mountain.

It is a long ridge of disintegrated rock,
flanked at either end by lower rounded tur-
rets, and at its highest part is no wider than a
New England stone wall. On the opposite
western side the cliffs fell away as on our own,
but they seemed shorter, were composed of
looser rock, and far down below we could see
steep slopes of shale meeting them part way.

The Ascent of Chief Mountain

After we had picked out our various landmarks in the wonderful outlook about us, and
I had made my record from compass and ba-
rometer, we pushed our way carefully along
to the highest point of the narrow ridge, in
order to mark it with a cairn of rocks. Just as
we reached it, the Indian, who was still in the
lead, suddenly stopped and pointed to the
ground. There, on the very summit of Chief
Mountain, safely anchored by rocks from the
effect of wind or tempest, lay a small, weather-
beaten bison skull. It was certainly one of
the very oldest I have ever seen. Even in the
pure air of that mountain top it had rotted
away until there was little else than the frontal
bone and the stubs on which had been the
horns. Billy picked it up and handed it to us
quietly, saying with perfect conviction, "The
old Flathead's pillow!"

We left the skull where it had been found.
Much as we should have treasured it as a
token of that day, the devotion of the old
warrior who had brought it was an influence
quite sufficient to protect this memorial of his
visit. We shared his reverence far too much
to allow us to remove its offering. And then,
too, as Billy suggested, we were still on top of

the Chief, and the Chief had certainly been very forbearing to us. Those long walls, now darkened by the afternoon shade, those narrow ledges whence the downward climber could no longer avoid seeing the stone he dislodged bound, after two or three lengthening jumps, clear to the pedestal below, loomed very suggestively before his mind. But the Chief still remained gracious, and Billy worked even more steadily and sure-footedly going down than in the morning. We had all gained confidence, and besides we were certain of our course. By 5 o'clock we had reached the last bad place—where Fox had left us—and, after avoiding that by swinging down hand over hand on the rope from a ledge above, it was only a few moments to the bottom.

That night, after we were all safe in camp, and the great cliff beamed down on us more kindly than ever in the moonlight, the Doctor and I decided that we had been more favored than the old Flathead warrior, for the spirit of our mountain had been with us even before we reached its top.

And for our success an explanation beyond our physical powers seemed necessary to others also; for, when a few days later we returned to the ranch in the St. Mary's Valley, Billy, who had preceded us, met us with the mien of the prophet who is denied by his own, and told us that his cousins, the Bloods from across the border, had suggested that, when next he returned from a trip to the range, he should bring them a likelier story than that he had climbed the east face of the Chief Mountain.

Henry L. Stimson.

The Cougar

It was upwards of twelve years ago that I
had been down to one of the Rio Grande River
towns herding up Mexicans, whom I expected
to aid me in discovering gold where none existed. On my way down I had run across a
mountain lion making off with a lamb, and
shot and secured him after a little strategic maneuvering. On the return journey, after I had
hired as many of the greasers as I desired, I
camped at night about twenty miles from
home, in a log cabin that had lost the door, the
roof and all the chinking from between the
logs.

There was no reason to fear wild beasts—
and the cabin would have been no protection
for me even if there had been; nor was the
structure any protection from the numerous
cut-throat, horse-stealing Mexicans who flour-
ished in that section of the country as thickly
as cactus. However, I lariated my horse and
threw down my blankets in this tumble-down

shack, and turned in. I have quite a habit of sleeping on my back, and I was awakened some time in the night by a feeling of oppression on my chest. Having been accustomed to life in a country where the Indians were rampant, and where the wise man on awakening looked about him before stirring, I opened my eyes without moving, and there, standing directly on my breast, looking me squarely in the face, was a skunk, with its nose not, I swear, six inches from my own.

It was a bright moonlight night, and I could see that the little devil was of the kind whose bite is said to convey hydrophobia. But that did not worry me; it was not the bite I feared. I realized perfectly that if I moved I might get myself into trouble. I knew that the only thing for me to do was to let the skunk gambol over me until he wearied of the pastime and went out of the cabin.

I have a lurking suspicion that that skunk knew I was awake and in mental agony; for, after looking me in the face, he ran down my body on one leg and then up again, actually smelling of one of my ears; and then he trotted off me on to the floor of the cabin, where he nosed about awhile, then up again on my body;

and, after sprinting a few seconds over my person, he went down and out of the cabin.

So soon as he had disappeared out of the door I jumped to my feet and, drawing my gun, rushed out after him. He was plainly visible just to the right of the cabin, and I blazed away. Immediately after I had shot him I regretted it, for I had to move camp.

The next day, on my way back to camp, I journeyed over a divide that was more or less noted as a den for mountain lions; though to designate any particular locality as a "den" for cougars is incorrect, for it is not an animal that remains in any one place for any great length of time. He is a wandering pirate, who makes no one district his home for any long period.

However, this especial divide was said to harbor more of them than any other; or, at least, there were more signs of them, and more were reported to be started from there by hunters than elsewhere in the territory. Be that as it may, on the particular day of which I write I accidentally ran across the only cougar I ever have killed which gave me a fight and stampeded my horse, so that I was obliged to foot it into camp.

The Cougar

I do not think the bronco is as fearful of the cougar as of the bear, at least my experience has not been such. I have had a mustang jump pretty nearly from under me on winding a bear, and I have wasted minutes upon minutes in getting him near the carcass of a dead one, that I might pack home a bit of bruin's highly-scented flesh, and I never had any similar experience where the cougar was concerned. I have had my pony evince reluctance to approach the slain lion, but not show the absolute terror which seizes them in the neighborhood of bear.

My experience at this particular time, as I say, was novel in two respects—first, the fright with which my bronco was stricken; and second, the fight shown by the cougar. I had reached the top of the divide, and was picking my way across the fallen timber, which so often blocks the trail over the tops of divides in New Mexico. I remember distinctly having gained a clear spot that was pretty well filled with wild violets, which grew in great profusion thereabouts, and was guiding my pony that I should not trample upon them; for in that God-forsaken district, 10,000 feet above the level of the sea, it seemed too bad to crush the life out of the dainty little flowers that hold up their heads to the New Mexico sunshine.

Without warning, my bronco, which was traveling along at a fox-trot, stopped suddenly, and looking up I saw, not more than fifty yards away, about as large a mountain lion as I had ever encountered, standing motionless and looking at us with utmost complacency. To throw myself out of the saddle and draw my Sharps-forty from the saddle holster was the work of a very few seconds. Throwing the bridle rein over my arm, I slipped in a cartridge, and was just pulling down on him when the cougar started off at a swinging trot to one side at right angles to where he had stood, and through some small quaking aspens. Without thinking of the bridle being over my arm, I knelt quickly in order to get a better sight of the animal, and almost simultaneously pressed the trigger.

As I did so my bronco threw up his head, which spoiled my aim, and, instead of sending the ball through the cougar's heart, as I had hoped to do, it went through the top of his shoulders, making a superficial wound— not sufficiently severe to interfere with his locomotion, as I immediately discovered; for, with a combined screech and growl, that lion wheeled in my direction, and made for me with big jumps that were not exactly of lightning rapidity, but were ground-covering enough to create discomfort in the object of his wrath.

My bronco, meanwhile, was jumping all over the ground, and I realized I could not hold him and make sure of my aim. To swing myself into the saddle and make away would have been simple, but I knew enough of the cougar to know that if I retreated, he, in his fury, would be sure to follow; and on that mountain side, with its fallen timber and rough going, I should have little chance in a race with him. I had no revolver to meet him in the saddle at short range, and a knife was not to my liking for any purpose, so far as an infuriated cougar was concerned, except for skinning him, once I had put sufficient lead into his carcass to quiet his nerves. There was nothing for me to do but fight it out on foot; therefore I dropped the bridle rein and turned the bronco loose (thinking he would run his fright off in a short distance), and gave myself up to the business of the moment,

which, with the beast getting nearer every
instant, was becoming rather serious. I do
not know how others have felt under like
conditions; but there is something about the
look of a cougar on business bent, with its
greenish, staring eyes, that produces a most
uncomfortable sensation. I have been sent
up a tree post-haste by a bear, and I have
had an old bull moose give me an unpleasant
quarter of an hour, but I am sure I never
experienced a more disagreeable sensation
than when I looked through my rifle sights
at that loping lion. He did not seem to be in
any feverish anxiety to reach me, but there
was an earnest air about his progression that
was ominous.

Under any circumstances, it is not altogether pleasing to have a mountain lion, on his
busy day, making for you, and with only about
fifteen to twenty yards between him and his
quarry. I presume the delicacy of the situation must have impressed itself upon me; for
my next shot, although I aimed for one of
those hideous eyes, missed far enough to clip
off a piece of skin from the top of his skull
and to whet his appetite for my gore. My
bullet seemed to give him an added impetus;

The Cougar

for, with almost a single bound and a blood-
chilling screech, by the time I had put another cartridge into my single-shot rifle, he was
practically on top of me. Fortunately, his
spring had landed him short, and in another
instant I had very nearly blown his entire
head off. He was a monster. I skinned him
and hung his pelt on a tree; and, on foot,
made my way into camp, after a fruitless
search for my bronco.

I have killed five cougars, and this is the
only one that ever gave me a fight. I record
it with much pleasure, for there is an uncertainty about the cougar's temperament and
an alacrity of movement that are altogether
unsettling. You never know in what mood
you find the mountain lion, and he does not
seem by any chance to be in the same one
more than once, for those I have shot have
evinced different dispositions; generally, however, bordering on the cowardly. At times
their actions are sufficient to characterize
them as the veriest cowards in the world,
and yet again, on very slight provocation,
they are most aggressive and cruelly ferocious. There are many well-authenticated stories, to be had for the asking of any old

mountaineer, of the unwonted craftiness and ferocity of the cougar, and I suppose I could fill a couple of chapters of this volume by recounting yarns that have been told me during my Western life.

Between ourselves, I do not think hunting the cougar is very much sport. It is an instructive experience, and one, I think, every hunter of big game should have; but, at the same time, in my opinion it does not afford the sport of still-hunting deer, antelope, elk, moose or bears. In the first place, there is really no time you can still-hunt the cougar except in winter, when there is a light snow on the ground, and at all times it is most difficult, because you are dealing with an animal that embodies the very quintessence of wariness, and is ever on the lookout for prey and enemies. You have to deal with an animal that knows every crevice and hole of the mountain side, that moves by night in preference to day, and rarely travels in the open; whose great velvety paws enable it to sneak about absolutely unheard, and that will crouch in its lair while you pass, perhaps within a dozen feet.

Yet there are only two ways of really hunting the mountain lion—by still-hunting and by baiting. I have tried baiting a number of times, but have never found it successful. Others, I understand, have found it so; but in a score of cases, where I have provided tempting morsels, and lain out all night in hopes of getting a shot at the marauder, in none have I been rewarded, and in only one or two have I got a glimpse of a pair of shining eyes, that disappeared in the gloom almost on the instant of my discovering them.

Probably the most successful method of getting a shot at this wary beast is by hunting it with dogs (though I never had the experience), for the mountain lion has small lungs and makes a short, fast race. With dogs on his trail he is likely to take to a tree after a not very long run, which rarely occurs when he is still-hunted on foot. Yet, if the hunter values the lives of his dogs, he must be sure of his first shot, for the cougar is a tough customer to tackle when in his death throes; and I have been told, by those who have hunted in this way, that many a young and promising dog has had the life crushed out of him by the dying lion. Their forelegs are short and very powerful; but, curiously enough, unlike the bear, they do not use them in cutting and slashing so much as in drawing the victim to them to crush out its life with their strong jaws.

I have said, one never knows how to take the cougar. Almost every mining camp in the West will produce somebody who has met and scared him to flight by a mere wave of the hand or a shout, and that identical camp will as like as not produce men that have had the most trying experiences with the same animal. It is this knowledge that makes you, to say the least, a little uncomfortable when you meet one of these creatures. I have had many trying experiences of one kind and another, and hunted many different kinds of game, but none ever harassed my soul as the cougar has. On one occasion I had been about five miles from camp, prospecting for gold, which I had discovered in such alluring quantities as to keep me panning until darkness put an end to my work and started me homeward. It was a pretty dark night, and my trail lay along the side of a mountain that was rather thickly wooded and a pretty fair sort of hunting country. I had left my cabin early in the morning, intent on finding one of the numerous fortunes that was confidently believed to be hidden away in those New Mexico gulches, and was armed only with pick, shovel and pan. I was sauntering along, beset by dreams of prospective prosperity, based on the excellent finds I had made, when suddenly in front of me—I am sure not more than twenty-five feet —two great balls of fire rudely awakened me and brought my progress to an abrupt halt. I dare say it took a second or two to bring me down to earth, but when the earthward flight was accomplished I immediately concluded that those balls of fire must belong to a mountain lion.

At that time my experience with the cougar had been sufficient to put me in an uncertain frame of mind as to just what to expect of the creature. I had not an idea whether he was going to spring at me or whether I could scare him away. However, on chance, I broke the stillness of the night by one of those cowboy yells, in the calliope variations of which I was pretty well versed in those days, and, to my immense relief, the two glaring balls of fire disappeared.

Trudging on my way, I had once more lost myself in the roseate future incidental to placers averaging three dollars in gold to the cubic yard, when, as suddenly as before, and as directly in front of me, those two glaring balls shone out like a hideous nightmare. This time, I confess, I was a little bit annoyed. I knew that, as a rule, mountain lions do not follow you unless they are ravenous with hunger or smell blood. I had not been hunting, and, consequently, my clothes and hands were free from gore, and I was therefore forced to the sickening conclusion that this particular beast had selected me as a toothsome morsel for its evening repast. I cannot honestly say I was flattered by the implied compliment, and, summoning all my nerve, I reached for a rock and hurled it at those eyes, to hear it crash into the dry brush, and, greatly to my peace of mind, to see the diabolical lights go out, for it was too dark to distinguish the animal itself.

Congratulating myself on the disappearance of the hideous will-o'-the-wisp, I set out at a five-mile-an-hour gait for camp. My castles in the air had by this time quite dissolved, and I was attending strictly to the business of the trail, wishing camp was at hand instead of a mile off, when once more those greenish lanterns of despair loomed up ahead of me—not more than a dozen feet away, it seemed. I presume the beast had been trailing me all the time, though, after its second visitation, I kept a sharp lookout without discovering it, but evidently it had kept track of my movements.

I had no proof of its being the same animals, of course, but I was pretty well persuaded of its identity, and I became thoroughly convinced that this particular cougar had grown weary of waiting for its supper, and was about to begin its meal without even the courtesy of "by your leave." The uncanny feature of the experience was that not a sound revealed its approach on any occasion, and I had no intimation of its call until it dropped directly in my path. I leaned against a friendly tree and thought pretty hard, watching the animal most intently to see that it did not advance. It stood there as still as death, so far as I could distinguish, not moving even its head, and the steady glare of its eyes turned full upon me.

I made up my mind that, if the animal was going to feast on me that evening, I would disarrange its digestion, if possible. My short-handled prospecting pick was the nearest approach I had to a weapon, and, summoning all my ancient baseball skill, and feeling very carefully all around me to see that there were no intervening branches to arrest its flight, I hurled that pick at those two shining eyes, with a fervid wish that it might land between them. My aim was true and it landed—just where I cannot say, but I do know that it struck home; for, with a screech calculated to freeze one's blood, and a subsequent growl, the lion made off. For the rest of the mile to camp I had eyes on all sides of the path at once, but I was not molested.

I have since often wondered whether hunger or pure malice possessed that brute. Owen Wister, to whom I told the story not very long ago, suggested curiosity, and I am half inclined to believe his interpretation; for, if hunger had been the incentive, it seems as if a tap on the nose with a prospecting pick would not have appeased it, though the cougar's propensity for following people, out of unadulterated wantonness to frighten them, is well known. At any rate, he showed his cowardly side that trip.

The cougar is a curious beast, capricious as a woman. One day he follows his prey stealthily until the proper opportunity for springing upon it comes; again he will race after a deer in the open; at one time he will flee at a shout, at another he will fight desperately. They are powerful animals, particularly in the fore quarters. I have seen one lope down a mountain side, through about six inches of snow, carrying a fawn by the nape of the neck in its jaws, and swinging the body clear.

In the West generally, I think, the lion is considered cowardly—a belief I share, though agreeing with Theodore Roosevelt, who in "The Wilderness Hunter" says cougars, and, in fact, all animals vary in moods just as much as mankind. Because of their feline strategy and craftiness, they are most difficult animals to hunt; I know none more so. Neither do I know of any beast so likely to still the tenderfoot's heart. Their cry is as terror-striking as it is varied. I have heard them wail so you would swear an infant had been left out in the cold by its mamma; I have heard them screech like a woman in distress; and, again, growl after the conventional manner attributed to the monarch of the forest. The average camp dog runs to cover when a cougar is awakening the echoes of the mountain. I should call it lucky, for those who hunt with dogs, that the lion does not pierce the atmosphere by his screeches when being hunted; for, if he did, I fear it would be a difficult matter to keep dogs on his trail. There seems to be something about his screeching that particularly terrorizes dogs.

Casper W. Whitney.

YAKS GRAZING.

Big Game of Mongolia and Tibet

From remote antiquity hunting has been a favorite pastime of the emperors of China, but at no time has it been conducted with such magnificence as under the Mongol dynasty in the thirteenth century and during the reigning Manchu one.

Marco Polo's account of a hunt of Kublai Khan reads like a fairy tale. The Emperor left his capital every year in March for a hunting expedition in Mongolia, accompanied by all his barons, thousands of followers and innumerable beaters. "He took with him," says Polo, "fully 10,000 falconers and some 500 gerfalcons, besides peregrines, sakers and other hawks in great numbers, including goshawks, to fly at the waterfowl. He had also numbers of hunting leopards *(cheetah)* and lynxes, lions, leopards, wolves and eagles, trained to catch boars and wild cattle, bears, wild asses, stags, wolves, foxes, deer and wild goats, and other great and fierce beasts.

"The Emperor himself is carried upon four elephants in a fine chamber, made of timber, lined inside with plates of beaten gold and outside with lions' skins. And sometimes, as they may be going along, and the Emperor from his chamber is holding discourse with the barons, one of the latter shall exclaim: 'Sire, look out for cranes!' Then the Emperor instantly has the top of his chamber thrown open, and, having marked the cranes, he casts one of his gerfalcons, whichever he pleases; and often the quarry is struck within his view, so that he has the most exquisite sport and diversion there, as he sits in his chamber or lies on his bed; and all the barons with him get the enjoyment of it likewise. So it is not without reason I tell you that I do not believe there ever existed in the world, or ever will exist, a man with such sport and enjoyment as he has, or with such rare opportunities."

In the latter part of the seventeenth century, during the reign of the Emperor K'ang-hsi, Father Gérbillon followed the Emperor several times on his hunting expeditions into Mongolia, and has told us in his accounts of these journeys of the enthusiasm and skill displayed by the Emperor in the pursuit of game, which he usually shot with arrows, though he also had hawks and greyhounds with him.

I find no mention of the use of firearms in these imperial hunts, nor do I believe that it has ever been considered, by the Tartars and Mongols, sportsmanlike to use them.

Coursing and hawking were probably introduced into China and Mongolia after the Mongol conquest of Western Asia, where those royal sports had then been in vogue for a long time. At present the Manchus keep great numbers of hawks, caught for the most part in the northern portion of the province of Shan-hsi, and with them they take hares and cranes. Greyhounds are no longer numerous in Mongolia and China, though they are much prized, and I have seen some among the Ordos Mongols and in Manchu garrisons. They were short-haired, of a clear tan color with black points, and showed good blood in their small tails and depth of chest.

Besides the great annual hunts on the steppes—which, leaving aside the sport and incidental invigorating influence on the courtiers, helped, by the vast numbers of troops which took part in them, to keep quiet the then turbulent Mongol tribes—the emperors

of China have had, at different times, great
hunting parks, inclosed by high walls, at convenient distances from their capital, or even in
close proximity to it, where they could indulge
their fondness for the chase. Several of these
parks (called *wei chang*) are still preserved
for imperial hunts, and one I visited in 1886,
to the north of Jehol and about six days'
travel from Peking, is some ninety miles long
from north to south, and over thirty miles
from east to west. It is well stocked with
pheasants, roebucks, stags, and, it is said, there
are also tigers and leopards in it. The park
is guarded by troops, and any person caught
poaching in it, besides receiving corporal punishment, is exiled for a period of a year and
a half to two years to a distant town of the
empire. During my visit to this park, I and
my three companions camped just outside one
of the gates, and, by paying the keepers a
small sum, we were able to get daily a few
hours' shooting in a little valley inside the
wall and near our camp. Though we had
no dogs, and lost all the winged birds and
wounded hares, we bagged in nine or ten days
over 500 pheasants, 150 hares, 100 partridges
and a few ducks.

Big Game of Mongolia and Tibet

A mile or so south of Peking is another famous hunting park, called the *Nan-hai-tzu*, in
which is found that remarkable deer, not
known to exist in a wild state in any other
spot, called *Cervus davidi*. Of late years a number of these deer have been raised in the imperial park of Uwino at Tokio, and also in the
Zoölogical Garden of Berlin, where a pair
were sent by the German Minister to China,
Mr. Von Brandt. This deer is known to the
Chinese as the *ssu-pu-hsiang-tzu*, "the four dis-
similarities," because, while its body shows
points of resemblance to those of the deer,
horse, cow and ass, it belongs to neither of
those four species—so say the Chinese.

The Chinese proper show but rarely any
great love for sport. They are fond of fishing,
and I have seen some very good shots among
them, especially at snipe shooting, when, with
their match-locks fired from the hip, they will
frequently do snap shooting of which any of
our crack shots might be proud. But the Chinese are essentially pot hunters, and have no
sportsmanlike instincts as have the Manchus
and Mongols, with whom sport is one of the
pleasures of life, though it is also a source of
profit to many Mongol tribes. In winter they

supply with game—deer, boars, antelope, hares, pheasants and partridges—the Peking market, bringing them there frozen from remote corners of their country.

Among the big game in the northern part of the Chinese Empire the first place properly belongs to tigers and leopards. In Korea tigers are quite common, and a special corps of tiger hunters was kept up until recently by the Government. The usual method of killing tigers is to make a pitfall in a narrow path along which one has been found to travel, and on either side of it a strong fence is erected. When the tiger has fallen into the pit, he is shot to death or speared. The skin belongs to the king, and the hunters are rewarded by him for each beast killed. The skins are used to cover the seats of high dignitaries, to whom they are given by the king, as are also the skins of leopards; and tigers' whiskers go to ornament the hats of certain petty officials.

Leopards are so numerous in Korea that I have known of two being killed within a few weeks inside of the walls of Seoul.

Tigers are also found in Manchuria, and, as before mentioned, in parts of northern and southeastern China. I have seen the skin of a small one hanging as an *ex voto* offering in a lama temple near the Koko-Nor, and was told that it had been killed not far from that spot. Colonel Prjevalsky, however, says that the tiger is not found in northwestern China; so the question remains an open one.

Leopards, at all events, are common in northeastern and northwestern China, in the hunting parks north of Peking, in the mountains of northwest Kan-su and to the south of Koko-Nor. Bears are common from northern Korea to the Pamirs. The Chinese distinguish two varieties, which they call "dog bear" or "hog bear," and "man bear." The first is a brown bear, and the latter, which is found on the high barren plateaus to the north of Tibet, where it makes its food principally of the little lagomys or marmots, which live there in great numbers, has for this reason been called by Colonel Prjevalsky *Ursus lagomyarius.* I killed one weighing over 600 pounds, whose claws were larger and thicker than those of any grizzly I have seen. Its color is a rusty black, with a patch of white on the breast.

Besides these two varieties of bears, there is another animal, which, though it is not properly a bear, resembles one so closely that it is classed by the Chinese and Tibetans in that family. It is known to the Chinese as *hua hsiung,* or "mottled bear," and Milne Edwards, who studied and described it, has called it *Ailuropus melanoleucus.* This animal was, I believe, discovered by that enterprising missionary and naturalist, Father Armand David (who called it "white bear"), in the little eastern Tibetan principality of Dringpa or Mupin, in western Ssu-ch'uan.* Five specimens have so far been secured of this very rare animal: three are in the Jardin des Plantes of Paris, the other two in the Museum at the Jesuits' establishment, at Zikawei, near Shanghai.

The stag or red deer ("horse deer" in Chinese) is found in Manchuria and northern Korea, and the Tibetan variety, called *shawo,* must be very abundant in portions of eastern Tibet, to judge from the innumerable loads of horns which I have passed while traveling through eastern Tibet on the way to China, in which latter country they are used in the preparation of toilet powder. There is also a small deer in the mountains of Alashan, in western Kansu and Ssu-ch'uan, and in the

*See *Nouvelles Archives du Museum de Paris,* X., pp. 18 and 20.

AILUROPUS MELANOLEUCUS.

Ts'aidam; but I know nothing concerning it save its Mongol name, *bura*, and its Chinese, *yang lu*, or "sheep deer." Prjevalsky, however, gives some interesting details concerning it. Some Chinese mention a third variety, called *mei lu*, or "beautiful deer," said to live in the Koko-Nor country.

The musk deer is found in most parts of the Himalayas and Tibet, and as far northeast as Lan-chou, on the Yellow River, in the Chinese province of Kan-su. It is hunted wherever found, and nearly all the musk ultimately finds its way to Europe or America, as it is not used to any great extent by either Tibetans, Chinese or any of the other peoples in whose countries it is procured; the Chinese only use a small quantity in the preparation of some of their medicines. They distinguish two varieties of musk deer: one, having tusks much larger than the other, is called "yellow musk deer."

Next in importance among the game of this region we find the *Antilope gutturosa* and the *Ovis burhil*, or "mountain goat," which range from eastern Mongolia to western Tibet. But more important than these from a sportsman's point of view is the *argali*, of which Col. Prjevalsky distinguishes two varieties: the *Ovis argali,* ranging along the northern bend of the Yellow River, between Kuei-hua Ch'eng and Alashan; and the white-breasted *argali,* or *Ovis poli,* ranging from the Ts'aidam and western Ssu-ch'uan to the Pamirs.

The name *argali* is, I think, an unfortunate one to give to this species, as it is a Mongol word solely used to designate the female animal, the male of which is called *kuldza.*

The *Antilope hodgsoni,* called *orongo* in Mongol, has about the same range as the *Ovis poli.* It is by far the most beautiful antelope of this region—the long, graceful, lyre-shaped horns, which it carries very erect when running, being frequently over two feet in length.

Although, to my mind, what are commonly regarded as cattle should no more be considered game when wild than when tame, still, as I am perhaps alone of this opinion, I must note, among the game animals of this part of Asia, yaks and asses, which are found in western Mongolia, Turkestan and in many parts of Tibet, especially the wild northern country, or Chang-t'ang.

The wild yak is invariably black, with short, rather slender horns (smaller than our buffalo's), bending gracefully forward. The head is large, but well proportioned, and the eyes quite large, but with a very wild look in them. The legs are short and very heavy, the hoofs straight and invariably black. The hair, which hangs down over the body and legs, the face alone excepted, is wavy, and on the sides, belly and legs is so long that it reaches within a few inches of the ground. The tail is very bushy and reaches to the hocks, all the hair being of such uniform length that it looks as if it were trimmed. When running, the yak carries its tail high up or even over its back, and when frightened or angered holds it straight out behind.

The calves have a grunt resembling that of the hog, hence the name *Bos grunniens*, but in the grown animal it is rarely heard; it is at best only a dull, low sound, unworthy of such a big, savage-looking beast. The bones of the yak are so heavy that it is nearly impossible to kill one except by shooting it through the heart or wounding it in some equally vital spot. Although I have shot a great many of these animals in northern Tibet, I have never bagged any except when shot as above mentioned, nor have I ever broken the limb of one. It is true that I have done all my shooting with a .44 caliber Winchester carbine, which was entirely too light for the purpose.

The yak is not a dangerous animal except in the case of a solitary bull, which will sometimes charge a few yards at a time, till he falls dead at the hunter's feet, riddled with bullets. When in large bands yaks run at the first shot, rushing down ravines, through snow banks and across rivers, without a moment's hesitation, in a wild stampede.

Mongol and Tibetan hunters say that one must never shoot at a solitary yak whose horns have a backward curve, as he will certainly prove dangerous when wounded; but the same beast may be shot at with impunity if in a band. In fact, the natives never shoot at yaks except when in a good-sized bunch. Natives usually hunt them by twos and threes, and, after stalking to within a hundred yards or even less, they all blaze away at the same time.

The number of yaks on the plateaus north of Tibet is very considerable, but there are no such herds as were seen of Buffaloes on our plains until within a few years. I have never seen over 300 in a herd, but Col. Prjevalsky says that when he first visited the country around the sources of the Yellow River, in 1870, he saw herds there of a thousand head and more. Yaks are enormous feeders, and, in a country as thinly covered with grass as that in which they roam, they must travel great distances to secure enough food. As it is, it is the rarest thing in the world to find even in July or August fine grazing in any part of this country; the yaks keep the grass as closely cut as would a machine.

In some of the wildest districts of western China a wild ox *(budorcas)* is still found. Father Armand David thus describes it *(Nouvelles Archives du Museum de Paris,* X., 17): "It is a kind of *ovibos,* with very short tail, black and sharp horns, with broad bases touching on the forehead; its ears are small, and, as it were, cropped obliquely. The iris is of a dirty yellow gold color, the pupil oblong and horizontal. The fur is quite long and of a dirty white color, with a dash of brown on the hind quarters."

The wild ass is no longer found, I believe, to the east of the Koko-Nor, but from that meridian as far west as Persia is met with in large numbers, and in the wilds to the north of

Tibet in vast herds, quite as large and numerous as those of yaks.

The wild ass (called *kulan* or *hulan* in Mongol) stands about twelve hands high, and is invariably of a tan color, with a dark line running down the back, and white on the belly, neck and feet. The tail is rather short, and thinly covered with hair; the head is broad, heavy, and too large for the body of the animal. It carries its head very high when in motion, and when trotting its tail is nearly erect. Its usual gait is a trot or a run. A herd always moves in single file, a stallion leading. As a rule, a stallion has a small band of ten or twelve mares, which he herds and guards with jealous care day and night. Frequently these bands run together and form herds of 500 or even of 1,000.

One often meets solitary jackasses wandering about; they have been deprived of their band of mares in a fight with some stronger male. These have frequently proved most troublesome to me; they would round up and drive off my ponies—all of which were mares—to add to the little nucleus of a band they had hidden away in some lonely nook in the hills. I have frequently had to lose days at a time hunting for my horses, and I finally made it a point to shoot all such animals that came near my camp; though I had a strong dislike to killing them—they looked so like tame asses—and I never could see any sport in it, though the meat was good enough—much better than yak flesh.

The *hulan* is very fleet and has wonderfully acute hearing, but it possesses too great curiosity for its own safety; it will generally circle around the hunter if not shot at, and come quite near to have a look at the strange, unknown animal.

It is said that wild camels and horses are found in some of the remoter corners of southwestern Turkestan and south of Lob-Nor, and specimens of them have been secured by Prjevalsky, Grijimailo and Littledale. The question is now whether these animals are domesticated ones run wild, or really wild varieties. Naturalists will probably disagree on this point. For the time being these animals are too little known for me to express an opinion on the subject, and, not having seen any, I can add nothing to what has been written on the subject.

My own shooting in Mongolia and Tibet has

always been under difficulties. Traveling without European companions, and my Asiatic one not knowing how to handle our firearms, I have been able to give but little time to sport. When pressed for food, however, I have killed yaks, asses, *argali*, mountain sheep and antelope; I have also bagged a few bears and leopards; but, as my only rifle was rather for purposes of defense than for shooting game, I never went much out of my way to look up these animals, though I felt great confidence in my good little Winchester, having killed the largest yak I ever shot at, and a fine bear, each with one shot from it.

The game I mostly shot while in Tibet was yak; but, as I never killed any save for meat— not believing in the theory of destroying animal life for the sake of trophies to hang upon the wall—I made no phenomenal bags, though big game was so plentiful in many sections of the country that even with a native matchlock it would have been possible to have killed many more animals than I did.

The yak I approached at first with considerable trepidation, as I had read in various books of their savageness and of the danger that the hunter was exposed to from one of

ELAPHURUS DAVIDIANUS.

these big animals when wounded; but now I am wiser, and I can reassure those who would kill these big beasts; they look more dangerous than they really are, and will hardly ever push their charge home, even when badly wounded. The first time I saw them we were traveling up a rather open valley beside a frozen rivulet, where, upon reaching the top of a little swell, some six or eight hundred yards off, were a couple of hundred yaks coming down toward the stream to try and find a water hole. I made signs to the men behind me to stop, and, jumping from my horse, I crawled along to within about 200 yards of them, when I blazed away at the biggest I could pick out, standing a little nearer to me than the rest of the herd. They paid hardly any attention to the slight report of my rifle; only the one at which I shot advanced a short distance in the direction of the smoke and then stopped, waving his great bushy tail over his back and holding his head erect. I fired again, when he and the rest of the herd turned and ran on to the ice, where I opened fire on them once more. They seemed puzzled by the noise, but my bullets did not seem to harm them. Finally one charged and then another, and at last the whole herd came dashing up in my direction; but "I lay very low," especially as at this seemingly critical moment I found that I had no more cartridges in my gun. After awhile they turned and trotted back to the river, and I made for my horse, much disappointed at my apparent failure to do any of them any injury.

In the meantime my men had pushed on about half a mile, and we stopped in a little nook to take a cup of tea. Having here supplied myself with cartridges, I thought I would try to get another shot at the yaks, some of which I could still see on the mountain side beyond the stream. My delight was great when, coming up to the place where I had last seen them, a big bull was lying dead, shot through the heart.

The only time I ever encountered a solitary bull he bluffed us so completely that I do not know but my reputation as a sportsman will suffer materially by mentioning the incident. One day, as we were rounding the corner of a hill, we saw an immense fellow, not 200 yards off; and my two big mastiffs, which by this time were getting hardly any food—as our stock of provisions was running very short, and

who passed most of their time while we were
on the march vainly chasing hares, marmots
and any other animals they could see—made a
dash for the yak and commenced snapping at
him. He trotted slowly off, but soon, becoming angry, turned on the dogs, who came back
to the caravan. He followed them until within
twenty yards of us. All my recollections of the
dangers encountered by Prejevalsky with yaks,
all his remarks of the extraordinary thickness
and impenetrability of their skulls, of the difficulty of killing these monstrous animals, and
of their ferociousness when wounded, came
vividly to my mind in an instant. I saw my
mules and horses gored and bleeding on the
ground, my expedition brought to an untimely
end, and a wounded yak waving his tail trium-
phantly over us, for I was certain that with my
light Winchester I could never drop him dead
in his tracks. We did not even dare so much
as look at him, but kept on our way, and the
yak walked beside us, evidently rejoicing in his
victory. The dogs, now thoroughly cowed,
took refuge on the side of the caravan furthest
from the infuriated animal, and so we marched
on for about half a mile, when, in utter disgust, he turned and trotted off to the hillside,

where he stood watching us, his bushy tail stretched out as stiff as iron behind him, pawing the ground, and thus we left him.

Shooting wild asses was much tamer business. We saw them sometimes in herds of five or six hundred. They would mix with our mules even when grazing around the camp, and often took them off five or six miles, when we had great difficulty in getting them back. We frequently, however, killed one for meat, which we found to be very savory; though most of my men, who were Mahomedans, would only eat it when very hard pushed by hunger, as their religion forbade them to eat the flesh of any animal without cloven hoofs. I always felt, however, in shooting these animals, as if I were destroying a domestic mule, and could never bring myself to look upon them as fit game for a sportsman. This was strongly impressed upon me one day when, desiring to get a fine specimen, whose skin and bones I could bring back for the National Museum, I shot a very large jack which was grazing some distance from our line of march, and broke its hind legs, and was then obliged to go up to the poor beast and put a ball into its head. After accomplishing this disagreeable duty in the interest of science—though to no purpose, as it turned out, for I was obliged to throw away the skin and bones a few days after, because I had no means of transporting them—I made a solemn promise to myself that I would never shoot a *kyang* again; and, I am pleased to say, I broke my promise but twice, and then I did so only to give us food, of which we stood in great need.

Shooting antelope in Tibet is not more exciting—or interesting, for that matter—than shooting them elsewhere, and I do not know that anything special can be said about this sport beyond the fact that the number of Hodgson antelope which we met in parts of northern Tibet was sometimes extraordinarily great. These animals suffer greatly, however, from some plague, which frequently sweeps off enormous numbers of them. I have passed over places where the bones of a hundred or more of them might be seen, one near the other; and districts which I had visited in 1889, and where I had found great numbers of them, were absolutely without a sign of one when I was there again in 1892.

Of bear-hunting I can say but little. On different occasions, in various parts of northern Tibet, I killed six or eight pretty good sized brown bears; but a man would have to be blind not to be able to hit one at twenty-five or thirty yards, and it is always possible to get as near them as that, even in the open country which they frequent. They have apparently no dens, but live in the holes in the ground which they dig to get the little marmots on which they feed. These bears are, however, very fleet, as I once or twice found out when trying to ride them down on horseback, and when they nearly proved a match for the best ponies I had. The natives stand in great dread of them, and will never attack them except when there are three or four men together, when they approach them from different directions and open fire all at the same time. They say these bears are man-eaters, and even when the men with me saw them lying dead they showed great repugnance to touch the body, or even to come near them; though they might have made eight or ten dollars by splitting them open and removing the gall—a highly-prized medicine among the Chinese, who also find a place for bears' paws in their pharmacopoeia.

On the whole, though Korea, Mongolia and

Big Game of Mongolia and Tibet

Tibet have plenty of big game, they are not countries for a sportsman, and unless he has some other hobby to take him there, he had better seek his fun elsewhere in more accessible quarters of the globe.

W. W. Rockhill.

Hunting in the Cattle Country

The little hunting I did in 1893 and 1894 was while I was at my ranch house, or while out on the range among the cattle; and I shot merely the game needed for the table by myself and those who were with me. It is still possible in the cattle country to kill an occasional bighorn, bear or elk; but nowadays the only big game upon which the ranchman of the great plains can safely count are deer and antelope. While at the ranch house itself, I rely for venison upon shooting either blacktail in the broken country away from the river, or else whitetail in the river bottoms. When out on the great plains, where the cattle range freely in the summer, or when visiting the line camps, or any ranch on the heads of the longer creeks, the prongbuck furnishes our fresh meat.

In both 1893 and 1894 I made trips to a vast tract of rolling prairie land, some fifty miles from my ranch, where I have for many years

enjoyed the keen pleasure of hunting the
prongbuck. In 1893 the pronghorned bands
were as plentiful in this district as I have ever
seen them anywhere. A friend, a fellow Boone
and Crockett man, Alexander Lambert, was
with me; and in a week's trip, including the
journey out and back, we easily shot all the
antelope we felt we had any right to kill; for
we only shot to get meat, or an unusually fine
head.

In antelope shooting more cartridges are expended in proportion to the amount of game
killed than with any other game, because the
shots are generally taken at long range; and
yet, being taken in the open, there is usually a
chance to use four or five cartridges before the
animal gets out of sight. These shots do not
generally kill, but every now and then they do;
and so the hunter is encouraged to try them,
especially as after the first shot the game has
been scared anyway, and no harm results from
firing the others.

In 1893, Lambert, who was on his first hunt
with the rifle, did most of the shooting, and I
myself fired at only two antelope, both of
which had already been missed. In each case
a hard run and much firing at long ranges, to-

gether with in one case some skillful maneuvering, got me my game; yet one buck cost
nine cartridges and the other eight. In 1894
I had exactly the reverse experience. I killed
five antelope for thirty-six shots, but each one
that I killed was killed with the first bullet,
and in not one case where I missed the first
time did I hit with any subsequent one.
These five antelope were shot at an average
distance of about 150 yards. Those that I
missed were, of course, much further off on an
average, and I usually emptied my magazine
at each. The number of cartridges spent
would seem extraordinary to a tyro; and a
very unusually skillful shot, or else a very
timid shot who fears to take risks, will of
course make a better showing per head killed;
but I doubt if men with much experience in
antelope hunting, who keep an accurate account of the cartridges they expend, will see
anything out of the way in the performance.
During the thirteen years I have hunted in
the West I have always, where possible, kept
a record of the number of cartridges expended
for every head of game killed, and of the distances at which it was shot. I have found
that with bison, bears, moose, elk, caribou, big-

horn and white goats, where the animals shot at were mostly of large size and usually stationary, and where the mountainous or wooded country gave chance for a close approach, the average distance at which I have killed the game has been eighty yards, and the average number of cartridges expended per head slain three: one of these representing the death shot and the others standing either for misses outright, of which there were not very many, or else for wounding game which escaped, or which I afterward overtook, or for stopping cripples or charging beasts. I have killed but one cougar and two peccaries, using but one cartridge for each; all three were close up. At wolves and coyotes I have generally had to take running shots at very long range, and I have killed but two for fifty cartridges. Blacktail deer I have generally shot at about ninety yards, at an expenditure of about four cartridges apiece. Whitetail I have killed at shorter range; but the shots were generally running, often taken under difficult circumstances, so that my expenditure of cartridges was rather larger. Antelope, on the other hand, I have on the average shot at a little short of 150 yards, and they have cost me about nine cartridges apiece. This, of course, as I have explained above, does not mean that I have missed eight out of nine antelope, for often the entire nine cartridges would be spent at an antelope which I eventually got. It merely means that, counting all the shots of every description fired at antelope, I had one head to show for each nine cartridges expended. Thus, the first antelope I shot in 1893 cost me ten cartridges, of which three hit him, while the seven that missed were fired at over 400 yards' distance while he was running. We saw him while we were with the wagon. As we had many miles to go before sunset, we cared nothing about frightening other game, and, as we had no fresh meat, it was worth while to take some chances to procure it. When I first fired, the prongbuck had already been shot at and was in full flight. He was beyond all reasonable range, but some of our bullets went over him and he began to turn. By running to one side I got a shot at him at a little over 400 paces, as he slowed to a walk, bewildered by the firing, and the bullet broke his hip. I missed him two or three times as he plunged off, and then by hard running down a water course got a shot at 180 paces and broke his shoulder, and broke his neck with another bullet when I came up. This one was shot while going out to the hunting ground. While there, Lambert killed four or five; most of the meat we gave away. I did not fire again until on our return, when I killed another buck one day while we were riding with the wagon.

The day was gray and overcast. There were slight flurries of snow, and the cold wind chilled us as it blew across the endless reaches of sad-colored prairie. Behind us loomed Sentinel Butte, and all around the rolling surface was broken by chains of hills, by patches of bad lands, or by isolated, saddle-shaped mounds. The ranch wagon jolted over the uneven sward, and plunged in and out of the dry beds of the occasional water courses; for we were following no road, but merely striking northward across the prairie toward the P. K. ranch. We went at a good pace, for the afternoon was bleak, the wagon was lightly loaded, and the Sheriff, who was serving for the nonce as our teamster and cook, kept the two gaunt, wild-looking horses trotting steadily. Lambert and I rode to one side on our unkempt cow ponies, our rifles slung across the saddle bows.

Our stock of fresh meat was getting low and we were anxious to shoot something; but in the early hours of the afternoon we saw no game. Small parties of horned larks ran along the ground ahead of the wagon, twittering plaintively as they rose, and occasional flocks of longspurs flew hither and thither; but of larger life we saw nothing, save occasional bands of range horses. The drought had been very severe and we were far from the river, so that we saw no horned stock. Horses can travel much further to water than cattle, and, when the springs dry up, they stay much further out on the prairie.

At last we did see a band of four antelope, lying in the middle of a wide plain, but they saw us before we saw them, and the ground was so barren of cover that it was impossible to get near them. Moreover, they were very shy and ran almost as soon as we got our eyes on them. For an hour or two after this we jogged along without seeing anything, while the gray clouds piled up in the west and the afternoon began to darken; then, just after passing Saddle Butte, we struck a rough prairie road, which we knew led to the P. K. ranch— a road very faint in places, while in others the wheels had sunk deep in the ground and made long, parallel ruts.

Almost immediately after striking this road, on topping a small rise, we discovered a young prongbuck standing off a couple of hundred yards to one side, gazing at the wagon with that absorbed curiosity which in this game so often conquers its extreme wariness and timidity, to a certain extent offsetting the advantage conferred upon it by its marvelous vision. The little antelope stood broadside, too, gazing at us out of its great bulging eyes, the sharply contrasted browns and whites of its coat showing plainly. Lambert and I leaped off our horses immediately, and I knelt and pulled the trigger; but the cartridge snapped, and the little buck, wheeling around, cantered off, the white hairs on its rump all erect, as is always the case with the pronghorn when under the influence of fear or excitement. My companion took a hasty, running shot, with no more effect than changing the canter into a breakneck gallop; and, though we opened on it as it ran, it went unharmed over the crest of rising ground in front. We ran after it as hard as we could pelt up the hill, into a slight valley, and then up another rise, and again got a glimpse of it standing, but this time further off than before; and again our shots went wild.

However, the antelope changed its racing gallop to a canter while still in sight, going slower and slower, and, what was rather curious, it did not seem much frightened. We were naturally a good deal chagrined at our shooting and wished to retrieve ourselves, if possible; so we ran back to the wagon, got our horses and rode after the buck. He had continued his flight in a straight line, gradually slackening his pace, and a mile's brisk gallop enabled us to catch a glimpse of him, far ahead and merely walking. The wind was bad, and we decided to sweep off and try to circle round ahead of him. Accordingly, we dropped back, turned into a slight hollow to the right, and galloped hard until we came to the foot of a series of low buttes, when we turned more to the left; and, when we judged that we were about across the antelope's line of march, leaped from our horses, threw the reins over their heads, and left them standing, while we stole up the nearest rise; and, when close to the top, took off our caps and pushed ourselves forward, flat on our faces, to peep over. We had judged the distance well, for we saw the antelope at once, now stopping to graze. Drawing back, we ran along some little distance nearer, then drew up over the same rise. He was only about 125 yards off, and this time there was no excuse for my failing to get him; but fail I did, and away the buck raced again, with both of us shooting. My first two shots were misses, but I kept correcting my aim and holding further in front of the flying beast. My last shot was taken just as the antelope reached the edges of the broken country, in which he would have been safe; and almost as I pulled the trigger I had the satisfaction of seeing him pitch forward and, after turning a complete somersault, lie motionless. I had broken his neck. He had cost us a good many cartridges, and, though my last shot was well aimed, there was doubtless considerable chance in my hitting him, while there was no excuse at all for at least one of my previous misses. Nevertheless, all old hunters know that there is no other kind of shooting in which so many cartridges are expended for every head of game bagged.

As we knelt down to butcher the antelope, the clouds broke and the rain fell. Hastily we took off the saddle and hams, and, packing them behind us on our horses, loped to the wagon in the teeth of the cold storm. When we overtook it, after some sharp riding, we threw in the meat, and not very much later, when the day was growing dusky, caught sight of the group of low ranch buildings toward which we had been headed. We were received with warm hospitality, as one always is in a ranch country. We dried our steaming clothes inside the warm ranch house and had a good supper, and that night we rolled up in our blankets and tarpaulins, and slept soundly in the lee of a big haystack. The ranch house stood in the winding bottom of a creek; the flanking hills were covered with stunted cedar, while dwarf cottonwood and box elder grew by the pools in the half-dried creek bed.

Next morning we had risen by dawn. The storm was over, and it was clear and cold. Before sunrise we had started. We were only some thirty miles from my ranch, and I directed the Sheriff how to go there, by striking east until he came to the main divide, and then following that down till he got past a certain big plateau, when a turn to the right down any of the coulees would bring him into the river bottom near the ranch house. We wished our-

selves to ride off to one side and try to pick up
another antelope. However, the Sheriff took
the wrong turn after getting to the divide, and
struck the river bottom some fifteen miles out
of his way, so that we reached the ranch a
good many hours before he did.

When we left the wagon we galloped
straight across country, looking out from the
divide across the great rolling landscape, every
feature standing clear through the frosty air.
Hour after hour we galloped on and on over
the grassy seas in the glorious morning. Once
we stopped, and I held the horses while Lambert stalked and shot a fine prongbuck; then
we tied his head and hams to our saddles and
again pressed forward along the divide. We
had hoped to get lunch at a spring that I knew
of some twelve miles from my ranch, but when
we reached it we found it dry and went on
without halting. Early in the afternoon we
came out on the broad, tree-clad bottom on
which the ranch house stands, and, threading
our way along the cattle trails, soon drew up
in front of the gray, empty buildings.

Just as we were leaving the hunting grounds
on this trip, after having killed all the game we
felt we had a right to kill, we encountered

bands of Sioux Indians from the Standing Rock and Cheyenne River reservations coming in to hunt, and I at once felt that the chances for much future sport in that particular district were small. Indians are not good shots, but they hunt in great numbers, killing everything, does, fawns and bucks alike, and they follow the wounded animals with the utmost perseverance, so that they cause great destruction to game.

Accordingly, in 1894, when I started for these same grounds, it was with some misgivings; but I had time only to make a few days' hunt, and I knew of no other accessible grounds where prongbuck were plentiful. My foreman was with me, and we took the ranch wagon also, driven by a cowboy who had just come up over the trail with cattle from Colorado. On reaching our happy hunting grounds of the previous season, I found my fears sadly verified; and one unforeseen circumstance also told against me. Not only had the Indians made a great killing of antelope the season before, but in the spring one or two sheep men had moved into the country. We found that the big flocks had been moving from one spring pool to another, eating the pasturage bare, while the shepherds whom we met—wild-looking men on rough horses, each accompanied by a pair of furtive sheep dogs—had taken every opportunity to get a shot at antelope, so as to provide themselves with fresh meat. Two days of fruitless hunting in this sheep-ridden region was sufficient to show that the antelope were too scarce and shy to give us hope for sport, and we shifted quarters, a long day's journey, to the head of another creek; and we had to go to yet another before we found much game. As so often happens on such a trip, when we started to have bad luck we had plenty. One night two of the three saddle horses stampeded and went back straight as the crow flies to their home range, so that we did not get them until on our return from the trip. On another occasion the team succeeded in breaking the wagon pole; and, as there was an entire absence of wood where we were at the time, we had to make a splice for it with the two tent poles and the picket ropes. Nevertheless it was very enjoyable out on the great grassy plains. Although we had a tent with us, I always slept in the open in my buffalo bag, with the tarpaulin to pull over me if it rained. On each night before going to sleep, I lay for many minutes gazing at the extraordinary multitude of stars above, or watching the rising of the red moon, which was just at or past the full.

We had plenty of fresh meat—prairie fowl and young sage fowl for the first twenty-four hours, and antelope venison afterward. We camped by little pools, generally getting fair water; and from the camps where there was plenty of wood we took enough to build the fires at those where there was none. The nights were frosty, and the days cool and pleasant, and from sunrise to sunset we were off riding or walking among the low hills and over the uplands, so that we slept well and ate well, and felt the beat of hardy life in our veins.

Much of the time we were on a high divide between two creek systems, from which we could see the great landmarks of all the regions roundabout—Sentinel Butte, Square Butte and Middle Butte, far to the north and east of us. Nothing could be more lonely and nothing more beautiful than the view at nightfall across the prairies to these huge hill masses, when the lengthening shadows had at last merged into one and the faint glow of the red sun filled the west. The rolling prai-

rie, sweeping in endless waves to the feet of
the great hills, grew purple as the evening
darkened, and the buttes loomed into vague,
mysterious beauty as their sharp outlines
softened in the twilight.

Even when we got out of reach of the
sheep men we never found antelope very
plentiful, and they were shy, and the country was flat, so that the stalking was extremely
difficult; yet I had pretty good sport. The
first animal I killed was a doe, shot for meat,
because I had twice failed to get bucks at
which I emptied my magazine at long range,
and we were all feeling hungry for venison.
After that I killed nothing but bucks. Of the
five antelope killed, one I got by a headlong
gallop to cut off his line of flight. As sometimes happens with this queer, erratic animal,
when the buck saw that I was trying to cut off
his flight he simply raced ahead just as hard as
he knew how, and, as my pony was not fast, he
got to the little pass for which he was headed
200 yards ahead of me. I then jumped off,
and his curiosity made him commit the fatal
mistake of halting for a moment to look round
at me. He was standing end on, and offered
a very small mark at 200 yards; but I made a

good line shot, and, though I held a trifle too high, I hit him in the head, and down he came. Another buck I shot from under the wagon early one morning as he was passing just beyond the picketed horses. The other three I got after much maneuvering and long, tedious stalks.

In some of the stalks, after infinite labor, and perhaps after crawling on all fours for an hour, or pulling myself flat on my face among some small sagebrush for ten or fifteen minutes, the game took alarm and went off. Too often, also, when I finally did get a shot, it was under such circumstances that I missed. Sometimes the game was too far; sometimes it had taken alarm and was already in motion. Once in the afternoon I had to spend so much time waiting for the antelope to get into a favorable place that, when I got up close, I found the light already so bad that my front sight glimmered indistinctly, and the bullet went wild. Another time I met with one of those misadventures which are especially irritating. It was at midday, and I made out at a long distance a band of antelope lying for their noon rest in a slight hollow. A careful stalk brought me up within fifty yards of them. I was crawling flat on my face, for the crest of the hillock sloped so gently that this was the only way to get near them. At last, peering through the grass, I saw the head of a doe. In a moment she saw me and jumped to her feet, and up stood the whole band, including the buck. I immediately tried to draw a bead on the latter, and to my horror found that, lying flat as I was, and leaning on my elbows, I could not bring the rifle above the tall, shaking grass, and was utterly unable to get a sight. In another second away tore all the antelope. I jumped to my feet, took a snap shot at the buck as he raced round a low-cut bank and missed, and then walked drearily home, chewing the cud of my ill luck. Yet again in more than one instance, after making a good stalk upon a band seen at some distance, I found it contained only does and fawns, and would not shoot at them.

Three times, however, the stalk was successful. Twice I was out alone; the other time my foreman was with me, and kept my horse while I maneuvered hither and thither, and finally succeeded in getting into range. In both the first instances I got a standing shot, but on this last occasion, when my foreman was with me, two of the watchful does which were in the band saw me before I could get a shot at the old buck. I was creeping up a low washout, and, by ducking hastily down again and running back and up a side coulee, I managed to get within long range of the band as they cantered off, not yet thoroughly alarmed. The buck was behind, and I held just ahead of him. He plunged to the shot, but went off over the hill crest. When I had panted up to the ridge, I found him dead just beyond.

One of the antelope I killed while I was out on foot at nightfall, a couple of miles from the wagon; I left the shoulders and neck, carrying in the rest of the carcass on my back. On the other occasion I had my horse with me and took in the whole antelope, packing it behind the saddle, after it was dressed and the legs cut off below the knees. In packing an antelope or deer behind the saddle, I always cut slashes through the sinews of the legs just above the joints; then I put the buck behind the saddle, run the picket rope from the horn of the saddle, under the belly of the horse, through the slashes in the legs on the other side, bring the end back, swaying well down on it, and fasten it to the horn; then I repeat the same feat for the other side. Packed in this way, the carcass always rides perfectly steady, and can not, by any possibility, shake loose. Of course, a horse has to have some little training before it will submit to being packed.

The above experiences are just about those which befall the average ranchman when he is hunting antelope. To illustrate how much less apt he is to spend as many shots while after other game, I may mention the last mountain sheep and last deer I killed, each of which cost me but a single cartridge.

The bighorn was killed in the fall of 1894, while I was camped on the Little Missouri, some ten miles below my ranch. The bottoms were broad and grassy, and were walled in by rows of high, steep bluffs, with back of them a mass of broken country, in many places almost impassable for horses. The wagon was drawn up on the edge of the fringe of tall cotton-woods which stretched along the brink of the shrunken river. The weather had grown cold, and at night the frost gathered thickly on our sleeping bags. Great flocks of sandhill cranes passed overhead from time to time, the air re-sounding with their strange, musical, guttural clangor.

For several days we had hunted persever-
ingly, but without success, through the broken
country. We had come across tracks of mountain sheep, but not the animals themselves, and
the few blacktail which we had seen had seen
us first and escaped before we could get within
shot. The only thing killed had been a whitetail fawn, which Lambert had knocked over by
a very pretty shot as we were riding through
a long, heavily-timbered bottom. Four men in
stalwart health and taking much outdoor exercise have large appetites, and the flesh of the
whitetail was almost gone.

One evening Lambert and I hunted nearly
to the head of one of the creeks which opened
close to our camp, and, in turning to descend
what we thought was one of the side coulees
leading into it, we contrived to get over the
divide into the coulees of an entirely different
creek system, and did not discover our error
until it was too late to remedy it. We struck
the river about nightfall, and were not quite
sure where, and had six miles' tramp in the
dark along the sandy river bed and through
the dense timber bottoms, wading the streams
a dozen times before we finally struck camp,
tired and hungry, and able to appreciate to the

full the stew of hot venison and potatoes, and afterward the comfort of our buffalo and caribou hide sleeping bags. The next morning the Sheriff's remark of "Look alive, you fellows, if you want any breakfast," awoke the other members of the party shortly after dawn. It was bitterly cold as we scrambled out of our bedding, and, after a hasty wash, huddled around the fire, where the venison was sizzling and the coffee-pot boiling, while the bread was kept warm in the Dutch oven. About a third of a mile away to the west the bluffs, which rose abruptly from the river bottom, were crowned by a high plateau, where the grass was so good that over night the horses had been led up and picketed on it, and the man who had led them up had stated the previous evening that he had seen what he took to be fresh footprints of a mountain sheep crossing the surface of a bluff fronting our camp. The footprints apparently showed that the animal had been there since the camp had been pitched. The face of the cliff on this side was very sheer, the path by which the horses scrambled to the top being around a shoulder and out of sight of camp.

While sitting close up around the fire finish-

ing breakfast, and just as the first level sun-
beams struck the top of the plateau, we saw on
this cliff crest something moving, and at first
supposed it to be one of the horses which had
broken loose from its picket pin. Soon the
thing, whatever it was, raised its head, and we
were all on our feet in a moment, exclaiming
that it was a deer or a sheep. It was feeding
in plain sight of us only about a third of a
mile distant, and the horses, as I afterward
found, were but a few rods beyond it on the
plateau. The instant I realized that it was
game of some kind I seized my rifle, buckled
on my cartridge belt, and slunk off toward the
river bed. As soon as I was under the protection of the line of cottonwoods, I trotted
briskly toward the cliff, and when I got to
where it impinged on the river I ran a little
to the left, and, selecting what I deemed to be
a favorable place, began to make the ascent.
The animal was on the grassy bench, some
eight or ten feet below the crest, when I last
saw it; but it was evidently moving hither and
thither, sometimes on this bench and sometimes on the crest itself, cropping the short
grass and browsing on the young shrubs.
The cliff was divided by several shoulders

or ridges, there being hollows like vertical gullies between them, and up one of these I scrambled, using the utmost caution not to dislodge earth or stones. Finally I reached the bench just below the sky line, and then, turning to the left, wriggled cautiously along it, hat in hand. The cliff was so steep and bulged so in the middle, and, moreover, the shoulders or projecting ridges in the surface spoken of above were so pronounced, that I knew it was out of the question for the animal to have seen me, but I was afraid it might have heard me. The air was absolutely still, and so I had no fear of its sharp nose. Twice in succession I peered with the utmost caution over shoulders of the cliff, merely to see nothing beyond save another shoulder some forty or fifty yards distant. Then I crept up to the edge and looked over the level plateau. Nothing was in sight excepting the horses, and these were closed up to me, and, of course, they all raised their heads to look. I nervously turned half round, sure that if the animal, whatever it was, was in sight, it would promptly take the alarm. However, by good luck, it appeared that at this time it was below the crest on the terrace or bench already mentioned, and, on creeping to the next shoulder, I at last saw it—a year-ling mountain sheep—walking slowly away from me, and evidently utterly unsuspicious of any danger. I straightened up, bringing my rifle to my shoulder, and as it wheeled I fired, and the sheep made two or three blind jumps in my direction. So close was I to the camp, and so still was the cold morning, that I distinctly heard one of the three men, who had remained clustered about the fire eagerly watching my movements, call, "By George, he's missed; I saw the bullet strike the cliff." I had fired behind the shoulders, and the bullet, of course going through, had buried itself in the bluff beyond. The wound was almost instantaneously fatal, and the sheep, after striving in vain to keep its balance, fell heels over head down a crevice, where it jammed. I descended, released the carcass and pitched it on ahead of me, only to have it jam again near the foot of the cliff. Before I got it loose I was joined by my three companions, who had been running headlong toward me through the brush ever since the time they had seen the animal fall.

I never obtained another sheep under circumstances which seemed to me quite so remarkable as these; for sheep are, on the whole, the wariest of game. Nevertheless, with all game there is an immense amount of chance in the chase, and it is perhaps not wholly uncharacteristic of a hunter's luck that, after having hunted faithfully in vain and with much hard labor for several days thorugh a good sheep country, we should at last have obtained one within sight and earshot of camp. Incidentally I may mention that I have never tasted better mutton, or meat of any kind, than that furnished by this tender yearling.

In 1894, on the last day I spent at the ranch, and with the last bullet I fired from my rifle, I killed a fine whitetail buck. I left the ranch house early in the afternoon on my favorite pony, Muley, my foreman riding with me. After going a couple of miles, by sheer good luck we stumbled on three whitetail—a buck, a doe and a fawn—in a long winding coulee, with a belt of timber running down its bottom. When we saw the deer, they were trying to sneak off, and immediately my foreman galloped toward one end of the coulee and started to ride down through it, while I ran Muley to the other end to intercept the deer. They were, of course, quite likely to break off to one side, but this happened to be one of the occasions when everything went right. When I reached the spot from which I covered the exits from the timber, I leaped off, and immediately afterward heard a shout from my foreman that told me the deer were on foot. Muley is a pet horse, and he enjoys immensely the gallop after game; but his nerves invariably fail him at the shot. He stood snorting beside me, and finally, as the deer came in sight, away he tore—only to go about 200 yards, however, and stand and watch us with his ears pricked forward until, when I needed him, I went for him. At the moment, however, I paid no heed to Muley, for a cracking in the brush told me the game was close, and in another moment I caught the shadowy outlines of the doe and the fawn as they scudded through the timber. By good luck, the buck, evidently flurried, came right on the edge of the woods next to me, and, as he passed, running like a quarter horse, I held well ahead of him and pulled the trigger. The bullet broke his neck and down he went— a fine fellow with a handsome ten-point head, and fat as a prize sheep; for it was just before the rut. Then we rode home, and I sat in a rocking-chair on the ranch house veranda, looking across the river at the strangely shaped buttes and the groves of shimmering cottonwoods until the sun went down and the frosty air bade me go in.

I wish that members of the Boone and Crockett Club, and big game hunters generally, would make a point of putting down all their experiences with game, and with any other markworthy beasts or birds, in the regions where they hunt, which would be of interest to students of natural history; noting any changes of habits in the animals and any causes that tend to make them decrease in numbers, giving an idea of the times at which the different larger beasts became extinct, and the like. Around my ranch on the Little Missouri there have been several curious changes in the fauna. Thus, magpies have greatly decreased in number, owing, I believe, mainly to the wolf-hunters. Magpies often come around carcasses and eat poisoned baits. I have seen as many as seven lying dead around a bait. They are much less plentiful than they formerly were. In this last year, 1894, I saw one large party; otherwise only two or three strag-

glers. This same year I was rather surprised
at meeting a porcupine, usually a beast of the
timber, at least twenty miles from trees. He
was grubbing after sagebrush roots on the
edge of a cut bank by a half-dried creek. I
was stalking an antelope at the time, and
stopped to watch him for about five minutes.
He paid no heed to me, though I was within
three or four paces of him. Both the luciver,
or northern lynx, and the wolverine have been
found on the Little Missouri, near the Kildeer
Mountains, but I do not know of a specimen
of either that has been killed there for some
years past. The blackfooted ferret was always rare, and is rare now. But few beaver
are left; they were very abundant in 1880, but
were speedily trapped out when the Indians
vanished and the Northern Pacific Railroad
was built. While this railroad was building,
the bears frequently caused much trouble by
industriously damming the culverts.

With us the first animal to disappear was
the buffalo. In the old days, say from 1870
to 1880, the buffalo were probably the most
abundant of all animals along the Little Missouri in the region that I know, ranging, say,
from Pretty Buttes to the Killdeer Mountains.

They were migratory, and at times almost all of them might leave; but, on the whole, they were the most abundant of the game animals. In 1881 they were still almost as numerous as ever. In 1883 all were killed but a few stragglers, and the last of these stragglers that I heard of as seen in our immediate neighborhood was in 1885. The second game animal in point of abundance was the blacktail. It did not go out on the prairies, but in the broken country adjoining the river it was far more plentiful than any other kind of game. It is greatly reduced in numbers now. Blacktail were not much slaughtered until the buffalo began to give out, say in 1882; but they are probably now not a twentieth as plentiful as they were in that year. Elk were plentiful in 1880, though never anything like as abundant as the buffalo and the blacktail. Only straggling parties or individuals have been seen since 1883. The last I shot near my ranch was in 1886; but two or three have been shot since, and a cow and calf were seen, chased and almost roped by the riders on the round-up in the fall of 1893. Doubtless one or two still linger even yet in inaccessible places. Whitetail were never as numerous as the other game, but they have held their own well. Though they have decreased in numbers, the decrease is by no means as great as of the blacktail, and a good many can be shot yet. A dozen years ago probably twenty blacktail were killed for every one whitetail; now the numbers are about equal. Antelope were plentiful in the old days, though not nearly so much so as buffalo and blacktail. The hunters did not molest them while the buffalo and elk lasted, and they then turned their attention to the blacktails. For some years after 1880 I think the pronghorn in our neighborhood positively increased in numbers. In 1886 I thought them more plentiful than I had ever known them before. Since then they have decreased, and in the last two years the decrease has been quite rapid. Mountain sheep were never very plentiful, and during the last dozen years they have decreased proportionately less than any other game. Bears have decreased in numbers, and have become very shy and difficult to get at; they were never plentiful. Cougars were always very scarce.

There were two stages of hunting in our country, as in almost all other countries similarly situated. In 1880 the Northern Pacific Railroad was built nearly to the edge of the Bad Lands, and the danger of Indian war was totally eliminated. A great inrush of hunters followed. In 1881, 1882 and 1883 buffalo, elk and blacktail were slaughtered in enormous numbers, and a good many whitetail and prongbuck were killed too. By 1884 the game had been so thinned out that hide hunting and meat hunting had ceased to pay. A few professional hunters remained, but most of them moved elsewhere, or were obliged to go into other business. From that time the hunting has chiefly been done by the ranchers and occasional small grangers. In consequence, for six or eight years the game about held its own—the antelope, as I have said above, at one time increasing; but the gradual increase in the number of actual settlers is now beginning to tell, and the game is becoming slowly scarcer.

The only wild animals that have increased with us are the wolves. These are more plentiful now than they were ten years ago. I have never known them so numerous or so daring in their assaults on stock as in 1894. They not only kill colts and calves, but full-grown steers and horses. Quite a number have been poisoned, but they are very wary about taking baits. Quite a number also have been roped by the men on the round-up who have happened to run across them when gorged from feeding at a carcass. Nevertheless, for the last few years they have tended to increase in numbers, though they are so wary, and nowadays so strictly nocturnal in their habits, that they are not often seen. This great increase, following a great diminution, in the number of wolves along the Little Missouri is very curious. Twenty years ago, or thereabouts, wolves were common, and they were then frequently seen by every traveler and hunter. With the advent of the wolfers, who poisoned them for their skins, they disappeared, the disappearance being only partly explicable, however, by the poisoning. For a number of years they continued scarce; but during the last four or five they have again grown numerous, why I cannot say. I wish that there were sufficient data at hand to tell whether they have decreased during these four or five years in neighboring regions, say in central and eastern Montana. Another curious feature of the case is that the white wolves, which in the middle of the century were so common in this region, are now very rare. I have heard of but one, which was seen on the upper Cannon Ball in 1892. One nearly black wolf was killed in 1893.

I suppose all hunters are continually asked what rifles they use. Any good modern rifle is good enough, and, after a certain degree of excellence in the weapon is attained, the difference between it and a somewhat better rifle counts for comparatively little compared to the difference in the skill, nerve and judgment of the men using them. Moreover, there is room for a great deal of individual variation of opinion among experts as to rifles. I personally prefer the Winchester. I used a .45-75 until I broke it in a fall while goat-hunting, and since then I have used a .45-90. For my own use I consider either gun much preferable to the .500 and .577 caliber double-barreled Express for use with bears, buffalo, moose and elk; yet my brother, for instance, always preferred the double-barreled Express; Mr. Theodore Van Dyke prefers the large bore, and Mr. H. L. Stimson has had built a special .577 Winchester, which he tells me he finds excellent for grizzly bears. There is the same difference of opinion among men who hunt game on other continents than ours. Thus, Mr. Royal Carroll, in shooting rhinoceros, buffalo and the like in South Africa, preferred big, heavy English double-barrels; while Mr. William Chanler, after trying these same double-barrels, finally threw them aside in favor of the .45-90 Winchester for use even against such large and thick-hided beasts as rhinoceros. There was an amusing incident connected with Mr. Chanler's experiences. In a letter to the London *Field* he happened to mention that he preferred, for rhinoceros and other large game, the .45-90 Winchester to the double-barrel .577, so frequently produced by the English gun makers. His letter was followed by a perfect chorus of protests in the shape of other letters by men who preferred the double-barrel. These men had a perfect right to their opinions, but the comic feature of their letters was that, as a rule, they almost seemed to think that Mr. Chanler's preference of the .45-90 repeater showed some kind of moral delinquency on his part; while the gun maker, whose double-barrel Mr. Chanler had discarded in favor of the Winchester, solemnly produced tests to show that the bullets from his gun had more penetration than those from the Winchester—which had no more to do with the question than the production by the Winchester people of targets to show that this weapon possessed superior accuracy would have had. Of course, the element of penetration is only one of twenty entering into the question; accuracy, handiness, rapidity of fire, penetration, shock—all have to be considered. Penetration is useless after a certain point has been reached. Shock is useless if it is gained at too great expense of penetration or accuracy. Flatness of trajectory, though admirable, is not as important as accuracy, and when gained at a great expense of accuracy is simply a disadvantage. All of these points are admirably discussed in Mr. A. C. Gould's "Modern American Rifles." In the right place, a fair-sized bullet is as good as a very big one; in the wrong place, the big one is best; but the medium one will do more good in the right place than the big one away from its right place; and if it is more accurate it is therefore preferable.

Entirely apart from the merit of guns, there is a considerable element of mere fashion in them. For the last twenty years there has been much controversy between the advocates of two styles of rifles—that is, the weapon with a comparatively small bore and long, solid bullet and a moderate charge of powder, and the weapon of comparatively large bore with a very heavy charge of powder and a short bullet, often with a hollow end. The first is the type of rifle that has always been used by ninety-nine out of a hundred American hunters, and indeed it is the only kind of rifle that has ever been used to any extent in North America; the second is the favorite weapon of English sportsmen in those grandest of the world's hunting grounds, India and South Africa. When a single-shot rifle is not used, the American usually takes a repeater, the Englishman a double-barrel. Each type has some good qualities that the other lacks, and each has some defects. The personal equation must always be taken into account in dealing with either; excellent sportsmen of equal experience give conflicting accounts of the performances of the two types. Personally, I think that the American type is nearer right. In reading the last book of the great South African hunter, Mr. Selous, I noticed with much interest that in hunting elephants he and many of the Dutch elephant hunters had abandoned the huge four and eight bores championed by that doughty hunter, Sir Samuel Baker, and had adopted precisely the type of rifle which was in almost universal use among the American buffalo hunters from 1870 to 1883—that is, a rifle of .45 caliber, shooting 75 grains of powder and a bullet of 550 grains. The favorite weapon of the American buffalo hunter was a Sharps rifle of .45 caliber, shooting about 550 grains of lead and using ordinarily 90 to 110 grains of powder—which, however, was probably not as strong as the powder used by Mr. Selous; in other words, the types of gun were identically the same. I have elsewhere stated that by actual experience the big double-barreled English eight and ten bores were found inferior to Sharps rifle for bison-hunting on the Western plains. I know nothing about elephant or rhinoceros shooting; but my own experience with bison, bear, moose and elk has long convinced me that for them and for all similar animals (including, I have no doubt, the lion and tiger) the .45-90 type of repeater is, on the whole, the best of the existing sporting rifles for my own use. I have of late years loaded my car-

tridges not with the ordinary rifle powder, but
with 85 grains of Orange lightning, and have
used a bullet with 350 grains of lead, and then
have bored a small hole, taking out 15 or 20
grains, in the point; but for heavy game I
think the solid bullet better. Judging from
what I have been told by some of my friends,
however, it seems not unlikely that the best
sporting rifle will ultimately prove to be the
very small caliber repeating rifle now found in
various forms in the military service of all
countries—a caliber of say .256 or .310, with
40 grains of powder and a 200-grain bullet.
These rifles possess marvelous accuracy and a
very flat trajectory. The speed of the bullet
causes it to mushroom if made of lead, and
gives it great penetration if hardened. Certain of my friends have used rifles of this type
on bears, caribou and deer; they were said to
be far superior to the ordinary sporting rifle.
A repeating rifle of this type is really merely a
much more perfect form of the repeating rifles
that have for so long been favorites with
American hunters.

But these are merely my personal opinions;
and, as I said before, among the many kinds of
excellent sporting rifles turned out by the best

Hunting in the Cattle Country

modern makers each has its special good points and its special defects; and equally good sportsmen, of equally wide experience, will be found to vary widely in their judgment of the relative worth of the different weapons. Some people can do better with one rifle and some with another, and in the long run it is "the man behind the gun" that counts most.

Theodore Roosevelt.

Wolf-Coursing

While wolf-coursing is one of the most thrilling and exciting sports to be enjoyed in this country, it is less indulged in than any other sport; this, too, in the face of the fact that no country offers such excellent opportunities for its practice. This is, no doubt, due to the fact that it is a sport requiring special preparation, a thorough knowledge of both the game and country, and is very trying on horse, rider and hound. Russia seems to be the only country in which it has a foothold and a permanent place in the hearts of its sportsmen. In fact, with the Russians it might be called a national pastime. However, did it require in this country the same outlay of money, time and preparation that it does in Russia, I doubt very much its advancement as a sport.

There are really but two species of wolf in this country—the timber wolf, generally called the gray, and the prairie wolf or coyote. In

THE WOLF THROWING ZLOEEM.

different sections one hears of other varieties; but these, I believe, are merely variations in color and size, and are not specific differences. While the habits of the coyote or prairie wolf are well known to a majority of sportsmen, it is not so with the timber or gray wolf, and a few words in regard to the latter will not be amiss. My experience is that the wolves of Montana and Wyoming are larger, stronger and fiercer than those further south, though it is a fact that the largest single wolf that I ever saw killed was in Arizona. However, he was an exception to the general run of them there. If we may judge of the Russian or European wolf from specimens to be seen in menageries and zoölogical gardens, the American wolf, while not so tall or leggy, is more compact, with heavier head, coarser muzzle, smaller ears, and perhaps a little heavier in weight— the American wolf standing from 29 to 36 inches at shoulder, and weighing from 85 to 125 pounds. I am also inclined to think that the American wolf is, when run down to a death-finish, a much more formidable foe for dogs than his European relative. I reached this conclusion only after hunting them with high-priced hounds, that had won medals in Russia for wolf-killing, but which demonstrated their utter inability even to hold American wolves.

Alive, the wolf is the enemy of man and beast, and when dead he is almost useless. His skin has but little commercial value, and even dogs refuse to eat his flesh. I have never known dogs to tear and mutilate a wolf's carcass, and verily believe they would starve to death before eating its flesh. And yet I have read accounts of hunters feeding their dogs upon wolf meat. I recall an effort I made to cultivate in my dogs a taste for wolf meat. I cut up a quantity of bear meat into small strips and tossed them to the dogs, which would gulp them down before they could fall upon the ground. Substituting a piece of wolf meat was of no avail; they detected it instantly, and those which were fooled into swallowing it immediately lost interest in the proceedings and walked away.

The wolf is by nature cowardly, being deficient in courage comparative to his strength and great size, but he often becomes courageous from necessity. When reduced to extremity by hunger, he braves danger, and has been known in numbers to attack man, though no such incident ever came under my personal observation. I have had them dog my footsteps throughout a long day's hunt, always managing to remain just beyond gunshot distance; and upon one occasion, when I had shot a pheasant, one actually carried it off in full view before I could reach it, and, notwithstanding I fired several shots that must have come uncomfortably close, he made off with his dangerously earned meal.

As a general thing, however, the wolf manifests a desire to run, rather than fight, for life, and when alone will frequently tuck his tail between his legs, and run like a stricken cur from a dog that he could easily crush out of existence. They are great believers in the maxim, "In union there is strength." The female, while apparently more timid than the male, seems to lose all sense of danger when hemmed in and forced to a fight, and attacks with intrepidity. I once shot a female at long range, the bullet from my Winchester passing through her hind quarters and breaking both legs. When I got up to her, she was surrounded by the ranch dogs—an odd assortment of "mongrel puppy, whelp and hound, and cur of low degree"—furiously attacking first one, then another of them as they circled around her; and, though she was partially paralyzed, dragging her hind quarters, she successfully stood off the entire pack until another bullet ended the struggle. When in whelp they fight with great obstinacy, and defend themselves with intrepidity, being seemingly insensible to punishment. When captured young they are susceptible of taming and domestication, though they are never free from treachery. Though I have heard it denied, I know it to be a fact that the dog has been successfully crossed upon the wolf. I saw any number of the produce around the old Spotted Tail agency. They closely resembled wolves, and were hardly distinguishable from them in appearance, though generally lacking the good qualities of faithfulness and attachment possessed by the dog.

The amount of damage a wolf can do in a horse or cattle country is almost beyond belief. He slaughters indiscriminately, carrying waste and destruction to any section he honors with his presence. When a pack of these nocturnal marauders come across an unprotected flock of sheep, a sanguinary massacre occurs, and not until they have killed, torn or mangled the entire flock will they return to the mountains. Thus the wolves become a scourge, and their depredations upon herds of sheep and cattle cause no inconsiderable loss to the rancher. They frequently plunder for days and nights together. I am not prepared to state whether it is owing to daintiness of appetite or pure love of killing, but as it is a fact that a single wolf has been known to kill a hundred sheep in a night, it would seem that this indiscriminate slaughter was more to satisfy his malignity than his hunger. It is a prevalent idea that the wolf will eat putrid meat. This I have not found to be true. He seldom if ever devours carcasses after they begin to putrify, choosing to hunt for fresh spoils rather than to return to that which he had half devoured, before leaving it to the tender mercies of the coyotes, who have an appetite less nice.

The coyote is a good scavenger, following in the footsteps of the wolf, and will pick bones until they glisten like ivory. His fondness for domestic fowl and his thieving propensity often embolden him to enter farmyards and even residences during the daytime; yet he often seems contented to dine upon corrupt flesh, bones, hair, old boots and saddles, and many remarkable gastronomic performances are credited to him. I had occasion to "sleep out" one night in the Powder River country, and, after picketing my horse, I threw my saddle upon the ground near the picket pin, and, placing my cartridge belt beneath the saddle—which I used as a pillow—I was soon sound asleep. Imagine my surprise at daybreak—knowing there was not a human being within fifty miles of me—to find that my cartridge belt was missing. After a short search I found the cartridges some few hundred yards away, and a few remnants of the belt. The coyotes had actually stolen this from under my head without disturbing me, devoured it and licked all the grease from the cartridges. I felt thankful that they had not devoured my rawhide riata.

Of all animals that I have hunted, I consider the wolf the hardest to capture or kill. There is only one way in which he can be successfully coped with, and that is with a pack of dogs trained to the purpose and thoroughly understanding their business. Dogs, as a rule, have sufficient combativeness to assail any animal, and, as a general thing, two or three of them can easily kill another animal of same size and weight; but the wolf, with his wonderful vitality and tenacity of life, combined with his thickness of skin, matted hair and resistant muscles, is anything but an easy victim for even six or eight times his number.

I spent the winter of 1874–75 in a portion of the Rocky Mountains uninhabited except by our own party. Wolves were very plentiful, and we determined to secure as many pelts as possible. Owing to the rough nature of the country and our inability to keep up with the dogs on horseback, we tried poisoning, but with only moderate success. While others claim it is an easy matter to poison wolves, we did not find it so. In a country where game is plentiful, it is almost impossible to poison them. We tried trapping them, with like results. Always mistrustful and intensely suspicious, they imagine everything unusual they see is a trap laid to betray or capture them, and with extreme sagacity avoid everything strange and new. When caught, they frequently gnaw off a foot or leg rather than be taken. Our cabin was surrounded by a stockade wall, over which we could throw such portions of deer carcasses as we did not use,

and at nightfall the wolves, attracted by the
smell of the meat, would assemble on the outside, and we shot them from the portholes.
It required a death shot; for, if only wounded,
no matter how badly, they would manage to
get far enough away from the stockade to be
torn into shreds by the survivors before we
could drive them off. I have always found
the wolf a most difficult animal to shoot. En-
dowed with wonderful powers of scent and
extremely cunning, it is almost impossible to
stalk them. Frequently, after a long stalk
after one, have I raised my head to find him
gone, his nose having warned him of my
approach.

The successful chase of the wolf requires
a species of knowledge that can be acquired
only by experience. It also requires men,
horses and dogs trained and disciplined for
the purpose; and woe to the man, horse or
dog that undertakes it without such preparation. The true sportsman is not a blood-
thirsty animal. The actual killing of an animal, its mere death, is not sport. Therefore,
upon several occasions, I have declined to join
a general wolf round-up, where men form a
cordon, and, by beating the country, drive

them to a common center and kill them indiscriminately. I have always preferred hunting them with hounds to any other method of extermination. The enjoyment of sport increases in proportion to the amount of danger to man and beast engaged in it, and for this reason coursing wolves has always held a peculiar fascination for me. A number of years spent in the far West afforded me ample opportunity to indulge my tastes in this line of sport, so my knowledge of wolf-hunting and the habits of the wolf has been derived from personal experience and from association with famous hunters.

The principal drawback to the pleasure of wolf-coursing is the danger to a good horse from bad footing, and the possible mutilation and death of a favorite dog—death and destruction of hounds being often attendant upon the capture and death of a full-grown wolf. I do not know that I can give a better idea of the sport than by describing a day's wolf-hunting I enjoyed in the early seventies near Raw Hide Butte, in Wyoming.

We had notified the cook, an odd character who went by the name of Steamboat, to call us by daybreak. As we sat up late talking about the anticipated pleasures of the morrow, it seemed to me that I had hardly closed my eyes when Steamboat's heavy cavalry boots were heard beating a tattoo on the shack door. I rolled out of my bunk, to find Maje and Zach, my companions in the hunt, dressed and pulling on their shaps. Hastily dressing, I followed them out to the corral just as the gray tints of earliest morning were gathering in the sky. The horses had been corralled the night before, and, with Steamboat standing in the door, using anything but choice language at our delay in coming to breakfast, we saddled up. Having ridden my own horse, a sturdy half-breed from Salt Lake, very hard the day before in running down a wounded antelope, I decided on a fresh mount; and, as luck would have it, I selected one of the best lookers in the band, only to find out later, to my sorrow, that I had fallen upon the only bucking horse in the lot. While we breakfasted upon antelope steak, flapjacks and strong coffee, Steamboat was harnessing a couple of wiry cayuses to a buckboard, and, as we came out, we found him with the strike dogs chained to the seat behind him, impatient to be off. The party consisted of Maje,

Wolf-Coursing

a long-legged, slab-sided, six-foot Kentuckian, mounted on a "States" horse; Zach, an out-and-out typical cowboy, who had come up from Texas on the trail, mounted on a pinto that did not look as though he had been fed since his arrival in the territory, but, as Zach knowingly remarked, "No route was too long or pace too hot for him"; Steamboat in the buckboard, holding with a pair of slips Dan, an English greyhound, and Scotty, a Scotch deerhound; while the other dogs, consisting of a pair of young greyhounds, a pair of cross-bred grey and deerhounds, and Lead, an old-time Southern foxhound, were making the horses miserable by jumping first at their heads, then at their heels, in their eagerness to facilitate the start; and myself on the bucking broncho.

While crossing the creek a few hundred yards above the ranch, I heard old Lead give mouth, a short distance ahead, in a chaparral rendered impenetrable by tangled undergrowth, and which formed secure covert for countless varmints. Knowing that he never threw his tongue without cause, I dug my spurs into my horse, with the intention of joining him. But I reckoned without my host,

and for the next few minutes all my energies were devoted to sticking to my horse,
who then and there in the creek bed proceeded to give an illustration of bucking that
would have put the wild West buckers to
shame. Lead had jumped a coyote that put
off with all the speed that deadly terror could
impart—all the dogs after him full tilt. It required quite a display of energy upon the part
of Zach and his pinto to whip the dogs off;
and, had it not been for the fact that Dan and
Scotty—who had jerked Steamboat literally
out of the buckboard and raced off together
with the slips dangling about their heels—ran
into a bush, and the slips catching held them
fast, we would have been called upon to par-
ticipate in a coyote and not a wolf-hunt—as,
when once slipped, no human power could
have stopped these dogs until they had tested
the metal of Brer Coyote. By the time Zach
and the dogs returned, I had convinced my
broncho that I was not a tenderfoot, having
"been there before," and he was contented to
keep at least two feet upon the ground at the
same time.

We rode probably five or six miles, carefully
scanning the trackless plains, without sighting

a wolf, when Maje, who had ridden off a mile to our right, was seen upon a butte wildly waving his hat. We instinctively knew that game was afoot, and, as he disappeared, we commenced a wild stampede for the butte. Steamboat, with slips and reins in one hand and blacksnake whip in the other, came thundering after us, lashing his team into a wild, mad run—and how he managed to hold himself and dogs on the bounding buckboard was a mystery to me. Reaching the butte, we espied Maje a mile away, riding for dear life. It did not take long to decide, from the general direction taken, that the wolf would shortly return to us. Keeping well back out of sight, we impatiently awaited his return, and, had it not been for the pure malignity of my broncho, the wolf would have doubled back within a few hundred yards of us, and a close race have resulted.

I had taken the dogs from Steamboat, and, with the release cord of the slips around my wrist, sat in the saddle ready to sight and slip the dogs. Becoming impatient under the restraint, the dogs ran behind my horse, and, as the strap of the slips got under his tail, he again commenced bucking, and before I could

control him we were in full view of the wolf,
which, upon sighting us, veered off to the left.
Although not over a half mile away, the dogs
failed to sight him. With a cheer to the loose
dogs, we pushed forward at top speed, the
cracking of the quirts upon our horses' flanks
being echoed in the rear by the incessant pop-
ping of Steamboat's whip as he lashed the
panting cayuses to the top of their speed in a
vain effort to keep up with us.

We joined Maje at the point where we had
last seen the wolf, which by this time had
disappeared. Going over a rise, we dropped
down into an arroyo, where the foxhound
again gave tongue, and started back on the
trail almost in the same direction in which
we had come. Thinking that for once he was
at fault, and back-tracking, I took the two dogs
in slips up the arroyo, while Maje, Zach and
the pack of dogs followed the foxhound, and
were soon out of sight and hearing. Circling
around for some distance and seeing no sign
of the wolf, I rode upon a high point, and,
searching the country carefully through my
glasses, I could see the party probably a mile
and a half away; and, from the manner in
which they were getting over the ground, I

knew they had again sighted. A hard ride of
two miles, in which the dogs almost dragged
me from my horse in their eagerness, brought
me within sighting distance of the dogs—the
voice of the foxhound, which was in the rear,
floating back to me in strong and melodious
tones across the plains. Slipping Dan and
Scotty, they went from the slips like a pair
of bullets and soon left me far behind. Upon
rounding a point of rocks, I saw one of the
young dogs lying upon the ground. A hasty
glance showed me, from the violent manner in
which he strained to catch his breath, that he
had tackled the wolf and his windpipe was
injured. It afterward developed that he had
become separated from the pack, and, in cutting across country, had imprudently taken
hold of the wolf, which, with one snap of his
powerful jaws, had utterly disabled him, and
then continued his flight. Like most wolves,
he seemed to be able to keep up the pace he
had set over all kinds of ground. It seemed
to him a matter of indifference whether the
way was up or down hill, and he evidently
sought the roughest and stoniest ground, following ravines and coulees—this giving him
a great advantage over horses and hounds.

My horse beginning to show signs of distress, I realized that, if the chase was to be a straightaway, I would see but little of it and probably not be in at the death anyway; so I again sought a high point that gave a commanding view over a large area of country, and determined to await developments. Every once in a while, with the aid of my glasses, I could see the pack, fairly well bunched, straining every muscle, running as though for life. I could catch occasional glimpses of the wolf far in advance, as he scurried through the sagebrush, showing little power of strategy, but a determined obstinacy to outfoot his relentless foes.

Fortune again favored me. By degrees the superior speed and stamina of the hounds began to tell, though both seemed to be running with undiminished speed. The wolf, finding that, with all his speed and cunning, they were slowly but surely overtaking him, circled in my direction, and I was soon again an important factor in the hunt, urging the dogs with shouts of encouragement. I was now near enough to note that one of the young greyhounds, which had evidently been running cunning by lying back and cutting across, was far in advance of the pack—not over 100 yards behind the wolf, and gaining rapidly. Striking a rise in the ground, he overtook the wolf and seized him by the shoulder. The wolf seemed to drag him several yards before he reached around, and with his powerful, punishing jaws gave him a slash that laid his skull bare and rolled him over on the prairie.

Slight as this interruption was, it encouraged Dan to greater effort, and the next minute he had distanced the pack, nailed the wolf by the jowl, and over they went, wolf on top. Scotty was but a few paces behind, and, taking a hind hold, tried to stretch him. With a mighty effort the wolf tore himself loose from both and started to run again. He had not gone thirty paces before Scotty bowled him over again. Rising, he sullenly faced his foes, who, with wholesome respect for his glistening ivories, seemed to hesitate while recovering their wind, as they were sadly blown after their long run, the day being an intensely hot one. At this point I rode up. The wolf lay closely hugging the ground, his swollen tongue protruding from foam-flecked chops, and with keen and wary eye he watched the maddened pack circling about looking for a vulnerable point.

Varied experience in the art of self-defense had taught him skill and quickness, and as each dog essayed to assail him he found a threatening array of teeth. Throwing myself from the saddle, I cheered them on. Dan and Scotty hesitated no longer, but rushed savagely at him, one on either side, and the whole pack, including the one recently scalped, regardless of his gaping wound, followed them.

For a few minutes the pile resembled a struggling mass of dogs, and the air seemed filled with flying hair, fur and foam, and the snapping of teeth was like castanets. At first the wolf seemed only intent upon shaking off his foes and escaping, but the punishment he was receiving could not long be borne; and from then on to the last gasp, with eyes flaming with rage, every power seemingly put forth, he fought like a demon possessed. As he tossed the dogs about, seemingly breaking their hold at will, I was singularly impressed with his enormous size and strength, his shaggy appearance and his generally savage look, and suggested to Maje and Zach, who had come up in the meantime, that we take a hand in the fray, as I doubted the ability of the dogs to finish him without serious loss. However, we decided to give them the opportunity, and ere long they had him *hors de combat*, stretched upon the ground, his body crimson with his own life's blood, in the last throes of death. He was one of the largest specimens I had ever seen, weighing not less than 120 pounds, the green pelt weighing twenty-four. His carcass, when stood up alongside of Scotty, seemed several inches taller, and I afterward measured the latter and found him to be thirty-one inches.

All of the dogs received more or less punishment; none escaped scathless, but really much less damage was done than I expected. This was owing to the fact that Dan and Scotty, two of the staunchest seizers I ever saw, engaged him constantly in front, while the other dogs literally disemboweled him. Scotty had a bad cut on the side of the neck, requiring several stitches to close, and the muscles of his shoulder were laid bare; while Dan's most serious hurt was a cut from dome of skull to corner of eye, from which he never entirely recovered, as he ever afterward had a weeping eye. One of the cross-breeds, whose pads were not well indurated, suffered from lacerated feet, and one of his stoppers was torn

almost off, necessitating removal. A wolf's
bite is both cruel and dangerous, and wounds
on dogs are obstinate and very hard to heal
—more so than those of any other animal.
While skinning the wolf, our horses were
standing with lowered heads, heaving flanks,
shaking and trembling limbs; my horse, much
to my satisfaction, evidently without a good
buck left in him.

After a full hour's rest for man and beast,
we started back to the ranch. Taking Steamboat with the buckboard, I went back to the
point of rocks with the intention of taking up
the injured dog. Upon arrival there no trace
of him could be found; he had mysteriously
disappeared. Thinking that he had recovered
sufficiently to make his way back to the ranch,
we increased our speed and soon joined the
others, who had been heading directly for
home. The ride home was devoid of incident,
the monotony being occasionally broken by
our frantic efforts to restrain the dogs from
chasing innumerable jack rabbits that bounded
away on three legs, in their most tantalizing
way, inviting us to a chase. We also got
within rifle shot of a band of antelope, seeming quite at ease, feeding and gamboling

sportively with each other, until a pistol shot at long range sent them skimming gracefully over the plains, finally vanishing like a flying shadow in the distance. While crossing the creek below, and within sight of the ranch, we again heard Lead give tongue in the chaparral above the ranch, and in a few minutes he had a coyote busy, doubtless the same one we had disturbed in taking a constitutional in the morning. The dogs, now a sorry looking set, had been jogging lazily along behind us, but in a moment were all life and action. Their spirits were contagious, and, though we had positively agreed under no circumstances to run a coyote, we very soon found ourselves flying after the vanishing pack in full pursuit. A pretty race ensued. When first dislodged the coyote appeared lame to such an extent that I thought his leg broken; but after warming up this affection entirely disappeared, and the pace was a hot one for the first mile. The dogs ran well together, and were gradually lessening the gap between them and their wily foe, who, realizing this, displayed tact in selecting the very worst possible ground for footing, and soon regained his lost vantage. It began to look as though the coyote would

again give us the slip, when one of the young
dogs, that Zach in his excitement had ridden
over several minutes before and presumably
killed, was seen to dash out from a draw and
bowl over the coyote. His hold was not a
good one, but he succeeded in turning the
coyote, who then made a straight line for a
bunch of cattle grazing near, becoming tempo-
rarily unsighted among the cattle. The dogs
again fell behind, and when again sighted the
coyote was making a bee line for the ranch.
By the time the creek was reached, he was in
evident distress and sorely pressed. With a
final effort he dashed through the creek up the
opposite bank, and, as he dodged into the
open corral gate, one of the greyhounds
flicked the hair from his hind quarters. It
was his last effort. By the time we reached
the corral, he was being literally pulled to
pieces. We could not see that he made additional wounds upon any of the dogs. In
the excitement of the finish of the chase I
had lost Maje, and it was only after the death
in the corral that I missed him. Going to the
adobe wall, I peered over and saw him some
distance away standing beside his horse.
Upon going back to him, we found that his

horse had stepped into a prairie dog hole, throwing him violently, and, turning a somersault, had landed upon him. The only damage to Maje was, he had been converted for the time being into a cactus pincushion; but his "States" horse had broken his fore leg at the pastern joint and had to be shot.

After the long run of the morning, this race afforded us ample scope for testing both the speed and staying qualities of the dogs as well as of our horses.

We were disappointed in not finding the injured dog at the ranch. In fact, he was never afterward heard of, and doubtless crawled away among the rocks and died alone. After sewing up Scotty's wounds, dressing the minor cuts of the other dogs and removing the cactus and prickly pear points from their feet (the latter not a small job by any means), we were soon doing full justice to Steamboat's satisfying if not appetizing meal.

In contrast to our simple preparations and equipment for this, an average wolf-hunt in that country, wolf-hunts in Russia, as described to me by my friend, St. Allen, of St. Petersburg, are certainly grand affairs; but when the two methods of hunting are compared, I cannot but believe that the balance of sport is in our favor.

I have frequently been asked what breed of dogs I consider best for wolf-hunting. Having tried nearly all kinds, experience and observation justify me in asserting that the greyhound is undoubtedly the best. In the first place, there is no question of their ability to catch wolves, and, when properly bred and reared, their courage is undoubted. It is a general supposition that the greyhound is devoid of the power of scent. This is a mistake, as can be attested by anyone who has ever hunted them generally in the West upon large game, especially wolves, which give a stronger scent than any other animal. Of course, this power is not as well developed in the greyhound as in other breeds, because the uses to which he is put do not require scent, and, under the law of evolution, it has deteriorated as a natural consequence. Unrivaled in speed and endurance, these qualities have been developed and bred for, while the olfactory organs have been necessarily neglected by restricting the work of the dogs to sight hunting. Experience has taught me that they are the only breed of dogs that, without special training or preparation, will take hold and stay in the fight with the first wolf they encounter until they have killed him. I have heard it said that this was because they did not have sense enough to avoid a wolf. At all events, it is a fact that they will unhesitatingly take hold of a wolf when dogs older, stronger and better adapted to fighting will refuse to do so. I have found that, while all dogs will hunt or run a fox spontaneously, with seeming pleasure, they have a natural repugnance and great aversion to the proverbially offensive odor peculiar to the wolf. I once hunted a pack of high-bred foxhounds, noted for their courage. They had not only caught and killed scores of red foxes, but had also been used in running down and killing sheep-killing dogs. Though they had never seen a wolf, I did not doubt for an instant that they would kill one. While they trailed and ran him true, pulling him down in a few miles, they utterly refused to break him up when caught. The following extract, from an article I wrote some years ago on the "Greyhound," for the "American Book of the Dog," expresses my views of the courage and adaptability of the greyhound for wolf-hunting:

"A general impression prevails that the greyhound is a timid animal, lacking heart and courage. This may be true of some few strains of the breed, but, could the reader have ridden several courses with me at meetings of the American Coursing Club which I have judged, and have seen greyhounds, as I have seen them, run until their hind legs refused to propel them further, and then crawl on their breasts after a thoroughly used up jack rabbit but a few feet in advance, the singing and whistling in their throats plainly heard at fifty yards, literally in the last gasp of death, trying to catch their prey, he or she would agree with me in crediting them with both the qualities mentioned."

In hunting the antelope, it is not an uncommon thing to see a greyhound, especially in hot weather, continue the chase until he dies before his master reaches him. An uninjured antelope is capable of giving any greyhound all the work he can stand, and unless the latter is in prime condition his chances are poor indeed to throttle. A peculiar feature of the greyhound is that he always attacks large game in the throat, head or fore part of the body. I have even seen them leave the line

344

of the jack rabbit to get at his throat. Old "California Joe," at one time chief of scouts with Gen. Custer, in 1875 owned a grand specimen of the greyhound called Kentuck, presented to him by Gen. Custer. I saw this dog, in the Big Horn country, seize and throw a yearling bull buffalo, which then dragged the dog on his back over rough stones, trampled and pawed him until his ears were split, two ribs broken, and neck and fore shoulders frightfully cut and lacerated, yet he never released his hold until a Sharps rifle bullet through the heart of the buffalo ended the unequal struggle. Talk about a lack of courage! I have seen many a greyhound single-handed and alone overhaul and tackle a coyote, and in a pack have seen them close in and take hold of a big gray timber wolf or a mountain lion and stay throughout the fight, coming out bleeding and quivering, with hardly a whole skin among them. In point of speed, courage, fortitude, endurance and fine, almost human judgment, no grander animal lives than the greyhound. He knows no fear; he turns from no game animal on which he is sighted, no matter how large or how ferocious. He pursues with the speed of the wind, seizes the instant he comes up with the game, and stays in the fight until either he or the quarry is dead. Of all dogs these are the highest in ambition and courage, and, when sufficiently understood, they are capable of great attachment.

In selecting dogs for wolf-killing, the most essential qualities to be desired are courage, strength and stamina to sustain continued exertion, with plenty of force and dash. Training is a matter requiring unlimited patience, coupled with firmness and judgment, and a large amount of love for a dog. It also requires constant watchfulness of a dog's every movement and mood to make a successful wolf-courser of him. Many a good dog has been ruined at the outset by not being fully understood.

They should receive their first practical work when about one year old, provided they are sufficiently developed to stand the hard work necessary. They generally have mind enough at this age to know what is expected of them. It is, of course, better to hunt a young dog first with older and experienced dogs, which will take hold of any kind of game. The larger and stronger the dog, the better; for it requires immense powers of endurance, hardihood and strength to hold, much less kill, a wolf. The latter are particularly strong in the fore quarters and muscles of the neck and jaw. As an evidence of their great strength, I saw a wolf, while running at full speed, seize the Siberian wolfhound Zlooem by the shoulder and throw him bodily into the air, landing him on his back several feet away, and yet this wolf did not weigh as much as the dog.

Particular care should be taken to see that a young dog gets started right in his practical training. Encourage him with your presence; do all you can to see that he is sighted promptly; spare no expense or pains in getting a good mount, and keep as close as possible during the fighting; enliven him with your voice, and encourage him to renewed effort; for his ardor increases in proportion to the encouragement and praise received. Ride hard, to be in early at the death. His confidence once gained, he will place implicit reliance in your assistance; but, let him be beaten off once or twice through lack of encouragement, and he will soon lose his relish for the sport and show a disposition to hang back; while he may seem to be doing his best, a practiced eye will soon detect a want of ardor and dash. A pack of hounds, with a good strike dog and confidence in their owner, will carry everything before them; by keeping them in good heart they always expect success to crown their efforts.

If from any cause in the final struggle the dogs are getting the worst of it, or the other dogs refuse to assist the seizers, one must not hesitate an instant about assisting them; this requires perfect coolness, self-control and presence of mind, so as not to injure the dog. To attempt the use of the pistol or gun is too dangerous. A well-directed blow with a good strong hunting knife, delivered between the shoulders, will generally break the spine, leaving the wolf entirely at the mercy of the hounds.

I would advise no one to attempt the Russian method of taping the jaws while the wolf is held by the seizers. I had an experience of this kind once. After a long chase, the wolf, in his efforts to escape, leaped a wall, and, in alighting upon the farther side, thrust his head and neck through a natural loop formed by a grapevine growing around a tree. Reaching

him as soon as the hounds, I fought them off;
but, although he was virtually as fast as if in
a vise, it required the united efforts of five of
us to bind his legs and tape his jaws, and this
was only accomplished after a severe struggle
of some minutes. I am sure I would not have
trusted any dog or dogs I ever hunted to have
held him during this operation.

One should always be provided with a spool
of surgeon's silk and a needle, for these will
assuredly be called into use. Old Major, a greyhound owned by Dr. Van Hummel and myself, full of years and honors, is still alive. He
was a typical seizer and afraid of nothing that
wore hair. His entire body is seamed with innumerable scars, and has been sewed up so
often that he resembles a veritable piece of nee-
dlework. As an evidence of his speed, strength
and early training, I recollect that, shortly
after I had hunted him in the West, I had him
at my home in Kentucky. The Doctor was on
a visit to me, and we had taken Major to the
country with us while inspecting stock farms.
At Wyndom Place, where we were admiring a
handsome two-year-old Longfellow colt, running loose in the field, the owner, before we
were aware of his intention, set Major after the

colt "to show his speed and style." We both instantly saw his error, but it was too late—we could not call the dog off. He soon overhauled the colt, and, springing at his throat, down they went in a heap—the colt, worth a thousand dollars, ruined for life.

One of the most glaring instances of improper training and handling of wolfhounds that ever came under my observation was the Colorado wolf-hunt that attracted so much attention in the sporting press of this country, England and Russia. Mr. Paul Hacke, an enthusiastic fancier, of Pittsburg, Pa., while in Russia attended a wolf-killing contest in which the barzois contested with captive wolves. He became so much enamored of the sport that he purchased a number of trained barzois and brought them to this country. They were a handsome lot and attracted much attention while being exhibited at the bench shows. I was one of the official judges at the Chicago Bench Show in 1892, and wolfhound classes were assigned me. While I admired them very much for their handsome, showy appearance, I expressed grave doubts as to their ability to catch and kill timber wolves, notwithstanding I had read graphic accounts of their killing coyotes in thirty-five seconds. This doubt was shared and expressed by others present who had had practical experience in wolf-hunting. This coming to the ears of Mr. Hacke, who is always willing to back his opinion with his money, he issued a sweeping challenge offering to match a pair of barzois against any pair of dogs in the United States for a wolf-killing contest, for $500 a side. His challenge was promptly accepted by Mr. Geo. McDougall, of Butte City, Montana.

I was selected to judge the match, and in the spring of 1892 we made up a congenial carload and journeyed to Hardin, in the wilds of Colorado, where our sleeper was sidetracked. Arrangements were made at an adjoining horse ranch, and every morning a band of horses was promptly on hand at daylight. On the night of our arrival at hardin, a fine saddle horse had been hamstrung in his owner's stable by wolves. It was a pitiful sight, and added zest to our determination to exterminate as many as possible.

We were awakened from our sound sleep the first morning by the familiar sounds of saddling, accompanied by the pawing and bucking of horses, swearing of men, and snarling and growling of dogs. After a hasty breakfast, eaten by lamplight, we were soon mounted and in motion for the rendezvous. We had hardly crossed the Platte River, near which our camp was located, before the advance guard announced a wolf in full flight. A glance through my field-glasses convinced me that it was an impudent coyote, and we continued our search. We had probably ridden an hour through sand and cactus before one of the hunters had a wolf up and going.

McDougall had selected Black Sam, a cross between a deerhound and a greyhound, as his first representative, and he was accordingly in the slips with a magnificent-looking barzoi representing Mr. Hacke. Porter, from Salt Lake, the slipper and an old-time hunter, had all he could do to hold them until the word to slip was given. They went away from the slips in great style, the barzoi getting a few feet the best of it; but in the lead up to the wolf the cross-breed made a go-by, and, overtaking the flying wolf, unhesitatingly seized and turned it. Before it could straighten out for another run, the barzoi was upon it, and unfortunately took a hind hold, which it easily broke. The cross-breed, without having received a cut or even a pinch, lost all interest in the proceedings, and stood around looking on as unconcerned as though there was not a wolf within a hundred miles; and, though the wolf assumed a combative attitude, at bay, ready to do battle, and made no effort to avoid her canine foes, neither dog could be induced to tackle her again. The barzoi acted as though he was willing if any assistance was afforded by the half-breed. Neither of these dogs showed any evidence of cowardice, in my opinion, though credited with it by representatives of the press present. The evidences of this feeling are unmistakable, and I have seen fear and terror too often expressed by dogs, when attacked or run by wolves, not to recognize it when present. They did not turn a hair, and walked about within twenty feet of the wolf with their tails carried as gayly as though they were on exhibition at a bench show. Very different was the action of a rancher's dog, evidently a cross between a St. Bernard and a mastiff, that came up at this stage of the game. As soon as he caught sight of the wolf, every hair on his back reversed, his tail drooped between his legs, and the efforts of three strong men could hardly have held him. This I call fear and coward-ice; the actions of the others, a lack of proper training and knowledge of how to fight. As the wolf was a female and apparently heavy with whelp, I at the time thought this was the cause of their queer actions; but later, when skinning the wolf for the pelt, I found no evidence of whelp, but a stomach full of calf's flesh. In the second course, Allan Breck, a big, powerful Scotch deerhound, and Nipsic, a lighter female of the same breed, were put in the slips and a male wolf put up. They read-ily overhauled him. Allan, leading several lengths in the run up, promptly took a should-er hold and bowled over the wolf; then, as though he considered his whole duty per-formed, quietly looked on, whle Nipsic kept up a running fight with the wolf, attacking him a score of times, but was unable alone to disable or kill him. It was only after the wolf and Nipsic were lassoed and dragged apart by horsemen that she desisted in her crude efforts to kill the wolf. She displayed no lack of courage, but a total lack of training and knowledge of how to fight. In the final course two grand specimens of the barzoi were placed in the slips; one of them, Zlooem, a magnificent animal, all power and life, who had won the Czar's gold medal in St. Petersburg in a wolf contest, impressed me forcibly with the idea that, if he once obtained a throat hold, it would be all over with the wolf. On this occasion I had a most excellent mount, a thoroughbred Kentucky race mare, and, as one of the conditions of the match was that I alone was to be allowed to follow the hounds, I determined to stay with them throughout the run at all hazards, and to be in at the death. The wolf was put up in the bottom land of the Platte River. The footing was excellent, and, as he had but a few hundred yards' start, I was enabled to be within fifty yards of them throughout the run and fighting. The wolf at first started off as though he had decided to depend upon speed to save his pelt, disdaining to employ his usual stratagem, and the hounds gained but little upon him. Finding that but one horseman and two strange-looking animals were following him, he slackened his pace, and in an incredibly short time Zlooem was upon even terms with him, and, seizing by the throat, over and over they went in a cloud of sand, from which the wolf emerged first, again on the retreat, with both hounds after him full tilt. Within a hundred yards they again downed him, only to be shaken off. This was repeated probably a half dozen times, and, though both the barzois had throat and flank holds, they were unable to "stretch him." After five minutes of fast and furious fighting, they dashed into a bunch of frightened cattle and became separated. Though I immediately cut the wolf out of the bunch of cattle and he limped off in full view, the dogs were too exhausted to follow, and their condition was truly pitiable. Zlooem staggered about and fell headlong upon his side, unable to rise. Both were so thoroughly exhausted from their tremendous efforts that they could not stand upon their feet; their tongues were swollen and protruding full length, their breath came in short and labored gasps, the whistle and rattle in their throats was audible at some distance, while their legs trembled and were really unable to sustain the weight of their bodies. At the expiration of ten minutes, I signaled the slippers to come and take the dogs up; and thus ended the bid of the Russian wolfhound for popularity in this country.

Wolf-Coursing

Upon our return to Denver we were waited upon by a ranchman who had heard of the failure of a pair of these dogs to catch and kill wolves. He stated that he had a leash of greyhounds that could catch and kill gray timber wolves, and deposited $500 to bind a match to that effect. He was very much in earnest, and I regretted that we could not raise a purse of $500, as I should like to have seen the feat performed—my experience being that it required from four to six to accomplish this, and that even then they have to understand their business thoroughly.

Roger D. Williams.

Game Laws

Laws for the preservation of wild animals are a product of civilization. The more civilized a nation, the broader and more humane will be these laws.

Our ancestors of the flint age were lawless. After the fall "thorns also and thistles" came forth, and man ceased from eating herb-bearing seed and fruit, and turned his hand to killing and eating flesh—"even as Nimrod, the mighty hunter before the Lord." Many great and dangerous animals then existed, and it was a necessity to kill off the cave bear, the cave tiger and the mastodon. The earliest of Chaldean poems indicates the equally great fishing of those days: "Canst thou draw out leviathan with an hook, or his tongue with a cord which thou lettest down?" All savage nations are still ruthless and wasteful in their destruction of animal life. An example is found on the plains, where a thousand buffalo were driven over the walls of a cañon that a tribe might have a feast, although the tribe might, and often did, starve during the coming winter.

With the slow progress of civilization, at first customs grew up, and then laws were enacted consonant with the degree of education of the lawmakers. In ancient Oriental nations only a few animals were protected for the use of the rulers. Thus the elephant, the cheetah and the falcon in the East came under royal protection. The Normans, when they were not at war, followed the chase with ardor, and passed laws for the protection of deer, wolves and the wild boar. The Saxons, like the Romans, guarded their forest preserves, but left the open country free for chase to all the people. After the Conquest the new Norman rulers applied their own stern and selfish laws over all England. Not only was the chase forbidden, but the bearing of arms used in the chase as well, and the conquerors thus preserved the game for their own use, and also kept in subjection the disarmed people. Their punishments were barbarous, and comprised maiming and death, and the killing of a deer or a wild boar was punished with putting out the eyes or death. No greater penalty was inflicted for the killing of a man.

The underlying principle maintained was that all wild game was the property of no one, and that to which no one had title belonged to the sovereign. So the king held all lands not apportioned, and granted permission to his chiefs to hunt therein. He also created the right of *free chase, warren* and *free fishery,* thus authorizing a designated person to protect game and to follow the chase on the land of others, or protect and take fish from rivers and streams that flowed over the properties of other men. These claims of right became numerous and so burdensome that they were subsequently restricted by Magna Charta. The fascination of the chase, indulged in for years, became so inwrought in the English mind that it formed the principal recreation of the people, shared in alike by nobles, priests and peasants, evoking a world of romance and legend in Robin Hood tales, and a sturdy, semi-warlike pride. The exercise formed a school of stalwart out-of-door men, whose descendants of like taste have invaded the remotest isles of the sea, and girdled the earth with the colonies of England. The taste made its fair mark on English verse from the early date of Chevy Chase, when,

> To chase the deer with hawk and hound
> Earl Percy took his way,

down to this present year of grace, when Conan Doyle's archer sings:

> So we'll drink all together
> To the grey goose feather,
> And the land where the grey goose flew.

The pomp and dignity of the chase, its pursuit by the highest clergy and the sad result of want of skill by an archbishop are quaintly disclosed in the trial of the Archbishop of Canterbury for accidentally killing a game-keeper instead of a deer in the forest of Bramshill in the year 1621, as reported at length in Vol. II. of Cobbett's State Trials.

The right in the crown to all wild game, thus claimed and established in England, became part of the common law, and was inherited by the American colonies; and thus wild game in our Republic became the property of the people, and the duty of its care and protection fell upon the different States of the Republic, and in the territories upon Congress.

It is unnecessary to enumerate the different game laws and the various cruel judgments entered therein in the English courts, or to refer to the many essays and orations written and delivered against the game laws of the various European States. They met the condemnation alike of philanthropists, statesmen and poets. Charles Kingsley wrote in 1848, on behalf of the people, the bold and pathetic song:

> The merry brown hares came leaping
> Over the crest of the hill.

It defended the poacher lad, but lost for the writer his lawn sleeves.

The great distinction to be ever borne in mind between the game laws of Europe and those of America is, that the former were passed for the protection of game for a class, while the laws of a republic are passed for the preservation of game for the use of all the people. The former encountered the hostility of all the people save the aristocracy; the latter should obtain the approbation of all the people, rich and poor, for they are passed and maintained for the good of the people at large.

The value of the fish and game to the people of the State of Maine is greater and brings into the State more money than its hay crop or its potato crop. The value of a mountain stream is nothing except as it may water people or kine. Stock and protect that river by suitable laws, and the fishing privileges may be rented for an annual rental that will pay all the taxes of every county through which it runs. Yet often it is that the inhabitant of that county complains of the injustice of preventing him from taking fish therein at his pleasure at any season of the year.

The earliest recorded game law is found in the twenty-second chapter of Deuteronomy, where it is forbidden to take a bird from her nest. The earliest law upon this subject in America that we find was the act of the Assembly of Virginia of 1699, II. William III., wherein the killing of deer between January and July was prohibited under a penalty of 500 pounds of tobacco. In Maryland an act was passed on the same subject in 1730, which recites the evils of constant shooting—"Which evil practice, if not put a stop to, may in a few years entirely destroy the species of deer, to the great damage of the good people of this province; be it enacted by the Right Honorable the Lord proprietary, by and with the consent of his Lordship's Governor and the upper and lower Houses of Assembly, that it should not be lawful that any person (Indians in amity with us excepted), between January first and July last, to kill any deer under the penalty of 400 pounds of tobacco." South Carolina followed in 1769 with an act prohibiting the killing of deer during the same period, "under a penalty of forty shillings proclamation money." Both of these acts prohibited night hunting with fire-light, as did also the Statutes of the Mississippi Territory.

The earliest laws upon this subject in Kentucky were passed in 1775 by the Legislature, appropriately holding its sessions under the greenwood trees, and their author was Daniel Boone.

The earliest law in the State of New York was passed in 1791 (2 Session Laws of 1791, p. 188), and it prohibited the killing of "heath hen, partridge, quail or woodcock" on Long Island, or "in the city and county of New York," under penalty of twenty shillings.

Laws upon this subject thereafter multiplied in New York, varying in their scope and character with every Legislature. Sometimes the prosecution was left to the county prosecutor;

sometimes it was permitted to the informer, who shared the penalty; sometimes the power of enacting laws was reserved to the State; sometimes it was delegated to the supervisors. In 1879, by the influence of the Society for the Preservation of Game, a complete act was passed, entitled "An Act for the Preservation of Moose and Wild Deer, Birds, Fish and other Game," which for many years was vigorously enforced by that Society, and became the model for like laws in many other States. This law made the possession of game during the close season the offense, and not *prima facie* evidence of killing, and also it removed from the various local supervisors the power of making laws upon this subject.

These two essential features of law cannot be too strongly insisted upon with all lawmakers. Under this statute hundreds of prosecutions were made and convictions had in the markets of the great cities. The bidding for game by wealthy cities is the incentive to unlawful killing, and the closing of the markets stops the poacher's business more thoroughly than the conviction of an occasional poacher. When the law permitted game killed in other States during the open season to be sold in the State of New York in the close season, there was no lack of evidence to show that every head of game was killed elsewhere and in the open season, and the petit jury always found in favor of the oppressed market man. When the law was changed so that all game, wherever killed, was decreed illegal, the defense was plead that such a law restricted commerce and was unconstitutional; and it was not until the Society carried the case of Royal Phelps, President of the Society for the Preservation of Game, against Racey, through to the court of last resort, as reported in 60th New York Reports, that this defense was decreed insufficient. That case was followed in Illinois (97 Ill., 320), and Missouri (1st Mo. App., 15), and in other States, until it became the established law of the land. The Supreme Court of the United States held (125 U. S., 465), that a State cannot prohibit the importation of merchandise from another State, but can the sale. That court also sustained the right of States to protect fisheries and destroy illegal nets (Lawton *vs.* Steel, 152 U. S.), and it affirmed the right of States to compel the maintenance of fishways in damn erected in rivers (Holyoke

Co. *vs.* Lyman, 82 U. S.). The United States
courts also maintained purchaser's title to
marsh lands and enjoined trespassers from
shooting thereon in Chisholm *vs.* Caines (U. S.
Circuit Court of the 4th District). Thus, step
by step, the game laws of the land were sustained, held to be constitutional and enforced.

The forms of defense which offenders
deem it righteous to make to game prosecutions are without number, and as fraudulent
as their trade is wasteful. One instance will
illustrate. The writer, as counsel for the Society for the Protection of Game, prosecuted
one Clark, a prominent poulterer in State
street in Albany, for having and offering
for sale several barrels of quail. The case
was tried at Albany, Hon. Amasa J. Parker
appearing for the defense. After the plain-
tiff's witnesses had proved the possession of
the birds, the offering for sale as quail, and
the handling of several of them by the witnesses, the defendant testified that these
birds were not quail at all, but were English snipe, and that their bills were pared
down and the birds were thus sold as quail,
as they brought a better price, and that he
frequently did so in his trade. Probably no

person in the court-room believed this evidence, but the jury found for the defendant.

The defense has been frequently interposed, that the birds in question were not the prohibited birds, but were some other or foreign variety, until it was found that it was necessary always to purchase and to produce in court, fresh or dried, some of the game in regard to which the suit was being tried.

Before leaving the litigation of the courts of the State of New York, and in order to show how early and ardently the gentlemen of the old school followed the diversions of the chase, it is well to cite the case of Post against Pierson, tried in 1805 before the venerable Judges Tompkins and Livingston, and reported in 3d Cain's New York Reports. It there appears that Mr. Post, a worthy citizen of that most traditional hunting ground, Long Island, organized a fox-hunt. The chase went merrily—

> An hundred hounds bayed deep and strong,
> Clattered an hundred [more or less] steeds along,

and they started a fox and had him in view, when one Pierson, of Hempstead, the defendant in the case, well knowing of the chase, yet with wicked and felonious mind intercepted, shot, killed and carried away the fox. Post brought suit for the value of the animal, and the injury to the outraged feelings of the members of the hunt. Counsel learned in the law declaimed, and the wise opinion of the court, citing all the authorities from Puffendorf down, covers five printed pages, and finally decided that, "However uncourteous or unkind the conduct of Pierson in this instance may have been, yet this act was productive of no injury or damage for which a legal remedy can be applied."

Probably to correct this ruling, the Statute of 1844 was passed, which provides that anyone who starts and pursues deer in the Counties of Suffolk and Queens shall be deemed in possession of the same.

A great responsibility is thrown upon the Government of the United States to protect the large game in the different national parks. In a few years they will contain the only remnants of the buffalo, elk, antelope and mountain sheep. Poachers, like wolves, surround these parks, killing only to sell the heads for trophies. Captain George S. Anderson and Scout F. Burgess have done a good work in the

Yellowstone Park in capturing poachers, which efforts were recognized by the Boone and Crockett Club. If authority should be given to the army to try and punish these poachers by martial law, it would save many a herd elsewhere, and also relieve the Government from great expense for the transporting and trial of offenders.

When we reflect how many and valuable races of animals in North America have become extinct or nearly so, as the buffalo and the manatee; how many varieties of birds that afforded us food, or brightened the autumn sky with their migrations, have been annihilated, as have been the prairie fowl in the Eastern States and the passenger pigeon in all our States, the necessity of these laws appears urgent. A few suggestions that experience has taught us in regard to these matters are worthy of record.

We must remember that in a republic no law is effective without public opinion to back it. Therefore, cotemporaneously with making our laws, we should by writing and speaking educate the public mind to appreciate and sustain them. Experience has taught that in these prosecutions the public prosecutor is a laggard.

He prefers noted criminal cases and neglects these, which he regards as trivial offenses. Therefore the law should authorize private prosecutors, on giving security for costs and damages, to make search and conduct prosecutions in their own names.

Next, it is to be remembered that a single private person will make himself odious in the community by bringing such prosecutions, and is often deterred by the fear of revenge. Therefore, societies should be formed, composed of many good citizens; they should employ their own counsel, and prosecute in the name of the society or its president.

Next, the law should definitely fix a penalty for having in possession, transporting or exposing for sale. This is more important than prohibiting the killing, as it is the marketing of dead game that incites the killing. It is the market hunter that has destroyed all feathered life on our prairies, and the cold storage process has enabled him to transport to other States or countries, and make his gains there. Close the market and the killing ceases.

Another step to success is the procuring of the conformity of the laws in neighboring

States. The laws of New York may prohibit the sale of quail, ruffed grouse and prairie fowl, and the societies may enforce them in New York city, and day by day see the monstrous wrong of carloads of prairie fowl and other valuable game brought into Jersey City, and sold to the population of that town and to the ocean vessels sailing from its docks. Our Western prairies are denuded of their birds, that are frozen in the close season and are afterward shipped to Europe, and sold in the markets there at a price often less than they would bring in New York city.

Again, laws on these subjects should be as simple as possible, including in the one open and close season as many kinds of game as possible, and creating a general public understanding that the shooting season opens at a fixed date, say October 1st, and that no shooting or possession of game is to be allowed prior to that date, and that the close season for all game should commence on another certain date, say February 1st.

Lastly, a defective law, that is permanent and uniform throughout the State, is more effective than a better and more detailed law varying in different counties and towns, and

372

frequently altered. In illustration of the vagaries of lawmakers in this respect, it is to be remembered that the law of 1879, passed by the Legislature of the State of New York, was a complete and well-studied statute, made after much consultation, and meeting the approval of all the societies of the State, as well as the market men, and operated in the main satisfactorily to all. Since that date members of the Legislature from the different localities introduced bills making some exception or addition to the act, to benefit their little town or locality, to prohibit fishing in certain waters, to protect certain other animals, to provide certain restrictions as to weapons of chase or means of fishing, or times and seasons; or giving powers to county supervisors to legislate in addition to the general legislation of the State. Two hundred and fourteen such acts and ordinances have been passed since 1879, until the general law has been obscured and brought into contempt. These acts and ordinances include, among other curiosities, the protection of muskrats and mink, the preservation of skunks and other vermin, the prohibition of residents of one county from fishing in another county, and protecting parts of certain lakes or rivers in a different manner or season from other parts. In some of the acts words are misspelled; in one it is enacted that "*wild birds* shall not be killed at any time." Another act was passed defining the word "angling," as used in the general statute, thus—"taking fish with hook and line and by rod held in hands," leaving the troller or the happy schoolboy, that drops his hand-line from the bridge, exposed to the dire penalties of the law. While writing in this year of grace, eighteen hundred and ninety-five, the Legislature has passed a law permitting the sale of game at any time in the year, providing it is shown to have been killed 300 miles from the State.

This most unreasonable law was procured largely through the influence of the Chicago market men. The States lying west of Chicago have been endeavoring to protect their game. Salutary laws have been passed prohibiting the killing and freezing of game, and the transportation of it outside of those territories. The markets of Chicago and the other great cities of the West being closed to the public sale of game, the dealers sought to open the markets of New York, and they have thus

done so by this law. The Governor was fully
advised of the purpose and effect of the law,
but the powerful societies of the market men
were promoting it and the bill was approved.
In a few years the conspicuous prairie fowl
will exist only in the naturalists' books.

In olden times laws upon these subjects
protected only animals which lent pleasure
to the chase, and also certain royal fish
which were deemed to belong to the king.
These old laws were selfish and severe, and
were enforced with the cruelty of the age. A
gentler spirit has since dawned upon the
world, and now most game laws shelter as
well the song bird as the wild boar and the
stag. The true hunter derives more pleasure
in watching the natural life around him than
in killing the game that he meets. His heart
feels the poetry of nature in the "wren light
rustling among the leaves and twigs," and in
the train of ducks as,

> Darkly seen against the crimson sky,
> Their figure floats along.

He stops to enjoy the guttural syllables where
"Robert of Lincoln is telling his name" in the
summer meadow. At early dawn and even-tide

he listens to the bugle call of the great migration in the skies and exclaims:

Thou hast no sorrow in thy song,
No winter in thy year.

He feels the love that is begotten by contact with nature, and he it is in these later days who has extended the laws to protect all birds of meadow and woods, while in return he is rewarded by a choir of songsters giving thanks in musical numbers,

Better than all measures
Of delightful sound,
Better than all treasures,
That in books are found.

Chas. E. Whitehead.

YELLOWSTONE PARK ELK.

Protection of the Yellowstone National Park

The first regular expedition to enter the region now embraced within the limits of the National Park was the Washburn party of 1870.

In the summer of 1871 two parties—one under Captain J. W. Barlow, U. S. Engineers, and the other under Dr. F. V. Hayden, U. S. Geological Survey—made pretty thorough scientific explorations of the whole area.

As a result of the reports made by these two parties, and largely through the influence of Dr. Hayden, the organic act of March 1, 1872, was passed, setting aside a certain designated "tract of land as a public park or pleasure ground for the benefit and enjoyment of the people." It further provided that this Park should be "under the exclusive control of the Secretary of the Interior, whose duty it shall be, as soon as practicable, to make and publish such rules and regulations as he may deem necessary or proper for the care and management of the same. Such regulations shall provide for the preservation from injury or spoliation of all timber, mineral deposits, natural curiosities or wonders within the Park.

"He shall provide against the wanton destruction of the fish and game found within said Park, and against their capture or destruction for the purpose of merchandise or profit.

"And generally shall be authorized to take all such measures as shall be necessary or proper to fully carry out the objects or purposes of this act."

It will be seen that "timber, mineral deposits, natural curiosities and wonders" were, by the terms of the *law,* protected from "injury or spoliation." The Secretary of the Interior must, by *regulation,* "provide against the wanton destruction of fish and game," and against their "capture for the purpose of merchandise or profit." The Park proper includes nearly 3,600 square miles, but under the act of 1891 a timber reserve was set aside, adding about twenty-five miles on the east and about eight on the south, making the total area nearly 5,600 square miles.

Protection of the Yellowstone National Park

By an order of the Secretary of the Interior, dated April 14, 1891, this addition was placed under the control of the Acting Superintendent of the Park, "with the same rules and regulations" as in the Park; it thus in every respect became a part of the Park itself.

Dr. Hayden drew the Park bill from his personal observations, made in the summer of 1871. At that time the territorial lines were not run, and their exact location was not known. He consequently chose for his initial points the natural features of the ground, and made his lines meridians and parallels of latitude. His selections seem almost a work of inspiration. The north line takes in the low slopes on the north of Mt. Everts and the valley of the East Fork of the Yellowstone, where the elk, deer, antelope and mountain sheep winter by thousands; it leaves outside every foot of land adapted to agriculture; also—and this is more important than all—it passes over the rugged and inaccessible summits of the snowy range, where the hardiest vandal dare not put his shack.

The east line might have been placed where the timber reserve line now runs without much damage to material interests;

but in that case the owners of prospect holes about Cooke City would have long since secured segregation. As the line runs, it is secured by the impassable Absarokas—the summer home of large herds of mountain sheep—and it includes not a foot of land of a dime's value to mortal man. Both south and west lines are protected by mountain heights, and they exclude every foot of land of any value for agriculture, or even for the grazing of domestic cattle.

The experiment was once made of wintering a herd of cattle in the lowest part of the Park —the Falls River meadows, in the extreme southwest corner—and, I believe, not a hoof survived. Their bones by the hundreds now whiten the fair valley.

Following the act of dedication, Mr. N. P. Langford was on May 10, 1872, appointed superintendent, without salary. He was directed to "apply any money which may be received from leases to carrying out the object of the act." He never lived in the Park, never drew a salary, and never, except by reports and recommendations, did anything for its protection. In his first report he suggests that "wild game of all kinds be protected by law," that trapping be prohibited, and that the timber be protected from the axman and from fires. Unfortunately I am unable to possess myself of any of his subsequent reports; but I know that he toiled earnestly and without pay—and to no results.

On April 18, 1877, Mr. P. W. Norris was appointed to succeed him. He also served for love until July 5, 1878, when appropriations began, and something was done for "Park protection." In his report for 1879 he speaks of having stopped the killing of bison, and says that other game, although "grown shy by the usually harmless fusillade of tourists," was in "abundance for our largest parties." He also protected the wonders by breaking them off with ax and crowbar, and shipping them by the carload to Washington and elsewhere. His men did their best to protect the forests from fires, and with only fair success. By this report (1879) it seems that "no white men have ever spent an entire winter at the Mammoth Hot Springs"; he strongly recommended game protection, but not the prohibition of hunting. There was then but a single game superintendent, and he without authority to act. As at present, the main trouble was with the "Clark's Fork" people. The regulations permitted hunting for "recreation" or "for food," which would always be made to cover the object of any captured poacher.

Major Norris was doubtless a valuable man for the place and the time; but, as he expressed it in a manifesto dated July 1, 1881, and headed "Mountain Comrades," "The construction of roads and bridle paths will be our main object," to which he added the work of "explorations and research." His entire force lived upon game, which was hunted only in season, and preserved, or jerked, for a supply for the remainder of the year. He was succeeded by Mr. P. H. Conger on February 2, 1882, but Mr. Conger did not arrive until May 22 following, when he seems to have fallen full upon the trials and the tribulations that have beset his successors. He reported the necessity for protecting the wonders and the game, but seems to have accomplished nothing in either direction. His reports are largely made up of lists of the distinguished visitors by whose handshake he was anointed. He was relieved in August, 1884, by Mr. R. E. Carpenter, who was removed in May, 1885, without accom-

plishing anything. Mr. David W. Wear was
next in succession, and remained until legislat-
ed out of office in August, 1886. Nothing of
value seems to have been done in these two
administrations. In the sundry civil appropriation bill for 1886–87 the item for the protection and improvement of the Park was
omitted. By the act of March 3, 1883, the
Secretary of War was authorized, on request
from the Secretary of the Interior, to detail
part of the army for duty in the Park, the
commander of the troops to be the acting superintendent. As there was no money appropriated to pay the old officers, they, of course, had
business elsewhere. Captain Moses Harris,
First Cavalry, was the first detailed under the
new regime. He arrived there on August 17,
1886, and assumed control on the 20th. From
this time on things assumed a different aspect.
He had the assistance of a disciplined troop of
cavalry, and he used it with energy and discretion. It very soon became unsafe to trespass
in the Park, winter or summer, and load upon
load of confiscated property testified to the
number of his captures. His reports show the
heroic efforts made to prevent and extinguish
fires, to prevent the defacement of the geysers

and other formations, and to protect the game. In his report for 1887 he pays his respects to our enemies from "the northern and eastern borders"—the same hand that has continued to depredate until this day. He speaks of the "immense herds of elk that have passed the winter along the traveled road from Gardiner to Cooke City," and he goes on to say that "but little efficient protection can be afforded to this species of game except upon the Yellowstone and its tributaries. He remained in charge until June 1, 1889, when he transferred his duties to Captain F. A. Boutelle, and in the three years of his rule he inaugurated and put in motion most of the protective measures now in use.

Captain Boutelle, in succession to Captain Harris, continued his methods, and protection prospered. Meantime, in 1889, an additional troop of cavalry was detailed for duty in the Park in the summer, and had station at the Lower Geyser Basin. The principal use of this troop was in protecting the formations and the forests, but the work was well done and the foundation was laid for future efficiency.

I came to the Park in February, 1891, in succession to Captain Boutelle. On his departure there was only one man left here familiar with the Park and its needs, and that was Ed. Wilson, the scout. He had been a trapper himself, and was thoroughly familiar with every species of game and its haunts and habits. He was brave as Cæsar, but feared the mysterious and unseen. He preferred to operate alone by night and in storms; he knew every foot of the Park, and knew it better than any other man has yet known it; he knew its enemies and the practical direction of their enmity. He came to me one morning and reported that a man named Van Dyck was trapping beaver near Soda Butte; that he spent his days on the highest points in the neighborhood, and with a glass scanned every approach; and that the only way to get him was to go alone, by night, and approach the position from the rear, over Specimen Mountain. To this I readily assented, and at 9 that night, in as bad a storm as I ever saw, Wilson started out for the forty-mile trip. He reached a high point near the one occupied by Van Dyck, saw him visit his traps in the twilight and return to his camp, where at daybreak the next morning Wilson came upon him while sleeping, photographed him with his own kodak, and then awakened him and brought him to the post. But, unfortunately for the cause of Park protection, Wilson disappeared in July of that year, and his remains were found a mile from headquarters in the June following. That left me unsupported by anyone who knew the place and its foes; I was fortunate, however, in having as his successor Felix Burgess, who for more than three years has ably, bravely and intelligently performed the perilous and thankless duties of the position.

But before going on with a description of my own work in the Park, I will say a few words of my predecessors. In looking over the list, I think I can, without disparagement of the rest, single out three for especial mention.

Langford was an explorer and pioneer; by his writings he made the Park known to this country and to the whole world. He was an enthusiast and his enthusiasm was contagious. Protection was not yet needed, but a knowledge of the place was, and to this he largely contributed. He was the proper man and he came at the proper time.

Next came Major Norris. To him protection

was a minor or unconsidered subject. His "usually harmless fusillade of tourists" reminds one of Paddy's remark to his master: "Did I hit the deer, Pat?" "No, my lord, but you made him l'ave the place." For his time he was exactly suited; he penetrated every remote nook and corner; built roads, blazed trails, and in general made accessible all the wonders written of and described by Mr. Langford. Protection was not yet due, but it was on the road and close at hand.

For this part of the work Major Harris was an ideal selection, and he came none too soon. Austere, correct, unyielding, he was a terror to evil doers. And, after all, is there anything more disagreeable than a man who is always right? I believe Major Harris was always *sure* he was right before he acted, and then no fear of consequences deterred him. He once arrested a man for defacing the formations at the Upper Basin. The man confessed that he had done it, but that it was a small offense, and that if put out of the Park for it he would publish the Major in all the Montana papers. He was put out, and the Major was vilified in a manner with which I am personally very familiar. The next year this same man was sent to the penitentiary for one year for "holding up" one of the Park coaches in the Gardiner Cañon. In 1891 I derived great assistance in the protection of the wonders and the forests from Captain Edwards, who, with his troop, had served in the Park before. Unfortunately he had to leave in the autumn, and I was again left alone with my ignorance and my good intentions.

In May, 1892, Troop D of the Sixth Cavalry was sent to my assistance. Captain Scott was in command, and he has remained until the present time. Hard as iron, tireless and fearless, he has been an invaluable assistant in all that pertains to Park protection.

In protecting the beauties and wonders of the Park from vandalism, the main things to be contended against were the propensities of women to gather "specimens," and of men to advertise their folly by writing their names on everything beautiful within their reach. Small squads of soldiers were put on guard at each of the geyser basins, and at other points where protection was needful, with orders to arrest and threaten with expulsion anyone found breaking off or gathering specimens. Only a few examples were needed to materially diminish this evil. Of course, it still continued in small degree, but those who indulged in it had to be at great pains to conceal their operations, and this of itself greatly reduced the destruction. I personally engaged in a long controversy with a reverend despoiler, whom I detected in the act of breaking off a specimen. A large part of his defense was that, as I had on no uniform, he did not know it was necessary to be watchful and careful in my presence.

The names of the vain glared at one from every bit of formation, and from every place where the ingenuity of vanity could place them. Primarily I ordered that every man found writing his name on the formations should be sent back and made to erase it. I once sent a man from the Mammoth Springs and once a man from the Cañon to the Upper Basin to scrub his autograph from the rocks; and one morning a callow youth from the West was aroused at 6:30 A. M. at the Fountain Hotel and taken, with brush and soap, to the Fountain Geyser, there to obliterate the supposed imperishable monument of his folly. His parents, who were present, were delighted with the judgment awarded him, and his fellow tourists by their taunts and gibes covered him with confusion as with a garment. But, notwithstanding the sharpest watch and greatest care, new names were constantly being added, and they could not easily be detected from the old ones on account of the number of names already there. So, in the early part of the season of 1892, with hammer and chisel, where necessary, the old names were erased and we started even with the world, and the geyser basins are practically free from this disfigurement to-day. The remedy was heroic and successful, as such remedies usually are.

The protection of the forests—perhaps of more material importance than any other form of Park protection—became a subject of study, care and attention. As a rule, fires originated in one of three ways: by carelessly left camp fires, by lightning, or by the rubbing together of two trees swayed by the wind. There is no way of preventing the last two forms of ignition; the only thing to be done is to keep a ceaseless watch, and, so far as practicable, prevent the fire from spreading. The extensive areas burned over in days evidently prior to the advent of white men make it very apparent that these two agencies of destruction were then at work, as it is certain they have been since. Camping parties are many of them from cities, and they know little, and care less, about the devastation a forest fire may create. They leave a small and apparently harmless bunch of coals where their camp fire was; after they have passed on, a wind springs up, fans the embers into flame, the dry pine needles are kindled, and at once the forest is ablaze, and no power on earth can put it out. When once the flame reaches the tree tops, if the wind be strong, a man on horseback can scarce escape before it. As the wind ceases the fire quiets down, only to spring up again next day on the appearance of the afternoon breeze. The only time to fight the fire is when the wind has gone down and the flames have ceased. Then water poured on smouldering logs, earth thrown on unextinguished stumps, and the clearing of a path before the line of fire in the carpet of pine needles are the effective means of extinguishment. After a fire is once got under control it is no unusual thing for it to reappear 500 yards from any of its previous lines, carried there as a spark through the air, and dropped in the resinous tinder ever ready to receive and spread it.

In the four seasons during which I have
been in the Park but one fire of any magnitude
has occurred. That broke out along the main
road, about a mile north of Norris, in July,
1893. As it did not break out near a camping
place, its origin could not be traced to camp
fires; nor could it be charged to lightning or
rubbing of trees. It was evidently started by a
match or other fire carelessly dropped by a
member of the road crew, then working near
there, or possibly by a cigar stump thrown
from a stage by a tourist. It was at once reported to me by telegraph. The troop was at
drill, and in less than twenty minutes a dozen
men, under charge of a sergeant, were on their
way, with shovels, axes and buckets, to the
scene of the trouble. An hour later the report
was that it was beyond control. I then sent out
the balance of the troop, under Lieutenant
Vance, and ordered Captain Scott down from
the Lower Basin with all available men of his
troop. Thus the whole of the two troops were
at the scene, and they remained there toiling
and fighting night and day for twenty days,
when a providential rain put an end to their
labors. The area burned over included some
exceptionally fine timber, was in extreme

length nearly six miles, and in breadth from a few feet in some places to near a mile in others.

A fire in pine woods may be successfully fought so long as it is kept confined to the ground, but once it gets a start in the tree tops no power on earth can cope with it; no effort is of the slightest avail. Campers who leave their fires unextinguished often make the excuse that they did not believe any damage could result, as the coals were nearly dead. Although such might be the case at the hour of their leaving, in the still air of morning, the afternoon wind is quite capable of blowing them into dangerous and destructive life. My rule has been to insist on the rigorous enforcement of the regulation requiring expulsion from the Park in such cases. One or two expulsions each year serve as healthy warnings, and these, backed by a system of numerous and vigilant patrols, have brought about the particularly good results of which we can boast. In 1892 a fire on Moose Creek was sighted from a point near the Lake, and reported to me that night by wire from the Lake Hotel. Before the next evening, Captain Scott was on the spot with his troop, and the fire was soon under control. In a few hours it would have been in the heavy timber on the shore of Shoshone Lake, and there is no limit to the damage it might have wrought.

As a last heading of my subject I shall touch on the protection of the game. This was never seriously attempted until Major Harris came to the Park, in 1886; but he attacked it with an earnestness and a fearlessness that has left a lasting impress. It is not probable that the Park is the natural home of bison, elk or deer, yet the last remnant of the first and great numbers of the last two are found here. The high altitude, great cold and extreme depth of snow make it a forbidding habitat for the ruminants. They remain here simply because they are protected. Protection was given by a system of scouting extended over the best game ranges, and throughout the season of probable game destruction. A good many captures were made; the poachers were turned loose and their property confiscated; this was all the law allowed. The depredating element of the community soon came to care very little for this menace to their business, for they entered the Park

A HUNTING DAY.

with an equipment that was hardly worth packing in to the post, and, if taken from them, occasioned but small loss.

The accumulation of this sort of property had become great, and, as I had no proper storage room for it, I began my work by making a bonfire of it. A first requisite to successful work was to become acquainted with the names, the haunts and the habits of those whom it was necessary to watch or to capture. Ed. Wilson was thoroughly familiar with all this, and many is the lesson I patiently took from him. He described to me the leaders among the poachers from the several regions —Cooke, Henry's Lake, Jackson's Lake and Gardiner. To begin with the Cooke City parties, he named to me three as particularly active and dangerous: these were Van Dyck, Pendleton and Howell. Van Dyck, he told me, was at that time trapping beaver near Soda Butte, but he had not been able to definitely locate him. He made two trips there through cold and storm, but to no purpose. Finally, on his third expedition, he caught him, as already stated, sleeping in his bed. His property was destroyed, and he was held in the guard house awaiting the instructions of the Secretary of the Interior, which for some reason were very slow in coming. At last he was released, and ordered never again to cross the Park boundary without permission.

The next year Pendleton made a trip in the Park in early May, and got out with two young bison calves, which he was carrying on pack animals in beer boxes. Of course, they died before he got them to a place where he could raise them in safety, and he soon started back to renew his evil work. He was arrested and confined, and his case took exactly the same course as Van Dyck's had taken.

The last of the trio was Ed. Howell. Knowing of him and his habits, I kept him as well under watch as possible. During a trip I made to the east side of the Park in October, 1893, I saw many old signs of bison in several localities. Howell having disappeared from public view for a month or two, I sent Burgess out in January, 1894, with orders to carefully scout this country. I indicated to him exactly where I expected him to find signs of the marauder. He encountered very severe weather, and was not able to make a full tour of the places indicated; but he did report having found, in the exact locality I had designated to him, tracks of a man on *skis* drawing a toboggan. These tracks were old and could not be followed, but they formed a valuable clue. I next sent to the Soda Butte station and had a thorough search made near that place. It was found that the same tracks had passed over the hill behind the station, going toward Cooke. Careful inquiry developed the fact that Howell had come in for provisions with his equipment, but that he had not brought any trophies with him. Calculating the time when he should be due again in the bison country, I gave Burgess an order to repeat his trip there, and stay until he brought back results. He left the Lake Hotel in a severe storm on March 11th, and camped the night of the 12th where he had seen the tracks on his previous visit. Next morning, when scarcely out of camp, he found a *cache* of six bison scalps suspended in a tree. The *ski* tracks near by were old, and he was not able to follow them. He possessed himself of the spoils and started down Astringent Creek toward Pelican. When near the latter stream, he found a lodge, evidently occupied at the time, and the tracks near it, fresh and distinct, pointing to the southward. Soon he heard shots, and far off in the distance he espied the culprit in the act of killing more of the game. The problem then arose as to how he was to make the capture. With him was only a single soldier, and the two had for arms only a .38 caliber revolver. It was certain that this was Howell, and it was known that he was a desperate character.

In giving Burgess his orders, I had told him that I did not send him to his death—that I did not want him to take risks or serious chances; I impressed upon him the fact that, as far as Howell was concerned, even if times were hard, the wages of sin had not been reduced. All this he knew well, but there was a desperate criminal armed with a rifle; as for himself, he might as well have been unarmed. However, fortune favored him, and soon Howell became so occupied in removing the scalp from one of his bison that Burgess, by a swift and silent run, approached within four or five yards of him undiscovered. It would have been easy enough to kill him then, but it was too much like cold-blooded murder to do so at that range; at 200 or 300 yards it would have seemed entirely different. Howell's rifle was leaning against a buffalo's carcass a few yards from him. He made a step toward it, when Burgess told him to stop or he would shoot. Howell then turned back and said, "All right, but you would never have got me if I had seen you sooner." He was found surrounded by the bodies of seven bison freshly killed, and, to illustrate more fully the wanton nature of the man, of the eight scalps brought in to the post, six were cows and one of the others was a yearling calf.

His case went through the same course as the others, and finally toward the last of April he was turned loose, with orders to quit the Park and never return. He, however, is cast in a different mold from some of the previous captures, and some time in July he reappeared with the most brazen and shameless effrontery. He was reincarcerated, tried, and sentenced for disobedience of the order of expulsion. His sentence was thirty days in jail and fifty dollars fine, and this he now has under appeal. Insufficient as is Howell's punishment, his crime has been of more service to the Park than any other event in its history; it created the greatest interest throughout the country, and led to the passage of the Park Protection

Act, which was signed by the President on May 7th. A strange coincidence in the cases of Van Dyck and Howell is that both were accompanied by their faithful watchdogs, and neither dog gave a sign of the approach of the enemy, and both men swore vengeance on their faithless protectors.

The preservation of elk, deer, antelope and the carnivora is assured. Their numbers elsewhere, their wide distribution within the Park, their relatively small commercial value, added to the danger attendant on killing them within the Park, is a sufficient protection. Moose and mountain sheep will probably increase for similar reasons, although they are less generally distributed and are of greater value to head hunters. With the bison it is different. They have entirely disappeared from all other parts of the country, and they are of sufficient money value to tempt the cupidity of the hunters and trappers who surround the Park on all sides. It is told that a fine bison head has been sold, delivered in London, for £200—nearly $1,-000 in our money. A taxidermist would probably be willing to pay $200 to $500 for such a scalp. Many a hardy frontiersman, who has no sentiment for their preservation and no respect for the law, will take his chances of capture for such a sum.

Another animal that is difficult of preservation is the beaver; the trouble in this case is entirely due to the ease with which traps may be set in places where it is impossible to find them, and the ease with which the pelts may be packed and carried out. Within the last four years beaver have increased enormously, so I feel justified in saying that their preservation is so far successful.

For the general protection of the Park there are stationed within its lines two troops of cavalry. They are both kept at the Mammoth Hot Springs for eight months of the year, and one of them is sent to the Lower Geyser Basin during the four months of the tourist season. Small outposts are kept at Riverside on the west, Snake River on the south, Soda Butte on the northeast, and Norris near the center. Besides these a winter station has been placed in the Hayden Valley, and summer stations are kept at the Upper Basin, Thumb, Lake and Cañon. Between these a constant stream of patrols is kept up, so that no depredator can do very much damage without detection. There is allowed but one civilian scout, who is over-worked and underpaid. With all this enormous territory to guard, with all that is beautiful and valuable to protect, with the last of the bison to preserve, it would seem that this rich Government should be able to expend more than a paltry $900 per year for scouts, and more than $500 (which it receives for rentals) for the other needs of the Park.

There are very few who appreciate the amount of work done here by the soldiers in summer and in winter, in cold and in storms, on foot, on horseback and on snowshoes—and all without murmur or word of complaint. Never before was it so well placed before the public as it was by Mr. Hough in his *Forest and Stream* articles summer before last. Should Congress be stirred to make a more liberal appropriation for the purpose of carrying out the provisions of the act of May 7th, to him, more than to any other man, will the credit be due.

Geo. S. Anderson.

The Yellowstone National Park
Protection Act

On May 7, 1894, President Cleveland approved an Act
"to protect the birds and animals in Yellowstone National Park, and to punish crimes in said Park, and for
other purposes."

This law, as finally enacted, owed much to the efforts
and labor of members of the Boone and Crockett Club,
who for many years had persistently struggled to induce
Congress to pass such necessary legislation. The final tri-
umph is a matter of congratulation to every sportsman
interested in the protection of game, and fulfills one of
the great objects sought to be attained by the foundation
of the Club. While the statute, in many of its details,
could readily be improved, it is still, in its general features, sufficient to serve the purposes of its enactment. To
those not conversant with the subject, the statement may
seem astonishing, that from the establishment of the Park
in 1872 to the passage of the Act in 1894 no law protecting
either the Park, the animals or the visitors was operative
within the Yellowstone Park—a region containing about
3,500 square miles, and larger than the States of Delaware
and Rhode Island. This condition of affairs was frequently brought to the notice of the National Legislature,
and in 1887 their attention was called to it by a startling
episode. A member of Congress, Mr. Lacey, of Iowa, was

a passenger in a stage which was "held up" in the Park and robbed. The highwaymen were afterward apprehended, but escaped the punishment suited to their crime because of the great doubt existing as to whether any law was applicable. As to game offenses, regulations were powerless for prevention in the absence of any penalties by law to enforce them.

The explanation of this anomalous situation is to be sought in the circumstances under which the Park had been set apart. The eminent scientists, who interested themselves in this important object, were surrounded with difficulties. The vastness of the tract proposed to be included, the question of expense, the selfish interests opposing the measure, were obstacles not easy to overcome. Congress was told, "Give us the Park; nothing more is needed than to reserve the land from public sale or settlement." Doubtless the remoteness and isolation of the region might have been thought, at the time, sufficient to insure protection. But it was the wonderful scenery and extraordinary objects of interest in the Park which were then thought of; the forests and the game did not enter much into the consideration of the founders. And so Congress passed the Act of 1872, merely defining the limits of the Park and committing it to the keeping of the Department of the Interior, which was empowered to make rules and regulations for its control.

A great work was accomplished when Congress was persuaded to forever dedicate this marvelous region as a National Park, for the benefit of the entire country; and it was hoped and expected that Congress would, in time, supplement the organizing Act by the needful additional legislation. But this was not to be had for many years to

Yellowstone Park Protection Act

come. For some time after the year 1872, the reservation
was occasionally visited by a few adventurous spirits or
Government parties on exploring expeditions. During
that period it became the refuge of the large game which
had gradually receded from the lower country before the
advance of settlement and railroads. The abundance of
game astonished all who beheld it. Bears, deer, elk, sheep,
moose, antelope, buffalo, wolverines and many other
kinds of wild beasts were collected within an area which
afforded peculiar advantages to each and all. Nowhere
else could such a gathering of game be found in one locality. It should be remembered that those who visited
the Park in the early days we have mentioned confined
their investigations to a limited portion of it. The great
winter ranges and breeding grounds were almost unknown. During this period, game killing was so slight
and the supply so great that restrictions, by those exercis-
ing a very uncertain authority in the reservation, were
hardly pretended to be enforced.

But from about the year 1878 the depredations on the
game of the Park attained alarming proportions. The
number of visitors had largely increased. The skin hunter
and the record hunter—twin brothers in iniquity—appeared on the scene, and their number grew from year to
year. It was then that regulations and prohibitions were
promulgated from the Department of the Interior, but
they were known to contain only vain threats, which
could be defied with impunity. And so the slaughter continued, and likewise other depredations. Learned associations, sportsmen's associations, visitors of all lands, show-
ered petitions upon Congress to pass some protective law.
All that Congress did, however, was in 1883 to confer au-

thority for the use of troops in the Park. This was something, and the effect of their presence was very beneficial, and insured the only protection the Park had until the present time. Congress seemed affected with an apathy which no appeals could change. The result was non-action.

Some Congressmen thought they were justified in declining to take any interest in the matter, because few, if any, of their constituents had ever visited the Park. Others thought that it should be a Wyoming or Montana affair, and should be turned over to one or the other of those then territories. A few seemed to labor under the impression that the Park was nothing but a private pleasure ground, resorted to by the wealthy class, and that it was no part of the Constitutional functions of a Republican Government to afford security to wild animals, or to incur any expense therefor. These narrow views were not shared by most of the principal men in Congress; among these we had many staunch friends, including especially several who held seats in the Senate. Chief among them was Senator Vest, of Missouri, who at all times was found ready to do everything in his power to promote the welfare of the Park. Senator Manderson, of Nebraska, and many others were quite as willing. It was largely due to the gentlemen we have named that the Senate, as a body, was imbued with their views, and on all occasions recognized the important national objects to be attained by the Park, not only as a great game preserve, but also as a great forest reservation of the highest economic importance.

With the assistance of some of the present members of the Boone and Crockett Club, a bill was framed which

Yellowstone Park Protection Act

afforded in its provisions ample protection to the Park, while it added largely to its area on the south and on the east, embracing the great breeding grounds of the elk. This bill was introduced by Senator Vest. But new difficulties now arose, more serious than any hitherto encountered. By the completion of the Northern Pacific Railroad a large influx of travel set in toward the Park. It was now thought money was to be made there. Railroads through it were talked about. Mines, situated near its northern border, were said to contain untold wealth, needing only a railroad for their development. A mining camp, called Cooke City, was started, and it was urged that a railroad could reach it only by going through the Park. Corporate influences made themselves felt. The bill introduced by Senator Vest again and again, in session after session, passed the Senate. The promoters of a railroad through the Park thought they saw their opportunity. Afraid to launch their scheme of spoliation before Congress as an independent measure, they sought to attach it as a rider to the Park bill. They reasoned that those who desired the passage of that bill regarded it as so important that they would be willing to consent to its carrying a railroad rather than see all legislation on the subject dropped or defeated. The plan was well conceived, but failed of execution. The friends of the bill recognized that it was wiser to leave the Park unprotected than to consent to what would be its destruction. They recognized that, once railroads were allowed within the Park, it would be a reservation only in name, and that before long the forests and the game would both disappear. They therefore refused the bait held out to them by the railroad promoters, who thereafter always blocked the passage of the Park bill. In return they were always defeated in their own scheme. The House Committee having the protection bill in charge never failed to burden it with the railroad right of way whenever it came to them, blandly ignoring the evident fact that a railroad was not an appropriate nor a relevant feature to a law for the protection of the Park. And so it happened that the bill which had been the child of affection became an object of dread, and was denounced as bitterly as it had before been advocated by its original friends. It was thought better to have it die on the calendar than to take the risk of its adoption by the House of Representatives with the obnoxious amendment incorporated by the committee.

Apart from that amendment, it was feared the bill would not only encounter an opposition instigated by pecuniary interests, but might itself fail to call to its support any counteracting influence. Those who opposed the railroad, and notably the members of the Boone and Crockett Club, who invariably appeared before the Public Lands Committee to argue against it, were at the very least stigmatized as "sentimentalists," who impeded material progress—as busybodies, who, needing nothing themselves, interfered to prevent other people from obtaining what was necessary and beneficial to commerce. With practical legislators such animadversions are frequently not lacking in force, for nothing more incurs their contempt than a measure which has not what they call a *practical object*, by which they mean a *moneyed object*. While throughout the country there was considerable general interest taken in the preserva-

Yellowstone Park Protection Act

tion of the Park, such influence was not sufficiently concentrated to make itself felt by Congress. The Park was everybody's affair, and in the House of Representatives no one could be found to take any special interest in it. And so the fight went on from year to year. In Congress after Congress the bill was passed in the Senate, and emerged from the House Committee on Public Lands weighted down by the burden of the railroad. Secretary after Secretary of the Interior protested against this feature of the bill, and so did every officer of the Government who had any part in the administration or exploration of the Park. But their protests were without effect on the committee, which in those days seemed to regard the railroad as the most important feature of the bill.

It was clearly shown that the railroad would not only be most harmful to the Park, but could serve no useful purpose; for it was quite possible for a railroad to reach the mines without touching the Park, whereas the projected route cut through the Park for a distance of some fifty miles. The public press throughout the country was almost unanimous in denouncing the threatened invasion of the reservation. But the railroad in interest had a strong lobby at work, and many of the inhabitants in the territories and States nearest the Park showed the most selfish indifference to its preservation, and a greedy desire to plunder it. The railroad lobbyists were very active. They saw the necessity of trying to avoid openly outraging public opinion. Accordingly they changed the bill, so that, instead of conferring a right of way through the Park, it segregated and threw out of the reservation that portion through which the railroad was to go. This was supposed to be a concession to public sentiment; but it must have been thought that the public were very easily deceived, for there was really no concession at all, save to the railroad interests. Instead of a *right of way* through a portion of the Park, they now asked, and were offered by the committee, the land itself. The Committee of the House proposed that this land should be thrown out of the Park, and any and all railroads be allowed to scramble for it. The area thus doomed is situated north of the Yellowstone River, and constitutes one of the most attractive portions of the Park. It includes the only great winter range of the elk. In the winter there can be seen there some 5,000 animals, and no one who has traveled over this region in summer has failed to observe the enormous number of shed horns, showing how extensively the range is resorted to by this noble animal. Here too can be fofound a large band of antelope at all times, numbering about 500, and a smaller, but considerable, band of mountain sheep.

The friends of the Park succeeded in stopping the proposed railroad legislation, but they could accomplish nothing else in Congress. They had more success with another branch of the Government. There was a statute authorizing the President to set apart any part of the public domain as a forest reservation. Taking advantage of this, certain members of the Boone and Crockett Club saw an opportunity of substantially obtaining the enlargement of the Park which they had been vainly endeavoring to obtain from Congress. They laid the matter before General Noble, then Secretary of the Interior. He recommended to President Harrison that the tract in question should be constituted a forest reserve. This was done. In 1891 the President issued a proclamation, establishing the Yellowstone Park Forest Reserve. It embraced some 1,800 square miles, abutting on the east and south boundaries of the Park. The Secretary afterward had the same regulations extended to the Reserve as had been put in operation in the Park. This important action was followed by further proclamations, instituting other forest reservations in different sections of the country. The Executive and its representative, the Department of the Interior, have at all times been most sympathetic and helpful in the movement for forest and game preservation. They have sternly resisted all assaults upon the Park.

The organization of the Boone and Crockett Club had been a great step toward Park protection. Its membership included those who had shown most interest in obtaining legislation. One of the main objects of the society was the preservation of the game and the forests. It brought together a body of men whose motives were entirely disinterested, and who were able to make their influence felt. To their efforts must be largely attributed the success which was ultimately attained. But that success might have been indefinitely deferred had not Congress been awakened to its duty by an event as shocking as it was unlooked for.

For years one of the cherished objects of the Park had been the preservation of perhaps the only surviving band of buffalo. It had sought refuge in the mountains. It was known to be on the increase and it was supposed that it would remain unmolested. Its number had been estimated as high as 500. Its habitat was a wild and rugged country, affording a seemingly secure asylum. For a long time these buffalo remained comparatively safe. In the summer it would have been of no use to slaughter them for their heads and hides. In the winter the snow was so deep and their haunts so remote as to render it well nigh impossible to pack heads or hides out to a market. But a desperate man was found to take desperate chances. The trouble came to the Park from the mining camp of Cooke. A notorious poacher named Howell made it his headquarters. Its proximity to the northeast boundary of the Park made it a convenient point from which to conduct his raids and to which he might convey his booty. If he killed even a single buffalo, and safely packed out of the Park its head or hide, he was sure of realizing a large sum. If he was captured while making the attempt, he knew he was safe from punishment, and that there was no penalty, even if there was an offense. A less lawless man might have indulged a flexible conscience with the idea that, as there was no punishment, there was no crime. A similar view of ethics had been indulged in by a prominent member of the gospel, who had killed game in the Park, and sought extenuation on the ground that he had not violated any law. But Howell was not a man who sought to justify his actions; it was sufficient for him that he incurred no risk. The time he selected for his deed of destruction he thought the most propitious for covering up his tracks. His operations were conducted in the most tempestuous weather in that most tempestuous month, March, in the year 1894. The snow then was deepest, and Howell felt there would be little chance of interference by scouting or other parties. Eluding the

IN YELLOWSTONE PARK SNOWS.

guard stationed in the northern portion of the Park, on stormy nights, he stole into the Park and built a lodge in the locality where the buffalo wintered. In it he stored his supplies, which he had conveyed on a toboggan. He traveled on *skis*, the Norwegian snowshoes, ten feet long, which are generally used in the Northwestern country. This enabled him to traverse the roughest mountain range with ease and great rapidity, even in the deepest snow. Once established, the killing was an easy matter. He had only to find the buffalo where the snow was deep. The ponderous, unwieldy animals had small chance of escape from his pursuit. His quarry was soon located, and he needed no assistance to make a surround; for, while the frightened, confused beasts were plunging in the snow, in a vain attempt to extricate themselves, the butcher glided swiftly around them on his snowshoes, approaching as close as he chose. With his rapid-firing gun he slaughtered them as easily as if they had been cattle in a corral. How many he killed will never be known. The remains of many of his victims will never be found.

But while the ruffian was busiest in his bloody work, a man was speeding over the snow toward him from the south. He too was on *skis*. He too was a mountain man, who thought as little of the obstacles before him as Howell did. But the object of his trip was not the buffalo, but Howell. It was human game he was pursuing. Howell had not covered up his tracks as well as he thought. The trailer had struck a trail which he never left till it brought him to the object of his pursuit. This man was Burgess, the Yellowstone Park scout. He had learned of Howell's presence in the Park, and was sent out, with the intention of apprehending him, by the energetic superintendent, Captain Anderson. He proceeded on his course as swiftly as a howling wind would permit, when he was surprised by seeing suspended from some trees six buffalo scalps. He now felt that he was in close vicinity to the man he was hunting, and that his business had become a serious one. He knew the man who had done that deed was prepared to resist and commit a greater crime. But this did not deter him and he again took the trail. He had proceeded only a short distance when he heard six shots. Hastening up a hill, he saw Howell engaged in butchering five buffalo, the victims of the six shots. Howell's gun was resting on the body of one of the slain animals, a few feet away from where he was engaged in removing a scalp from another of the bison. So occupied was he in his work that he did not perceive the scout, who had emerged in plain view, and who silently glided to the weapon, and, securing it, had Howell at his mercy. The demand to throw up his hands was the first intimation Howell had that he was not alone in the buffalo country. It must have been difficult for the scout at that moment not to forget that ours is a Government of law, and to refrain from making as summary an end of Howell as Howell had made of the buffalo.

The poacher accepted his capture with equanimity, casually remarking that if he had seen Burgess first he never would have been captured. He was conveyed to the post headquarters. As soon as the Secretary of the Interior heard of his arrest, he ordered his discharge, as there was no law by which he could be detained or otherwise punished. Howell was proud of his achievement and of the notoriety it gave him, boasting that he had killed altogether eighty of the bison. This statement may only have been made for the purpose of magnifying his crime and so enhancing his importance. It may, however, be true. Besides those actually known to have been slaughtered by him, the remains of thirteen other bison, it is said, have been found in the Park. It is probable they were all killed by him.

When the intelligence of what had happened reached the country, much indignation was manifested. The public, which after all did have a vague sense of pride in the Park, and a rather loose wish to see it cared for, was shocked and surprised to discover that no law existed by which the offense could be reached. They were aroused to the knowledge that the Park was the only portion of our domain uncontrolled by law. The Boone and Crockett Club took prompt advantage of this awakened feeling, and redoubled its efforts to secure action by the National Legislature. Congress had long been deaf to the appeals of the few individuals who, year after year, endeavored to obtain a law; but now, at last, they realized that some action was really needed if they desired to save anything in the Park. Mr. Lacey, of Iowa, the gentleman whom we have mentioned as having had a practical experience of the condition of affairs in the Park, was naturally the first to take hold of the opportunity which public opinion afforded. He willingly adopted the chief jurisdictional and police features contained in the Park bill to which we have so frequently referred as repeatedly passing the Senate. He readily acquiesced in all the amendments which were proposed by members of the Boone and Crockett Club. The Club pushed the matter vigorously. The aid of many prominent members of the House of Representatives was enlisted. Before the hostile railroad party knew of the movement, the bill was presented to the House, unanimous consent for its consideration obtained, and it was passed. In the Senate the bill was among its friends, and Senator Vest was again instrumental in securing its passage. The promoters of the railroad scheme thought it more prudent not to meddle with the bill in the Senate, as they would have been certain to have encountered defeat.

The Act provides penalties and the means of enforcing them, and thus secures adequate protection. It makes the violation of any rule or regulation of the Secretary of the Interior a misdemeanor. It prohibits the killing or capture of game, or the taking of fish in an unlawful manner. It forbids transportation of game, and for the violation of the Act or regulations it imposes a fine not to exceed $1,000, or imprisonment not to exceed two years, or both. It also confiscates the traps, guns and means of transport of persons engaged in killing or capturing game. Finally a local magistrate is appointed, with jurisdiction to try all offenders violating the law governing the Park, and it specifies the jurisdiction over felonies committed in the Park. By a happy coincidence the new system was inaugurated by the trial and conviction of the first offender put on trial, and it was Howell who was the first prisoner in the dock. He had returned to the Park after the passage of the law, and was tried and convicted of violating the order of the Secretary of the Interior, by which he was expelled after he had slaughtered the buffalo. This was retributive justice indeed. The Club had

Yellowstone Park Protection Act

desired that the law should be extended by Congress over the Yellowstone Park Forest Reserve, but legal difficulties were encountered, so that this protection had to be deferred. It is to be hoped that in the near future this important adjunct to the Park may have the same law applied to it.

The Park is now on a solid foundation, and all that is necessary for its future welfare is the prevention of adverse legislation cutting down its limits or authorizing railroads within it. In the winter of 1894–95 the railroad scheme, now disguised under the form of a bill to regulate the boundaries of the Park, came up again. This was the old segregation plan. It aimed not only to cut off from the Park that valuable portion already described, and embracing 367 square miles north of the Yellowstone, but also to make extensive cuts in the Forest Reserve for railroad and other purposes, amounting to 640 square miles. This spoliation was not permitted. Congress seemed at last to be determined to support the Park intact, and the Committee of the Fifty-fourth Congress in the House having the Park legislation in charge manifested this disposition by adverse reports on all the bills to authorize railroads and on the segregation bill as well.

The present boundaries only need marking on the ground—a mere matter of departmental action. There is no need of legislation on the subject. The boundaries, especially on the north, afford such natural features as constitute the best possible barrier to prevent depredation from without, and to insure the retention of the game within, the Park. Notwithstanding the inadequacy of the protection in former years, the game has increased largely, especially since the military occupation. Competent authority has estimated the number of elk as high as 20,000, though this is probably too large a figure. Moose are frequently encountered. Mountain sheep and antelope are found in goodly numbers. It is doubtful now whether there are over 200 buffalo left. Bears of the different varieties are very plentiful and deer are also quite abundant. The animals thoroughly appreciate their security. They have largely lost their fear of man. Antelope and sheep can be seen in the vicinity of the stage roads, and are not disturbed by constant travel. Wild geese, ducks and other birds refuse to rise from the water near which men pass.

But bears show the most indifference for human presence. Attracted by the food obtained, they frequent the neighborhood of the hotels in the Park. The writer of these notes, together with some companions, had a good opportunity, in the latter part of August, 1894, to observe how bold and careless these generally wary animals may become if not hunted.

When we reached the Lake Hotel, the clerk asked us if we wished to see a bear, as he could show us one after we had finished dinner. We went with him to a spot some 200 feet back of the hotel, where refuse was deposited. It was then a little after sunset. We waited some moments, when the clerk, taking his watch out of his pocket said, "It is strange he has not come down; he is now a little overdue." Before he had replaced his watch, he exclaimed, "Here he comes now," and we saw descending slowly from a hill close by a very large black bear. The bear approached us, when I said to the clerk, "Had not we better get behind the timber? He will be

ON THE SHORE OF YELLOWSTONE LAKE.

frightened off should he see us." He answered, "No, he will not be frightened in the least," and continued to converse with us in a loud voice. We were then standing in the open close by a swill heap and the bear was coming toward us, there being no timber intervening. We did not move, but continued talking. The bear came up to us without hesitation, diverging slightly from his direct route to the swill heap so as to approach nearer to where we were. He surveyed us leisurely, with his nose in the air, got our scent, and, seeming content that we were only harmless human beings, turned slowly away and went to the refuse, where he proceeded to make a meal. We watched him for quite a while, when a large wagon passing along the road nigh to where we stood, the bear stopped feeding and turned toward the hotel in the direction in which the wagon was traveling. Our guide exclaimed, "He has gone to visit the pig sty," and in a little while we were satisfied this was so by hearing a loud outcry of "b'ar, b'ar," which we afterward found proceeded from a Chinaman, one of whose special duties it was to keep bears out of the pig sty.

After the departure of the black bear we retraced our steps, but before getting to the hotel I suggested to one of my companions, Del. Hay, that if we returned to the refuse pile we might see another bear. We accordingly went back on the trail to within a few yards of where we stood before. When we stopped we heard, in the timber near by, a great noise, as if dead pine branches were being smashed, and there emerged into the open a large grizzly. Although he was not quite so familiar as the black bear, he showed no hesitation, but walked straight toward us and the object of his visit—the swill. Before reaching his destination, however, he stopped and squatted on his haunches, calmly surveying the scene before him. The reason why he stopped became at once apparent. From the same hill down which the black bear had come we saw another grizzly, larger than the first, moving toward us at a rapid gait, in fact, on a lope, while the first grizzly regarded him with a look not altogether friendly or cordial. The second bear did not stop an instant until he reached the swill heap, where he proceeded to devour everything in sight, without any regard to us or to his fellow squatted near by. The latter apparently had had some experience on a former occasion which he was not desirous of repeating.

Three men coming through the timber toward us made a considerable racket, and the two bears moved off at no rapid gait in opposite directions; but they went only a short way. Until we left the spot we could see them on the edge of the timber, looking toward us, and, no doubt, waiting for more quiet before partaking of the delights before them. It was not easy to realize the scene before us was actual. The dim twilight, the huge forms of the bears pacing to and fro through the whitened dead timber, made it appear the creation of a disordered fancy. It did not seem natural to be in close proximity with animals esteemed so ferocious, at liberty in their native wilds, with no desire to attack them and with no disposition on their part to attack us. When the three men joined us and were talking about the bears, one of them shouted, "Here come two more," and before we could realize it we saw two good-sized cinnamons at the feast. They paid no attention whatever to us, but were entirely absorbed in finishing up what the other bears had left.

Yellowstone Park Protection Act

By this time it was fast becoming dark and we returned to the hotel. I should have said that we measured the distance from the nearest point from the black bear to where we stood, and found it to be exactly twenty-one feet. The other bears were but a few yards further.

When we returned to the house we entertained our friends with an account of what we had seen, and had there not been many eye-witnesses we probably would have been entirely disbelieved.* As we were narrating our story a man came into the room and said, "If you want some fun, come outside; we have a bear up a tree." We went outside of the hotel, and not over forty feet from it found a black bear in a pine tree. It seems that the wagon, already mentioned, had been stopped at the pine tree and the horses had been taken out. The owner, returning to his wagon, found the bear in it, and this was the explanation why the bear had so suddenly taken to the tree.

The animal was considerably smaller than the one we had seen earlier; in fact, it was not more than half as large, but still full grown. Quite a number of packers and teamsters stood about, amusing themselves by making the bear climb higher, till at last one of them asked our driver, Jim McMasters, why he did not climb the tree

---

*Colonel John Hay, of Washington, was one of the spectators of this curious scene. Captain Albrecht Heese, of the German Embassy, tells us that in July, 1895, while stopping at the Lake Hotel, he saw a very large bear eating out of a trough in the daytime while a number of tourists were present; and that the bear was finally chased away from the trough by a cow. At the Upper Geyser Basin a bear was domiciled in the hotel; it took food from the hands of the hotel keeper, following him around like a dog.

and shake the bear out. It was quite dark, and McMasters replied that he would not mind doing so if there were enough daylight for him to see. His companions continuing to banter him, he finally said, "I believe I'll go up anyhow," and up he went, climbing, however—instead of the tree the bear had ascended—a companion tree which grew alongside of the other, the trunks of the two not being more than a foot or so apart and the branches interlaced. We soon lost sight of McMasters and of the bear also; for, as Jim climbed the bear would climb too, until at last they both had reached the top of their respective perches, when we heard Jim cry out, "Boys, he's got to come down; I can reach him." With that he proceeded to break off a small branch of his tree, and we could hear him whack the bear with it, and also could hear the bear remonstrating with a very unpleasant voice, at times approaching a roar. But at last the bear seemed to have made up his mind that it was better to come down than stay up and be whacked with a pine branch, so down he came, but not with any great rapidity, stopping at every resting place, until Jim came down too and gave him a little persuading.

We could now see the action, but its dangerous features were lost sight of in its amusing ones. Jim had climbed into the tree down which the bear was descending, and when he was not persuading the bear he was pleading with us somewhat as follows: "Now, boys, don't throw up here, and don't none of you hit him until he gets down. If he should make up his mind to come up again he'd clean me out, sure." After each speech of this sort he would move down to where the bear was and apply his branch, whereupon both the man and the animal would descend a few pegs lower. At last the bear was almost near the ground. We all formed a circle around the tree, prepared to give both man and beast a reception when they should alight. The beast came first, and every fellow who had anything in the way of wood in his hand gave the bear a blow or two as a warning not to return to the wagon again. Bruin made off into the timber with great precipitancy. Jim, when he got down, did not seem to think that he had done anything more than if the bear had been a "possum," which he had shaken out of the tree.

Head-Measurements of the Trophies at the Madison Square Garden Sportsmen's Exhibition

During the week beginning May 14, 1895, there was held in Madison Square Garden, New York, a Sportsmen's Exhibition. There was a fair exhibit of heads, horns and skins, for which the credit largely belongs to Frederick S. Webster, the taxidermist.

At the request of the managers of the Exhibition, three of the members of the Boone and Crockett Club—Messrs. Theodore Roosevelt, George Bird Grinnell and Archibald Rogers—were appointed a Committee on Measurements. There were heads and skins of every kind of North American big game. Many of them were exhibited by amateur sportsmen, including various members of the Boone and Crockett Club, while many others were exhibited by furriers and taxidermists.

Some of the measurements are worth recording. For convenience we tabulate, in the case of each animal, the measurements of the specimens exhibited by amateur sportsmen who themselves shot the animals. For purposes of comparison we add the measurements of a few big heads exhibited by taxidermists or furriers; also for purposes of comparison we quote the figures given in two

Head-Measurements of Trophies

works published with special reference to the question of horn measurements. One is the "Catalogue and Notes of the American Hunting Trophies Exhibition" at London in 1887. The moving spirit in this exhibition was Mr. E. M. Buxton, who was assisted by all the most noted English sportsmen who had shot in America. The result was a noteworthy collection of trophies, almost all of which belonged to animals shot by the exhibitors themselves. Very few Americans took part in the exhibition, though several did so, one of the two finest moose heads being exhibited by an American sportsman.

The other big game book quoted is Rowland Ward's "Measurements," published in London in 1892. This is a very valuable compilation of authentic records of horn measurements gathered from many different sources. In many cases it quotes from Mr. Buxton's catalogue. The largest elk head, for instance, given by Ward is the one mentioned in the Buxton catalogue. But in most instances the top measurements given by Ward stand above the top measurements given in the catalogue, because the latter, as already said, contains only a record of the trophies of amateur sportsmen, whereas many of Ward's best measurements are from museum specimens, or from picked heads obtained from furriers or taxidermists, who chose the best out of those presented by many hundreds of professional hunters.

At the Madison Square exhibition there were numerous bear skins, polar, grizzly and black, submitted by men who had shot them. There were a few wolf and cougar skins and one peccary head; but there was no satisfactory way of making measurements of any of these. The peccary's head, which was submitted by Mr. Roose-

velt, of course, had the tusks in the skull, so that it was
not possible to measure them; for the same reason it was
not possible to measure the skulls which were in the
heads of the bear, wolf and cougar skins exhibited by Mr.
Roosevelt.

There were few Oregon blacktail deer heads exhibited,
and these were not large. The one exhibited by Mr.
Roosevelt, for instance, had horns 21 inches in length, 4
inches in girth and 17 inches in spread.

In measuring most horns it is comparatively easy to
get some relative idea of the size of the heads by giving
simply the girth and length. The spread is often given
also; but this is not a good measurement, as a rule,
because, in mounting the head, it is very easy to increase
the spread; and, moreover, even where the spread is
natural, it may be excessive and out of proportion to the
length of the horns, in which case it amounts to a de-
formity. The length is in every case measured from the
butt to the tip along the outside curve of the horn. The
girth is given at the butt in the case of buffalo, sheep,
goat and antelope; but in the case of deer it is given at the
narrowest part of the horn, above the first tine; in elk this
narrowest part comes between the bay and tray points;
in blacktail and whitetail deer it comes above the "dog-
killer" points, and below the main fork in the horn.
Even in the case of elk, deer, sheep and buffalo the
measurements of length and girth do not always indicate
how fine a head is, although they generally give at least
an approximate idea. The symmetry of the head cannot
be indicated by these measurements. In elk and deer
heads, extra points, though sometimes mere deformities,
yet when large and symmetrical add greatly to the

Head-Measurements of Trophies

appearance and value of the head, making it heavier and grander in every way, and being a proof of great strength and vitality of the animal and of the horn itself. In consequence, although the measurements of length and girth generally afford a good test of the relative worth of buffalo, elk, sheep and deer heads, it is not by any means an infallible test.

With moose and caribou heads the test of mere length and girth is of far less value; for many of them have such extraordinary antlers that the measurements of length and girth mean but little, and give hardly any idea of the weight and beauty of the antlers. With moose a better idea of these qualities can be obtained by measuring the extreme breadth of the palmation, and the extreme length from the tip of the brow point backward in each horn. Caribou horns are often of such fantastic shape that the actual measurements, taken in any ordinary way, give but a very imperfect idea of the value of the trophies. Very long horns are sure to be fine specimens, and yet they may not be nearly as fine as those which are much shorter, but more branched, and with the branches longer, broader and heavier, and at the same time more beautiful. Thus, at the Madison Square Garden, C. G. Gunther's Sons, the furriers, exhibited one caribou with antlers 50 inches long, of the barren ground type, with 43 points. These horns were very slender, and would not have weighed more than a third as much as an enormous pair belonging to a woodland caribou, which were some 10 inches shorter in extreme length, and with rather fewer points, but were more massive in every way, the beam being far larger, and all of the tines being palmated to a really extraordinary extent.

Hunting in Many Lands

TABULATED SERIES

With name of owner, and locality and date of capture.

BISON BULL.

	Girth.	Length.
1. P. Liebinger, Western Montana, '93	12½	19
2. Theodore Roosevelt, Medora, N. D., Sept., '83. . . .	12¾	14
3. Theodore Roosevelt, S. W. Montana, Sept., '89. . .	12½	17½

No. 2 was an old stub-horn bull, the animal being bigger in body than No. 3, which, like No. 1, was a bull in the prime of life.

F. Sauter, the taxidermist, exhibited a head killed in Montana in 1894, which measured 14 inches in girth and 18 inches in length.

In Ward's book the horns of the biggest bison given measure 15 inches in girth and 20⅞ inches in length.

BIG-HORN SHEEP.

	Girth.	Length.	Spread.
4. Geo. H. Gould, Lower Cal., Dec., '94 . .	16¼	42½	25¾
5. G. O. Shields, Ashnola River, B. C. . . .	16¼	37¾	22½
6. Arch. Rogers, N. W. Wyoming	16	34	17
7. Arch. Rogers, N. W. Wyoming	15½	33½	23
8. T. Roosevelt, Little Mo. River, N. D. . .	16	29½	18½

No. 4 had the tip of one horn broken; it is on the whole the finest head of which we have any record.

No. 5 was a very heavy head, the horns huge and with blunted tips.

A head was exhibited by C. G. Gunther's Sons which measured 17¾ inches in girth, although it was but 33½ inches in length.

In Buxton's catalogue the three biggest rams exhibited by English sportsmen had horns which measured respectively, in girth and length, 15¾ and 39 inches, 16⅜ and 38¼ inches, and 16½ and 31 inches.

In Ward's catalogue the biggest specimen given had

Head-Measurements of Trophies

horns which were 17¼ inches in girth and 41 inches in length.

WHITE GOAT.

	Girth.	Length.
9. Walter James, Swift Current River, Mont., '92	5¾	10½
10. T. Roosevelt, Big Hole Basin, Mont., Aug., '89	5¹⁄₁₆	9¹⁄₁₆
11. Theodore Roosevelt, Heron, Mont., Sept., '86	5	9¾

No. 11 was a female; as the horns of the female white goat always are, these horns were a little longer and slenderer than those of No. 10, which was a big-bodied buck.

In Buxton's catalogue the biggest horns given were 5 inches in girth and 8¼ inches in length. The two biggest specimens given in Ward's were 5 inches in girth by 10⅛ inches, and 5½ by 9½ inches.

MUSK OX.

There was no musk ox head exhibited by an amateur sportsman. One, which was exhibited by W. W. Hart & Co., had horns each of which was 29¾ inches by 20 ½ inches; the height of the boss was 13 inches. One of the members of the Boone and Crockett Club, Mr. Caspar W. Whitney, has this year, 1895, killed a number of musk ox; but he did not return from his winter trip to the Barren Grounds until June.

PRONGBUCK.

	Girth.	Length.
12. Theodore Roosevelt, Medora, N. D., Sept., '84	6½	16
13. A. Rogers	6	12½
14. A. Rogers	6¼	10⅞

No. 13 measured from tip to tip 6⅛ inches. The greatest width inside the horns was 8⅝ inches; the corresponding figures for No. 14 were 7¾ and 10¼ inches.

Hunting in Many Lands

In Buxton's catalogue the largest measurements given were for a specimen which girthed 5⅛ inches, and was in length 15¾ inches.

In Ward's catalogue the two biggest specimens given measured respectively 15¾ inches in length by 6¼ inches in girth, and 12⅞ inches in length by 6½ inches in girth.

WAPITI OR ROUND-HORN ELK.

	Girth.	Length.	Spread.	Points.
15. A. Rogers, Northwestern Wyoming. .	8	64¼	48	7+7
16. G. O. Shields, Clark's Fork, Wyo. . .	8¼	51⅜	50	6+7
17. T. Roosevelt, Two Ocean Pass, '91 . .	6⅞	56½	46⅜	6+6
18. T. Roosevelt, Two Ocean Pass, '91. .	7¾	50¾	47	6+6
19. P. Liebinger, Indian Creek, Mont. . .	6⅛	50½	54	8+8

No. 15, as far as we know, is the record head for amateur sportsmen in point of length.

No. 16 has very heavy massive antlers; though these are not so long as the antlers of No. 17, yet No. 16 is really the finer head.

In Buxton's catalogue the three finest heads measure respectively 8 inches in girth by 62½ inches in length by 48½ inches spread, with 7+9 points; and 7⅞ inches in girth by 60¾ inches in length by 52 inches spread, with 6+6 points; and 8½ inches in girth by 55 inches in length by 41¼ spread, with 6+6 points.

These are also the biggest heads given in Ward's catalogue.

MULE OR BLACKTAIL DEER.

	Girth.	Length.	Spread.
20. T. Roosevelt, Medora, N. D., Oct., '83 . .	5	26⅞	28½
21. P. Liebinger, Madison R., Mont., '89 . . .	4¾	25½	25½

No. 20 is an extremely massive and symmetrical head with 28 points.
No. 21 has 35 points.

Head-Measurements of Trophies

A still heavier head than either of the above, with 34 points, was exhibited by the furriers, C. G. Gunther's Sons; it was in girth 5¼ inches, length 26 inches and spread 28¼ inches.

In Buxton's catalogue the length of the biggest mule deer horn exhibited was 28½ inches.

In Ward's catalogue the biggest heads measured respectively: girth 4½ inches by 28⅝ inches length, and girth 5 ¼ inches by 27 inches length; they had 10 and 11 points respectively.

WHITETAIL OR VIRGINIA DEER.

	Girth.	Length.	Spread.
22. G. B. Grinnell, Dismal River, Neb., '77 .	4⅝	24	19½
23. T. Roosevelt, Medora, N. D., '94	4	22½	15¾

No. 22 is a very fine head with 18 points; very symmetrical.

No. 23 has 12 points.

In Ward's measurements the biggest whitetail horns are in girth 5⅜ inches, and in length 27⅝ inches.

MOOSE.

	Girth.	Length.	Points.
24. Col. Haselton, Chesuncook, Me., '87. . . .	8½	41	27
25. A. Rogers	7	31¾	14
26. T. Roosevelt, Bitter Root Mt., Mont., '89	5½	30	22

No. 24, a pair of horns only, is, with the possible exception of a head of Mr. Bierstadt's, the finest we have ever seen in the possession of an amateur sportsman. The measurements of the palm of one antler were 41½ by 21¾ inches.

No. 26 has a spread of 40½ inches, and the palm measured 29 by 13 inches.

In Buxton's catalogue the biggest moose given had horns which in girth were 8½ inches and in length 35½ inches; the palm was 41 by 24 inches; the spread was 65 inches. These measurements indicate a head about as fine as Col. Haselton's, taking everything into consideration.

The largest head given by Ward was 6½ inches in girth by 39⅞ inches in length and 51⅜ inches spread. It had 25 points, and the breadth of the palm was 15¾ inches.

For the reason given above, it is difficult in the case of moose, and far more difficult in the case of caribou, to judge the respective merits of heads by the mere record of measurements.

CARIBOU.

	Girth.	Length.	Points.
27. A. Rogers	4¾	41¼	16
28. T. Roosevelt, Kootenai, B. C., Sept., '88 .	5½	32	14

Neither of these is a big head. C. G. Gunther's Sons exhibited one caribou with 43 points. Its horns were 5⅞ inches in girth by 50 inches in length. They also exhibited a much heavier head, which was but 37 inches long, but was 6½ inches in girth, with all of the tines highly palmated; one of the brow points had a palm 17½ inches high.

In Buxton's catalogue the biggest caribou antler given girthed 5½ inches and was in length 37½ inches. The biggest measurements given by Ward are 5⅝ inches in girth by 60 inches in length for a specimen with 37 points.

National Park Protective Act

An Act to protect the birds and animals in Yellowstone National Park, and to punish crimes in said Park, and for other purposes.

Be it enacted by the Senate and House of Representatives of the United States of America in Congress assembled, That the Yellowstone National Park, as its boundaries now are defined, or as they may be hereafter defined or extended, shall be under the sole and exclusive jurisdiction of the United States; and that all the laws applicable to places under the sole and exclusive jurisdiction of the United States shall have force and effect in said Park: *Provided, however,* That nothing in this Act shall be construed to forbid the service in the Park of any civil or criminal process of any court having jurisdiction in the States of Idaho, Montana and Wyoming. All fugitives from justice taking refuge in said Park shall be subject to the same laws as refugees from justice found in the State of Wyoming.

Sec. 2. That said Park, for all the purposes of this Act, shall constitute a part of the United States judicial district of Wyoming, and the district and circuit courts of the United States in and for said district shall have jurisdiction of all offenses committed within said Park.

Sec. 3. That if any offense shall be committed in said Yellowstone National Park, which offense is not prohibited or the punishment is not specially provided for by any law of the United States or by any regulation of the Secretary of the Interior, the offender shall be subject to the same punishment as the laws of the State of Wyoming in force at the time of the commission of the offense may provide for a like offense in the said State; and no subsequent repeal of any such law of the State of Wyoming shall affect any prosecution for said offense committed within said Park.

SEC. 4. That all hunting, or the killing, wounding, or capturing at any time of any bird or wild animal, except dangerous animals, when it is necessary to prevent them from destroying human life or inflicting an injury, is prohibited within the limits of said Park; nor shall any fish be taken out of the waters of the Park by means of seines, nets, traps, or by the use of drugs or any explosive substances or compounds, or in any other way than by hook and line, and then only at such seasons and in such times and manner as may be directed by the Secretary of the Interior. That the Secretary of the Interior shall make and publish such rules and regulations as he may deem necessary and proper for the management and care of the Park, and for the protection of the property therein, especially for the preservation from injury or spoliation of all timber, mineral deposits, natural curiosities, or wonderful objects within said Park; and for the protection of the animals and birds in the Park from capture or destruction, or to prevent their being frightened or driven from the Park; and he shall make rules and regulations governing the taking of fish from the streams or lakes in the Park. Possession within the said Park of the dead bodies, or any part thereof, of any wild bird or animal shall be *prima facie* evidence that the

National Park Protective Act

person or persons having the same are guilty of violating this Act. Any person or persons, or stage or express company or railway company, receiving for transportation any of the said animals, birds or fish so killed, taken or caught shall be deemed guilty of a misdemeanor, and shall be fined for every such offense not exceeding three hundred dollars. Any person found guilty of violating any of the provisions of this Act, or any rule or regulation that may be promulgated by the Secretary of the Interior with reference to the management and care of the Park, or for the protection of the property therein, for the preservation from injury or spoliation of timber, mineral deposits, natural curiosities or wonderful objects within said Park, or for the protection of the animals, birds and fish in the said Park, shall be deemed guilty of a misdemeanor, and shall be subjected to a fine of not more than one thousand dollars, or imprisonment not exceeding two years, or both, and be adjudged to pay all costs of the proceedings.

That all guns, traps, teams, horses, or means of transportation of every nature or description used by any person or persons within said Park limits, when engaged in killing, trapping, ensnaring or capturing such wild beasts, birds, or wild animals, shall be forfeited to the United States, and may be seized by the officers in said Park and held pending the prosecution of any person or persons arrested under charge of violating the provisions of this Act, and upon conviction under this Act of such person or persons using said guns, traps, teams, horses, or other means of transportation, such forfeiture shall be adjudicated as a penalty in addition to the other punishment provided in this Act. Such forfeited property shall be disposed of and accounted for by and under the authority of the Secretary of the Interior.

Sec. 5. That the United States circuit court in said district shall appoint a commissioner, who shall reside in the Park, who shall have jurisdiction to hear and act upon all complaints made, of any and all violations of the law, or of the rules and regulations made by the Secretary of the Interior for the government of the Park, and for the protection of the animals, birds and fish, and objects of interest therein, and for other purposes authorized by this Act. Such commissioner shall have power, upon sworn information, to issue process in the name of the United States for the arrest of any person charged with the commission of any misdemeanor, or charged with the violation of the rules and regulations, or with the violation of any provision of this Act prescribed for the government of said Park, and for the protection of the animals, birds and fish in the said Park, and to try the person so charged; and, if found guilty, to impose the punishment and adjudge the forfeiture prescribed. In all cases of conviction an appeal shall lie from the judgment of said commissioner to the United States district court for the district of Wyoming, said appeal to be governed by the laws of the State of Wyoming providing for appeals in cases of misdemeanor from justices of the peace to the district court of said State; but the United States circuit court in said district may prescribe rules of procedure and practice for said commissioner in the trial of cases and for appeal to said United States district court. Said commissioner shall also have power to issue process as hereinbefore provided for the arrest of any person charged with the commission of any felony within the

Park, and to summarily hear the evidence introduced, and, if he shall determine that probable cause is shown for holding the person so charged for trial, shall cause such person to be safely conveyed to a secure place for confinement, within the jurisdiction of the United States district court in said State of Wyoming, and shall certify a transcript of the record of his proceedings and the testimony in the case to the said court, which court shall have jurisdiction of the case: *Provided,* That the said commissioner shall grant bail in all cases bailable under the laws of the United States or of said State. All process issued by the commissioner shall be directed to the marshal of the United States for the district of Wyoming; but nothing herein contained shall be construed as preventing the arrest by any officer of the Government or employee of the United States in the Park without process of any person taken in the act of violating the law or any regulation of the Secretary of the Interior: *Provided,* That the said commissioner shall only exercise such authority and powers as are conferred by this Act.

SEC. 6. That the marshal of the United States for the district of Wyoming may appoint one or more deputy marshals for said Park, who shall reside in said Park, and the said United States district and circuit courts shall hold one session of said courts annually at the town of Sheridan, in the State of Wyoming, and may also hold other sessions at any other place in said State of Wyoming or in said National Park at such dates as the said courts may order.

SEC. 7. That the commissioner provided for in this Act shall, in addition to the fees allowed by law to commissioners of the circuit courts of the United States, be paid an annual salary of one thousand dollars, payable quarterly, and the marshal of the United States and his deputies, and the attorney of the United States and his assistants in said district, shall be paid the same compensation and fees as are now provided by law for like services in said district.

SEC. 8. That all costs and expenses arising in cases under this Act, and properly chargeable to the United States, shall be certified, approved and paid as like costs and expenses in the courts of the United States are certified, approved and paid under the laws of the United States.

SEC. 9. That the Secretary of the Interior shall cause to be erected in the Park a suitable building to be used as a jail, and also having in said building an office for the use of the commissioner; the cost of such building not to exceed five thousand dollars, to be paid out of any moneys in the Treasury not otherwise appropriated upon the certificate of the Secretary as a voucher therefor.

SEC. 10. That this Act shall not be construed to repeal existing laws conferring upon the Secretary of the Interior and the Secretary of War certain powers with reference to the protection, improvement and control of the said Yellowstone National Park.

Approved May 7, 1894.

Constitution of the Boone and Crockett Club

Article I.

This Club shall be known as the Boone and Crockett Club.

Article II.

The objects of the Club shall be—

1. To promote manly sport with the rifle.

2. To promote travel and exploration in the wild and unknown, or but partially known, portions of the country.

3. To work for the preservation of the large game of this country, and, so far as possible, to further legislation for that purpose, and to assist in enforcing the existing laws.

4. To promote inquiry into, and to record observations on the habits and natural history of, the various wild animals.

5. To bring about among the members the interchange of opinions and ideas on hunting, travel and exploration; on the various kinds of hunting-rifles; on the haunts of game animals, etc.

439

Article III.

No one shall be eligible for membership who shall not have killed with the rifle in fair chase, by still-hunting or otherwise, at least one individual of one of the various kinds of American large game.

Article IV.

Under the head of American large game are included the following animals: Bear, buffalo (bison), mountain sheep, caribou, cougar, musk-ox, white goat, elk (wapiti), wolf (not coyote), pronghorn antelope, moose and deer.

Article V.

The term "fair chase" shall not be held to include killing bear, wolf or cougar in traps, nor "fire-hunting," nor "crusting" moose, elk or deer in deep snow, nor killing game from a boat while it is swimming in the water.

Article VI.

This Club shall consist of not more than one hundred regular members, and of such associate and honorary members as may be elected.

Article VII.

The Committee on Admissions shall consist of the President and Secretary and the Chairman of

Constitution, Boone and Crockett Club

the Executive Committee. In voting for regular members, six blackballs shall exclude. In voting for associate and honorary members, ten blackballs shall exclude. Candidates for regular membership who are at the same time associate members shall be voted upon before any other.

Article VIII.

The Club shall hold one fixed meeting a year, to be held the second Wednesday in January, and to be called the annual meeting.

Article IX.

This Constitution shall not be changed, save by a four-fifths vote of the members present.

Officers
of the Boone and Crockett Club
1895

President.

Theodore Roosevelt,   New York.

Secretary and Treasurer.

George Bird Grinnell,   New York.

Executive Committee.

W. A. Wadsworth,	Geneseo, N. Y.
Archibald Rogers,	Hyde Park, N. Y.
Winthrop Chanler,	New York.
Owen Wister,	Philadelphia, Pa.
Charles Deering,	Chicago, Ill.

Editorial Committee.

Theodore Roosevelt,	New York.
George Bird Grinnell,	New York.

442

List of Members
of the Boone and Crockett Club

*Deceased.

Lieut. Henry T. Allen,	Washington, D. C.
Capt. Geo. S. Anderson,	Yellowstone Park, Wyo.
F. H. Barber,	Southampton, L. I.
D. M. Barringer,	Philadelphia, Pa.
Hon. T. Beal,	Washington, D. C.
Albert Bierstadt,	New York.
W. J. Boardman,	Cleveland, Ohio.
Wm. B. Bogert,	Chicago, Ill.
Hon. Benj. H. Bristow,	New York.
Wm. B. Bristow,	New York.
A. E. Brown,	Philadelphia, Pa.
Major Campbell Brown,	Spring Hill, Tenn.
Col. John Mason Brown,*	Louisville, Ky.
W. A. Buchanan,	Chicago, Ill.
H. D. Burnham,	Chicago, Ill.
Edw. North Buxton,	London, Eng.
H. A. Carey,*	Newport, R. I.
Royal Carroll,	New York.
Judge John Dean Caton,*	Ottawa, Ill.
J. A. Chanler,	New York.

443

Hunting in Many Lands

W. A. Chanler,	New York.
Winthrop Chanler,	New York.
Frank C. Crocker,	Portland, Me.
A. P. Gordon-Cumming,	Washington, D. C.
Chas. P. Curtiss,	Boston, Mass.
Paul J. Dashiell,	Annapolis, Md.
E. W. Davis,	Providence, R. I.
Chas. Deering,	Chicago, Ill.
H. C. de Rham,	New York.
W. B. Devereux,	Glenwood Springs, Colo.
Col. Richard Irving Dodge,	Washington, D. C.
Dr. Wm. K. Draper,	New York.
J. Coleman Drayton,	New York.
Capt. Frank Edwards,	Washington, D. C.
Dr. D. G. Elliott,	Chicago, Ill.
Maxwell Evarts,	New York.
Robert Munro Ferguson,	New York.
J. G. Follansbee,	San Francisco, Cal.
Frank Furness,	Philadelphia, Pa.
W. R. Furness, Jr.,	Jekyll Island, Brunswick, Ga.
Jas. T. Gardiner,	Albany, N. Y.
John Sterett Gittings,	Baltimore, Md.
George H. Gould,	Santa Barbara, Cal.
De Forest Grant,	New York.
Madison Grant,	New York.
Gen. A. W. Greely,	Washington, D. C.
Geo. Bird Grinnell,	New York.

List of Members

Wm. Milne Grinnell,	New York.
Arnold Hague,	Washington, D. C.
Hon. Wade Hampton,	Columbia, S. C.
Howard Melville Hanna,	Cleveland, Ohio.
Major Moses Harris,	Washington, D. C.
Maj. Gen. W. H. Jackson,	Nashville, Tenn.
Dr. Walter B. James,	New York.
Col. Jas. H. Jones,	New York.
Clarence King,	New York.
C. Grant La Farge,	New York.
Alex. Lambert,	New York.
Dundas Lippincott,*	Philadelphia, Pa.
Hon. Henry Cabot Lodge,	Washington, D. C.
Francis C. Lowndes,	New York.
Frank Lyman,	Brooklyn, N. Y.
Geo. H. Lyman,	Boston, Mass.
Chas. B. Macdonald,	Chicago, Ill.
Prof. John Bache MacMasters,	Philadelphia, Pa.
Henry May,	Washington, D. C.
Col. H. C. McDowell,	Lexington, Ky.
Dr. C. Hart Merriam,	Washington, D. C.
Dr. J. C. Merrill,	Washington, D. C.
Dr. A. Rutherfurd Morris,	New York.
J. Chester Morris, Jr.,	Chestnut Hill, Pa.
H. N. Munn,	New York.
Lyman Nichols,	Boston, Mass.
Jas. S. Norton,	Chicago, Ill.

Hunting in Many Lands

Francis Parkman,*	Boston, Mass.
Thos. Paton,	New York.
Hon. Boies Penrose	Philadelphia, Pa.
C. B. Penrose,	Philadelphia, Pa.
R. A. F. Penrose,	Philadelphia, Pa.
W. Hallett Phillips,	Washington, D. C.
Col. W. D. Pickett,	Meeteetse, Wyo.
H. C. Pierce,	St. Louis, Mo.
John J. Pierrepont,	Brooklyn, N. Y.
Capt. John Pitcher,	Washington, D. C.
A. P. Proctor,	New York.
Hon. Redfield Proctor,	Washington, D. C.
Prof. Ralph Pumpelly,	Newport, R. I.
Percy Pyne, Jr.,	New York.
Hon. Thos. B. Reed,	Portland, Me.
Douglas Robinson, Jr.,	New York.
Hon. W. Woodville Rockhill,	Washington, D. C.
Archibald Rogers,	Hyde Park, N. Y.
E. P. Rogers,*	Hyde Park, N. Y.
Elliott Roosevelt,*	Abingdon, Va.
John Ellis Roosevelt,	New York.
J. West Roosevelt,	New York.
Hon. Theo. Roosevelt,	New York.
Elihu Root,	New York.
Bronson Rumsey,	Buffalo, N. Y.
Lawrence Rumsey,	Buffalo, N. Y.
Dean Sage,	Albany, N. Y.

List of Members

Alden Sampson,	Boston, Mass.
Hon. Carl Schurz,	New York.
Philip Schuyler,	Irvington, N. Y.
M. G. Seckendorf,	Washington, D. C.
Dr. J. L. Seward,	Orange, N. J.
Gen. Phil. Sheridan,*	Washington, D. C.
Gen. W. T. Sherman,*	New York.
Chas. F. Sprague,	Boston, Mass.
Henry L. Stimson,	New York.
Hon. Bellamy Storer,	Washington, D. C.
Rutherfurd Stuyvesant,	New York.
Frank Thompson,	Philadelphia, Pa.
B. C. Tilghman,	Philadelphia, Pa.
T. S. Van Dyke,	San Diego, Cal.
Hon. G. G. Vest,	Washington, D. C.
W. A. Wadsworth,	Geneseo, N. Y.
Samuel D. Warren,	Boston, Mass.
Jas. Sibley Watson,	Rochester, N. Y.
Maj. Gen. W. D. Whipple,	Norristown, Pa.
Chas. E. Whitehead,	New York.
Caspar W. Whitney,	New York.
E. P. Wilbur, Jr.,	South Bethlehem, Pa.
Col. Roger D. Williams,	Lexington, Ky.
R. D. Winthrop,	New York.
Owen Wister,	Philadelphia, Pa.
J. Walter Wood, Jr.,	New York.